FOREWO

KNOWLEDGE IS THE FOUNDATION
Lord Jamar – Brand Nubian

My full name is Lord Jamar Allah. You might know me from my roles on TV shows like *Oz* or *Law and Order*, or from my voiceover work with ESPN. Most likely though, you know me for my music. Together with Sadat X and Grand Puba, I came to the consciousness of the American public as Lord Jamar of Brand Nubian. During the 1990s – the "Golden Age of Hip Hop" – Brand Nubian captivated the streets with classics like "All for One" and "Slow Down." Meanwhile, we were making the American mainstream increasingly aware of the Nation of Gods and Earths. Throughout our reign in the music industry, we brought a lot of people into the desire for the knowledge of themselves. Though we received a lot of flack for what we said, it was worth it.

It's been 10 years since we recorded "Don't Let it Go to Your Head" and a lot has changed since then, both in the music industry and society as a whole. However, one thing is sure to outlast all change: The need for our people to have Knowledge of Self. That foundation is essential no matter what else is happening. It's the reason why I've prospered where others failed, and it could be the most important difference in your life as well. It's why I put out *The 5% Album* in 2006. And it's why this book is so essential.

I've had knowledge of self for about wisdom power (25) years, since about build understanding ('83), when I was knowledge power (15) years old. Before I got knowledge, I was basically a savage living in the pursuit of happiness, just running wild in New Rochelle, New York. A brother by the name of Barkim, who had just come home from being incarcerated up north, had returned to the community and was working as a guard at a mall in our city. A lot of us would hang out at the mall, looking for girls, trying to steal, or whatever else we wanted to do. And Barkim would pull certain ones of us to the side and start dropping little jewels on us, like, "Did you know the Black man is God?" or "You know why you shouldn't eat swine?"

All that stuff resonated with me somehow. I felt the vibrations of truth. But in my city at that time, there weren't many other Gods to build with. And Barkim was staying in tune with me, but he was beginning to deal with the Nation of Islam. So he had the magnetic of God knowledge, but he was coming with more of an NOI approach. There was an NOI mosque in Medina (Brooklyn) and he took me out there a few times. I definitely liked what I was hearing, but as a youth, I was still running wild and I wasn't trying to put that suit on. I was still smoking weed, doing what I wanted to do, crime and everything else. The knowledge was attractive to me, but I wasn't trying to be with the Nation of Islam, passing the collection plate around. I ain't had no money to be putting in a collection plate every time they passed it, and they were passing it around a lot, you know? So that kept me away, until a brother named True King Allah moved into my community from Queens.

I was a DJ at that time, and he used to DJ and MC, so we got together on a musical basis. And him being the true and living God that he is, he began striving to civilize me. He started building with me, and I was coming back at him with things I'd learned from Barkim. He was like, "Wow, you already know about Yacub and all that? God, you already got knowledge of self. You might as well just take the next step. Stop eating that swine, take that earring out your ear, and get with the Gods, you know what I mean?" And it's been strong ever since!

"One word can change a nation." - 5% proverb

You see, it was the vibration of truth. Words have power. People don't realize that they hold energy. Truth holds energy, and lies hold energy. If you are in tune with yourself, you are able to feel those vibrations and be in tune with those vibrations of truth or falsehood. Growing up, my old Earth was a Jehovah's Witness. She had us in that cipher pretty much since we were young children, and I'd always felt a vibration of falsehood there. There were so many things that didn't make sense, which they were telling me to accept on face value. So once I came into the knowledge of myself and that vibration of truth hit me, it opened doors for me. I saw the light, the blindfold was lifted off me and I saw the true reality of what life is about, and our purpose here on this planet.

For me, Supreme Mathematics is a blueprint for how to live your life. It shows you that everything comes in a certain order and if you don't follow that order, things can go wrong fast. For example, if you put the two (wisdom: words or actions) before the one (knowledge: thought), you're going to get a bad three (understanding: result or realization). You're going to get a misunderstanding instead of a proper understanding.

Mathematics has kept me strong. It's kept me focused and on the right path. When I was young, knowing the Supreme Mathematics and Supreme Alphabets, knowing that I was God and the master of my destiny - that kept me from allowing outside influences to master me. I came up in the era of the crack epidemic, and a lot of my friends fell victim to crack, whether selling it or smoking it. It was mathematics that kept me focused, instead of becoming another crackhead, or trying to become the next *Scarface*. Because when I was selling drugs, I was trying to figure out how to be the biggest crack dealer in my community. And in order to do that, I would've had to take the lives of the same brothers I went to school with. Now, had I not had knowledge of self, I probably would've went full-fledged into that plan. However I said to myself, "I can't do that to my own. These are my people. I can't do that to my people." I had to draw the line somewhere. Then I started seeing a lot of my friends getting indictments. I was surprised I didn't get one, and I knew that this music thing was something that I was destined to do. Even back then, my lyrics were righteous, so I knew that I had a job to do, and I couldn't ruin it by getting locked up.

When we came out as Brand Nubian, we were coming behind people like Public Enemy, KRS-1, and Rakim, so having something pro-Black to say was kinda popular at the time. That's not why we did it, but we were fortunate to come in at a time where it was accepted. Now once things changed, that's when people had to decide, are you going to flip it now, or are you going to stick to what you've been doing? My thing is, if it ain't broke, don't fix it – you know what I mean? I see the power and the influence that we've had on people through our music, and the positive responses we've got, and that by itself is worth way more than any gold or platinum to me. I've had people telling me that our music is what got them through college. Some of the testimonials I've received from people are just ridiculous. Knowing that the music is deeper than just making somebody dance – I guess that helps to keep you on the path too – but just being true to yourself is bigger. For me, that's the basic thing, just being true to yourself. And I don't know if there's just a defining moment that made me say, "Oh, I'm going to stick to this way of life." I think that's just kind of in my character. I'm a loyal dude, so if you're loyal to me, then I'm loyal to you. And this mathematics, this culture, this way of life has always been loyal to me. It's not really a debate in my mind. You can't do or not do something because you're worried about what other people are going to say. It all goes back to mathematics, and it all starts with knowledge. Knowledge is you. It starts with you and everything else comes after that. You can't start with wisdom, you can't start with culture. You don't start building a house from the fourth floor and work your way down. You start from the foundation and work your way up. A lot of people look for things outside of themselves, instead of inside themselves, looking for what help or relief they can get from outside. That can take many forms, and none of them are helpful to you. We don't teach that. Knowledge of Self begins with you *knowing that everything starts with you.*

CONTENTS

FOREWORD 3
INTRODUCTION..8
IDENTITY CRISIS 10
    LOVE, HELL, OR RIGHT...10
    THE GREATNESS IN MAN 18
    LOST IN THE WILDERNESS 21
    BLACK GOD 23
    BLACK IS BEAUTIFUL..26
    BLACKS IN CHINA?..27
    SOMOS ORIGINALES 30
    FROM HERU TO "HOW YOU DOIN?" 36
    EM-POWER-U 39
    VANILLA IS BLACK 41
    "MISS INDEPENDENT"...43
    RIGHTEOUSNESS AND RESPONSIBILITIES................48
    MURDERING FOUR DEVILS 52

THOUGHT MANIFESTED...54
    THE MIND IS THE MASTER KEY 54
    THE PRINCIPLES OF LEARNING...............................56
    IDEAS AND REALITY...57
    IS BEAUTY ONLY SKIN DEEP? 58
    DID I DO THAT? 61
    WHAT DO YOU FEAR?...65
    WISDOM IS THE WAY...66
    ARE YOU A RELUCTANT MESSIAH?.........................67
    GOD HAS NO RELIGION 69
    BELIEVE IN JESUS AND LOSE YOUR MIND 71
    PRAY AND IT WON'T COME 76
    THE BEAUTY OF KNOWLEDGE.................................77
    KNOWLEDGE VERSUS BELIEF 79
    THE POWER OF THE MIND..82
    DROPPING SCIENCE 84

THE BIRTHRIGHT 86
    WHY IS THE BLACK MAN GOD? 86
    THE CULTURE OF I-GOD..94
    THE SURE REALITY 95
    WHAT GOD IS AND WHAT GOD IS NOT 96
    THE TRUE AND LIVING GOD 98
    C.R.I.P. 99
    FROM INMATE TO GOD 102
    EARTH BY NATURE 104
    AN EARTH'S JOURNEY 108
    MARRIED AT THE AGE OF SIXTEEN 112
    SO...THEN WHO IS THE DEVIL? 114
    THE BUILD 120

CULTURE 132
    WHAT WE TEACH.. 132
    WHAT WE WILL ACHIEVE... 132
    WHO IS THE 5%?.. 133
    ALLAH THE FATHER 142
    FREE THE DUMB 146
    FROM K.O.S. TO 120° 149
    A GOOD NAME IS… 150
    WHAT'S IN A NAME: SELF DEFINITION 152
    NO PORK ON THE FORK.. 155
    THE UNIVERSAL FLAG 157
    IS THE NGE A MUSLIM COMMUNITY? 158
    HOLY VS. RIGHTEOUS 163
    CIVILIZATION STUDIES 158
    WHAT DOES IT MEAN TO BE GOD?....................................... 164
    CHANGE THE WORLD 166
    THOSE WERE THE DAYS 167
    SERVING JUSTICE 168
    ALLAH AND INDIGENOUS ANARCHY 174
    THIS IS NOT JUST A PHILOSOPHY 178
    ALLAH AIN'T RAISE NO PUNKS.. 182

TEACHING 184
    THE FATE OF THE MANY… 184
    WHY I AM A POOR RIGHTEOUS TEACHER........................... 185
    EDUCATING OUR YOUTH.. 188
    SAVE THE BABIES.. 191
    THE SWORD MY SON 193
    27 LESSONS... 194
    PROTECT YOUR COMMUNITY 196
    RESPONSIBILITY 197
    TO BE OR BORN THE EARTH 200
    FOR THE REVOLUTIONARIES... 204
    PEDAGOGY OF THE FIVE PERCENT 206
    THE P.E.A.C.E. COURSE 207

THE UNIVERSE 212
    WHY I DON'T BELIEVE IN A MYSTERY GOD 212
    WHAT HAPPENS WHEN WE DIE? 215
    LIFE AFTER LIFE?.. 222
    THE POWER OF THE QUEEN IN CHESS................................. 225
    THE GOD IN MAN 227
    QUANTUM PHYSICS AND THE BLACK GOD 229
    THE KINGDOM OF GOD IS WITHIN YOU 232
    BIAN XING 233
    'TIS THE SEASON 242
    WHAT DO YOU LOVE? 244
    OPTICS 245
    THE INTERNET: A BLESSING AND A CURSE 248
    CHOOSING A POOR RIGHTEOUS TEACHER 250

AFTERWORD 252
FAQ... 254
GLOSSARY... 257

INTRODUCTION

It has been written on the walls of temples since man's earliest history: *Know Thyself!* Knowledge of Self isn't some New Age, Hippie, feel-good philosophy. Nor is it an ancient, religious doctrine of some kind. No one is asking you to burn incense, grow dreadlocks, make animal (or human) sacrifices, wear sandals, do yoga or drink cyanide-laced Kool-Aid for a charismatic leader. No, fortunately, that isn't what Knowledge of Self is about. You don't have to beg, pray, meditate, fast, or give your money or things away in order to obtain knowledge of self. All that is required is that you be sincere, courageous and that you pay attention.

To know one's self is a gift that all of humanity deserves to be presented with. To be imparted with the awareness to constantly explore one's ideas in the most empowering manner. To delve into one's nature truthfully and share in a way that betters all. To have the greatest weaponry available to identify and protect oneself from any enemy's oppressive measures. These are achieved supremely with the knowledge of self.

The Nation of Gods and Earths teaches we are the creators of our entire universe and subsequent reality. Yet it did not begin with us. Since the earliest recorded times, many of our ancestral cultures and civilizations have shared the idea of man as God, the woman as the Earth, and the mathematical nature of the universe. Throughout history, this teaching has emerged, been repressed, and reemerged again. In this way, the element of the "Five Percent" in society is a timeless reality. However, the Nation of Gods and Earths truly adds on a unique perspective in many enlightening ways.

First, these great teachers did not search or wait for the "right" student to present themselves and their revolutionary ideas. Rather, they presented themselves to the world as God or Earth - without fear or hesitation - and allowed potential students from any and all walks of life to inquire. This is a departure from the nomadic Sufis imparting insight in the worlds of fundamentalist Islam, and then slipping away to see another day, or the Taoist masters who lived as mountain men, away from society's ill. The Gods and Earths have openly shared their understanding regardless of the consequences. The consequences have been great, from the risk of self-contradiction and hypocrisy, to being ostracized from one's family and community, from direct oppression and harassment by the existing power structure, to outright assassination. Still, the Gods and Earths continued to teach.

Second, the foundation of the teachings - the Supreme Mathematics - made such a complex subject as the universe and its workings, impressively simple to understand. This innovation and insight into the science of everything in life produced a methodology ready for application by anyone of any age group. This process also elevates the insightful teachings of the Nation of Islam, extracted and refined as our 120 lessons, into a mathematical system of study and development. In fact, though the truth we study is certainly ageless, the development of the Five Percent into the Nation of Gods and Earths as it exists today exemplifies the exact development most needed today. That is, a culture that makes sense of our identity, the reality of God, nature, and mathematics, and need for sweeping social change, yet goes about this work without the trappings of belief and religious thinking. Thus, the "science" of everything in life.

Third, we learn that we are the truth we seek in each and every problem or inquiry. A knowledge of self becomes the most empowering tool known because it is an actualizing of what is otherwise only factual information. The Original man is God/The Original woman is the Earth. This is true. Yet, through the living process of knowledge of self, I am this truth, and I prove it true. What is within us that enables us to survive and thrive? Knowing oneself, the answer presents itself. It is the intention of the editors of this book that, in reading, you will come to find answers of your own. More importantly, you will come upon more questions. And in the actions you take thereafter, you will discover the science of everything in life.

There are thousands, possibly hundreds of thousands of Gods and Earths who live and teach the principles named above. In the pages that follow, you will get a chance to explore some of their perspectives. This text is the first of its kind because it not a history book, biography, ethnography or how-to guide, but an anthology, or collection, of writings from individuals representing nearly every walk of life encompassed in our Nation. Young and old, male and female, free and incarcerated, high school dropout and postdoctoral researcher. This may be considered a "Black book," but in this culture, "Black" is inclusive of the Puerto Rican, Dominican, Iranian, Bengali, Native American, and Chinese authors you'll meet within these pages. This is a Nation of great diversity, in thought and experience. Thus, you will find many differing perspectives and methods of presentation. Some will resonate with you more than others. As the editors, it has been our goal to provide you with the most comprehensive picture of who we are and what we teach as a Nation. It is up to you, the reader, to "take the best part" for yourself. Even in doing so, however, read every word. Understanding will come in time, and will come sooner if you should *follow up* after your reading as recommended by the authors. In the intense experience that is to follow these pages, you may just begin to discover the "science of everything in life."

Peace,
The Editors

ೞ 1 ೞ
IDENTITY CRISIS

LOVE, HELL, OR RIGHT
Intelligent Tarref Allah - Interior Cipher (New York)

LOVE

I grew up with my parents and older brother in the crime-infested Brooklyn neighborhoods of East New York and Brownsville. My parents were from the South, but they were not the stereotypical Southern "church folk." I remember attending church twice, once with my grandmother, and once with my friends as I pursued a girl whose "Sunday best" fit too tight for "The Lord's House." In my home, the word "God" was usually trailed by the obscenity "damn." There were no Michelangelo depictions

of a pale Christ, or wooden crosses adorning my walls like I saw in the homes of my friends. The only symbol that hung in my home that was remotely related to religion was the infamous picture of Malcolm X clutching a rifle, and a smiling portrait of the late Nation of Islam spokesman and human rights activist. A love for Malcolm X and Elijah Muhammad spawned my father's use of the name "Allah" in lieu of "God." My parents had a belief and concept of God, but they never force-fed it to their children.

My parents had been "home schooling" me before it became fashionable or I set foot in a classroom. There was no formal curriculum, just daily instruction on reading, writing, math, history, and current events—mostly verbal tutoring in the tradition of ancient African griots.

HELL

I excelled in daycare and elementary school, so those classroom settings were heaven from the beginning to the end. But junior high was hell at first sight. I.S. 292 was a fashion show, boxing ring, and dating service rolled into one. The sidewalk in front of the school was a runway for students-turned-fashion-models on the first day of the school year. After the day-one outfits were hung up, true style was defined by the few students whose parents could afford wardrobes of Calvin Klein and Guess, or those pupils who had a collection of Polo and Gap, courtesy of crime. Fights erupted in the gym, lunchroom, halls, and classes, but the traditional after-school bouts drew the most attention and blood. Couples spent time hugging, rubbing, and kissing in the lunchroom, but a rare breed with raging hormones and huge hearts transformed a deserted doorway near the auditorium into a bedroom. Me being in the smartest classes each year in elementary school was cool to most of the students and all of my teachers there. Yet in junior high, to many, intellect was like a contagious disease with no cure. I was a leper among the pure—purely problematic.

Junior high exposed me to just enough personalities to help birth my identity crisis. While deciding whether to follow in the footsteps of my badboy brother, I battled the allure of fashion and females pulling me towards the in-crowd. In a rhyme I wrote called "The Autobiography," I rapped:

I was smart in school/
But I ain't want to be a nerd/
Badboys got girls/
Chicks flew past birds/

A bird is slang for a lame or loser, and trying to balance books and bravado was causing me to develop feathers and a beak. I had been the brunt of students' jokes, producing a distress within me that was more destructive than a nuclear weapon. No matter what game you play, everybody likes a winner. The students in my school were no different.

It only took months before I solved my identity crisis by flaunting the mask of thug, fashion icon, and ladies' man. I was the youngest and newest member among a crew of troublemakers who were players in The Game that's not a game. The drug game, stickup game, gun game, and other criminal activities of the street culture are collectively known as "The Game." Drug dealers "ball" (show off), stickup kids steal money like bases, gunslingers gamble with lives, and pimps are "players." But The Game is not a sport designed for fun. Gunshot wounds, dead comrades, life sentences, and kidnapped family members are realities of The Game that's not a game. I had stepped into this pot of warm water which was so slowly reaching a boiling point that I could not sense the heat.

By 1991, a month after I turned 15, I found myself in Spofford Juvenile Detention Center charged with murder. The jealousy and hate of a rival crew member caused my false incarceration. I was the collateral damage in a street war that was brewing. It would take 14 months to win my freedom after trial.

Some months after my incarceration, my father sent me a copy of Elijah Muhammad's *A Message to the Blackman in America*. One thing that stood out in the book was the Nation of Islam's concept of Master Fard Muhammad being God in the flesh. I had read this earlier in Malcolm X's autobiography, but within the isolated confines of my small white room at Spofford, the notion seemed different. I was fascinated enough to question my atheist views, but not compelled to believe in the existence of a God in any form. Traditional or non-traditional, in the flesh or spirit, any concept of God seemed totally irrational and supported solely by belief. I needed evidence before I could dedicate my life to any concept or person.

One night after perusing a chapter in *A Message to the Blackman in America*, I thought of Malcolm X's autobiography. Paraphrasing him, he mentioned being told to take one step towards Allah and Allah would take two steps towards him. Although Elijah Muhammad said Master Fard Muhammad was God in the flesh, he also spoke of Allah with connotations of a supernatural being external from man. I was confused. I was a skeptic, but if I could rationalize the existence of the supernatural, I would have to accept that as truth. Also, because my father idolized Malcolm X, and I accepted both of them as knowledgeable and logical thinkers, I yearned to know: how could they believe in God?

I paced my cell, wondering if I had it all wrong about God. I needed to find out. I dropped to my knees, closed my eyes, and prayed for the first time in my life. I took one step, as Malcolm X said, asking for forgiveness and a sign of the existence of Allah, thirsting to see if Allah would take two steps towards me. I begged something to the effect of, "Please forgive me. Just give me one sign. Please." After about fifteen minutes of repeating and rewording my request, I lay on my bed and stared at the ceiling.

Minutes later, I gazed out of the window into the dark night. Maybe there was a God, but his name was Jesus. I knew that more people believed in Jesus than Allah. I shut my eyes, kneeled, and repeated similar requests as I did earlier. When I did not receive a single signal, I opened my eyes and began wondering why I had allowed people to influence me to second-guess my logic. I put Elijah Muhammad's book beneath my bed. It remained there until I went home.

After I returned home, things were constantly changing. My crew had diminished to a group of about nine. We were spending less time getting into trouble, but the war between us and the rival crew was alive. We, however, were focused on making money illegally, partying at clubs, and trying to get record deals as rappers. I was involved in a relationship with a female named Cathy, so spending time with her in Williamsburg, Brooklyn, where she lived, kept me off the streets of East New York, where trouble haunted me. I was also enrolled in a GED program and receiving training in building maintenance under the tutelage of an independent contractor in Harlem.

Forty-one days before my 18th birthday, I crossed paths with the rival crew, including my tormenter who had me arrested. He noticed me before I saw him. I believe that we were the only two armed. He made the first move, but after seconds that seemed like eternity, I was the last man standing. My choice to become a player in The Game that's not a game had changed my life forever.

There is only one thing that feels worse than being locked up for murder: that's being falsely incarcerated for murder, then rearrested for killing the person who accused you of murder.

I had only been home from Spofford for 17 months and three days, when I was shackled, cuffed, and thrown in a precinct cell. My next trip led me to a cell in Brooklyn Supreme Court. With each step I took, and each second I observed my surroundings, my anger heightened. The sight of 30 grown men crammed into a 10-man cell made my blood boil. The sound of court officers barking orders, detainees telling war stories, and the jingle of keys, handcuffs, and shackles assaulted my ears. The stench of the mildewed clothes on the homeless man feet away made me nauseous. Back then, I kept blaming the deceased for starting the beef that led to my incarceration. Now, I recognize that he had only handed me the rope. I had hung myself the day I decided to trade in school for the streets.

I ended up in C-74, the Adolescent Reception Detention Center, on the world's largest penal colony—Riker's Island. Someone coined the phrase "C-74, adolescents at war." It fit perfectly for the single building that caged some of the most dangerous 16-to-19-year-olds in New York City. I knew some of the outlaws from my stay at Spofford, others had stomped through the streets with me. My ties to old associates and the new thugs I was introduced to made my ride relatively safe. Unfortunately, most new faces in C-74 crashed head-first into injuries and extortion. I had my share of drama, but I navigated the maze of madness without a homemade icepick puncturing my body or a razor gracing my face.

My body was locked up, but my mind was in society. My family were supportive and certain that I would be vindicated in court, because I had defended myself. Their thoughts were destroyed when we found out that the gun the deceased had possessed never made it to the precinct evidence locker. Possibly, one of the deceased's friends had taken it, or it was removed by the deceased's uncle, who worked in the precinct. The deck was stacked against me. I would end up pleading guilty to murder and receive 19 years to life.

My brother and a few guys from my crew had been visiting me regularly on Riker's Island. Several months after I was arrested, they had become members of The Nation of Gods and Earths, a God-centered cultural group commonly known as The Five Percent Nation. My brother told me not to call him Moe anymore, because his new name was Uneeke Understanding Allah. The rest of my crew had adopted names like Wise and Victorious that reflected positive attributes of themselves.

"I'm trying to keep a low profile," my brother told me inside of the crowded visiting room. He leaned back in the small red chair and said, "I'm on another level now. I'm God."

I held back my laughter and wondered if he had lost his mind. To me, anything involving God was insane. I switched the subject to avoid debate.

After the visit my mind remained on my brother, so when I got back to my dorm I mentioned him to Sharief. Sha, as we called the older brother for short, was also a member of The Nation. He began explaining how The Nation was started by a man who was an understudy of Malcolm X in the Nation of Islam. His name was Clarence 13X, but he changed it to Allah and was known as The Father after leaving the Nation of Islam. He parted from the group based on Master Fard Muhammad being considered the sole personification of God, though Elijah Muhammad also taught, to a lesser degree, that all Black men were God. I immediately remembered the time in Spofford when I was confused by the Nation of Islam's conflicting views on God.

"Ain't no God," I told Sha, as I leaned back on my bed, staring at Sha's narrow light-skinned face. "Not the Black man or Master Fard Muhammad. And it definitely ain't nobody in the sky that's controlling everything."

Sha smiled, as he sat on the small locker connected to my bed. "You don't believe in a supernatural God, right?"

"You know that," I responded to the rhetorical question.

"So who or what is greater than man?"

I replied, "Nothing."

Sha smiled again, nodding his bald head. "So if there is nothing greater than man, what does that make man?"

"What?" I shrugged my shoulders.

"Listen," Sha said, "God means the supreme being. Supreme means the most high. Being means to exist. So if you don't believe in something that exists that is on a higher level than man, then subconsciously, you already understand that man is God. The Black man. They say that God is the originator. Well, anthropology and history proves that the Black man was the first on the planet. They say that God created man. Well, science proves that all races derive from the Black man. They say God gave us land to live on and fruit for food. Well, the Black man was the first to have thriving civilizations where we cultivated the land and lived off it." Sha kept going for at least ten minutes, quoting book after book to support his claims. He even made reference to the Bible mentioning "Ye are gods."

I was silent, pondering what Sha said and how he could quote so much history and science. I had known other members of The Nation, but I had never heard anyone expound on their concept of God in such simple and logical terms.

"So if the Black man is God," I said, "What's up with the white man?"

Sha asked, "Do you know what duality is?"

"No," I responded.

Sha started talking about the Yin and Yang, explaining that positive and negative were principles that exist everywhere and in everybody. He said that God represented positivity and the devil represented negativity, and the Black man was God and the white man was devil. "On earth," he stated, "overall, the white man has been associated with negativity and destruction from antiquity until now. And the Black man has had a positive history overall."

My mind flashed back to Elijah Muhammad's book, where he spoke of the white man being the devil, and a speech of Malcolm X I had seen where he said the same. They both cited the historical atrocities white people had inflicted on people all over the world who were not white. But I was in an argumentative mood, so I said, "You did negativity, that's why you're here. Me too, and I'm Black. Plus a Black man tried to kill me."

Sha grinned again. "That's duality," he said. "There is positive and negative in everybody. It doesn't matter what your race is. Being God doesn't mean that the Black man can't do anything negative. Just like the white man being devil doesn't mean that he can't do anything positive." He began explaining that The Nation was not pro-Black nor anti-white, but pro-righteousness and anti-devilishment, meaning they championed the cause of any person doing righteous acts and they were against any person involved in negativity. Race was not an issue. Then he mentioned how Allah and The Nation had worked with the late Mayor Lindsey, who was white, to help fund different institutions and activities for The Nation. He also mentioned how New York magazine had run a cover story about how Allah and The Nation helped stop Black Harlemites from destroying their community out of their anger over the assassination of Dr. Martin Luther King Jr.

Sha said, "Being God is about balancing the negative and positive elements within you so you can become in tune with your higher self." He eased off of the locker onto my bed. "That's what we taught each other in Egypt, before we were stripped of our culture and the knowledge of ourselves and brought to America." Sha went on and on about The Nation. Years later I would learn about ancient religious men from the Middle East like the Hurifi founder Fazl Allah, and al-Hakim of the Druze, who asserted they were God. There were others from various religions who saw themselves as God, giving rise to the concept of incarnation.

RIGHT

As the months passed, my conversations about The Nation with Sha, my brother, and my crew began to sway me towards their views. I learned that Sha was born into The Nation and his full name was Intellectual Sharief Allah. His mother was an Earth, which is what female members of The Nation are referred to as. Symbolically, they traditionally dress in headwraps and long dresses that cover three-fourths of their bodies, like the earth is covered by three-fourths of water. About six months after my arrest, I joined The Nation under the tutelage of Sha. After a three-day fast,

I was given the name Intelligent Tarref Allah. Intelligent is a reflection of one of the strongest of my attributes.

I had ceased eating pork as a prerequisite for joining The Nation. Sha had schooled me on pork parasites, including the tapeworm, fluke, and trichina, some of which grow to 21 feet long inside the human body. I also learned that pork was forced upon Black people during slavery before becoming a staple of contemporary soul food cuisine. In antiquity in Kemet, renamed Egypt, swineherds were considered impure and not allowed to enter temples of their native land, nor marry people who were not swineherds. I was greedier than a pig, but learning these and other factors helped me stop eating the pig.

Eliminating pork from my diet enhanced my health and spiritual awareness. I became stronger mentally, and motivated to make positive changes in my life. Sha had stressed to me the need to constantly grow and learn new things.

Coming to my personal understanding of spirituality was something new. It took me years, because I considered spirituality tantamount to religion. But through learning in The Nation to simplify things and study etymology, I discovered that the word spirit derives from the Latin word spiritus, which meant "breath." I associate breath with life, thus making spirituality an innate energy that generates life. So spirituality is about becoming in sync with an internal energy that complements your mental and physical being.

Allah had devised a numerical system called Supreme Mathematics. I would later learn that the ancient people of Kemet and the Kabbalistic Jews had a numerical system called Gematria, and certain Muslims used a mathematical system called Abjad. Supreme Mathematics are principles that correspond to the numerical system of one through nine and zero. The first principle is knowledge, and it is first because a person should have knowledge before speaking or acting. That was a principle I began to live out immediately, because speaking and acting without knowledge of situations had caused me problems in the past.

Allah also devised a system called the Supreme Alphabet, which involves unique principles that correspond to the English alphabet. They work in conjunction with Supreme Mathematics. The twelfth degree is Love, Hell, Right, which shows that life is filled with cycles of us experiencing Love and Hell in order to emerge Right. I identified that with the Love I received from my family, the Hell I experienced on the streets, and me emerging Right after joining The Nation and changing my life. The more I used these principles and other teachings of The Nation, the more I began to grow.

After 16 months on Riker's Island, I was transferred to Downstate Correctional Facility. Spending most of my day alone in an empty cell provided me with a solitude that was foreign. I was a sociable person who was regularly busy with family, girlfriends, and comrades. My newfound solitude caused me to face myself and consciously begin my lifelong process of introspection. I thought of how Sha would always praise me for being smart, and how he was the first person I met who reveled in his own intellect. I wondered if my life would have been the same had I crossed paths with Sha before I became a player in The Game that's not a game.

As I was transferred from prison to prison, I met members of The Nation who were pivotal in my growth and development. Powerful Ruler Nation Allah taught me to write effectively through penning complaints that challenged the conditions of my imprisonment. Subsequently, I ventured into writing articles, editorials, essays, and fiction. Powerful Ruler Nation Allah also provided me with instruction on civil law and helped me file the lawsuit against DOCS on behalf of The Nation. After a federal trial in which I was victorious, members of The Nation are now provided certain constitutional protections while incarcerated in New York State. Divine Allah exposed me to litigating my criminal case, when I thought I had no recourse since I pled guilty. King Allah encouraged me to become health-conscious, by constant conversations and providing me with books on diet and nutrition. *African Holistic Health* was the book which led me to stop eating poultry and beef.

The more I learned externally from members of The Nation and the books they encouraged me to read, the more I began to develop internal discipline. I rid fish from my diet and stopped smoking weed. I had learned that nearly everything I consumed had an ill effect on me. Since I could not change everything I took in, I eradicated the worst things. I even stopped eating dairy products and eggs. To increase my willpower, I stopped eating sweets like pies, cookies, cakes, and junk food. I had begun exercising regularly. By stepping out of the pit of my lower desires, I elevated myself to higher levels of consciousness. Because I saw myself as God, I could not allow anything to have control over me.

I also began to reflect heavily on negative things I had done, because I had developed a respect for others. Although I was defending myself, I began empathizing with the deceased's family. I made a vow to be life-giving in my future endeavors and to control my destiny.

My sense of empathy also led me to be more understanding with other people's concepts of God, unlike my days as an atheist. I learned that everyone needs something from which to garner motivation and focus in life. For me it is The Nation. Your connection to the God of your choice is a personal one. I also recognized some life-giving principles found in many religions, and I apply some in my life. Just a year ago, my empathy also caused me to forgive the people who deserted me, because the prison walls had become a hurdle. I understand their positions and my responsibility for being in my predicament and all it entails.

I am constantly looking for new ways to elevate above my bodily desires and become more in tune with my higher self. Because knowledge is infinite, my journey will be life long. And I look forward to the possibilities that lie in the future.

Intelligent Allah is a graduate of the Writer's Digest School's Novel Writing Workshop. His writings have been published in books like *Classroom Calypso* and *The Immortal Birth*, as well as numerous websites. He has been contracted for copywriting by companies like Cinobe Publishing. He is the co-editor of books such as Wahida Clark's #1 National Best Selling novel *Thug Matrimony*. He is certified by the Department of Labor as a counseling aide, and has lectured to incarcerated people and civilians throughout his stay in numerous prisons in Upstate New York. He has also served in the leadership of prison organizations such as the NAACP Prison Branch, African Cultural Awareness Organization, and the Lifers' and Long-Termers' Organization.

THE GREATNESS IN MAN
Supreme Understanding Allah - Allah's Garden (Atlanta, GA)

"He who experiences the unity of life sees his own Self in all beings, and all beings in his own Self, and looks on everything with an impartial eye."- The Buddha

Do you realize there is a conscious intelligence that is running every system in your body right now? As you read this, this innate intelligence is ensuring the smooth operation of your body's 11 systems:

1. Circulatory system
2. Digestive system
3. Nervous system
4. Skeletal system
5. Reproductive system
6. Endocrine system
7. Immune system
8. Lymphatic system
9. Muscular system
10. Respiratory System
11. Urinary System

On Ghostface Killah's *Ironman* album, Popa Wu explains:

> See, some people don't have no direction God, because they don't know the science of they self. See, the science of life is the science of you – all the elements that it took to create you. Cause everything in the universe God - that created the universe God - exists within you. You see what I'm saying? And that's the mind that you can't see. Don't you know that if a man could take and flip himself inside out God, he'd fall out and die, if he sees the sh*t that goes on, inside?

This "mind that you can't see," this innate intelligence keeps your heart beating and your lungs breathing without you even having to think about it. How else could all those processes go on inside of you without a glitch? But there's nothing spooky about it. This intelligence is definitely within you. It's even within your control. You simply don't know about it. You see, there are actually five "stages" (or frequencies) to the mind: (1) Conscious,

(2) Subconscious, (3) Superconscious, (4) Magnetic Conscious, and (5) Infinite Conscious.

Most people are only aware of the base stage - their conscious thoughts. They are reminded of their subconscious thoughts when they dream at night or have fantasies, but even then they don't realize that their mind is functioning on more than one level. A computer works the same way. There are processes that happen on the desktop screen (like the program I used to type this book), and processes that happen in the background (like the computer managing its memory so it doesn't slow down while I type).

If you were to start investigating your subconscious thoughts, you could learn a lot about yourself. You could learn "what makes you tick" as they say. You could understand what you're REALLY thinking about or why you REALLY did something you did.

It's not that hard to do: It begins with looking past the basics, and asking questions like "Why?" about everything. If you ask yourself what everything means, even the little things you do, you'll begin to see clearly in no time. Unfortunately, most of us function solely on the conscious level: satisfying our most basic needs (food, clothing, shelter, sleep, and sex). We don't know why people (including us) do what they do, nor do we try to learn and find out. I'm hoping you're not like that, because I'm about to take you deep into the rabbit hole.

Remember that conscious intelligence that runs every system in your body without pause? Remember how I said that intelligence is within you?

"O Lord, our Lord, how majestic is Your name in all the earth,
who have displayed Your splendor above the heavens!" - Psalms 8:1

Think about the following:
The spiral found in the human fingerprint is the same spiral found everywhere throughout nature, from a common shell to the shape of our galaxy. The human brain cell is structured almost exactly like the structure of our universe.

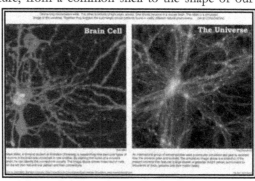

The Earth's surface is 75% water, the human body is 75% water, and the human brain is 75% water. And just as the most powerful natural forces on the Earth (and in the universe) involve electricity and magnetism, your body has its own magnetic field, and your brain operates using electricity.

It takes the same amount of time for blood to circulate from your heart throughout your body as it does for light to travel from the Sun to the Earth (8 minutes, 20 seconds). Melanin, the chemical substance that gives you your skin color is present in the brain as neuromelanin, and throughout the blackness of space. Carbon, a black element, is fundamental to all life…and your melanin.

Religious people often look at the birth process as proof of a miracle-working unseen God. God IS in the details, but is - as the Qur'an describes - "nearer to you than your jugular vein." In a woman's body, the egg can be found in only one fallopian tube at a time. A man's sperm, upon reaching the woman's uterus, consciously decides which way to turn, and picks the correct path 90% of the time. This sperm has almost nothing in it, except DNA. That's your mind still at work. Why do you think you get tired when she's the one pregnant? A human fetus then progresses through several stages, which resemble the different points in human evolution, once again reminding us of the brilliance of our design.

"As above, so it is below" - Ancient Egyptian maxim

The Ancient Egyptians understood all this, which is why they reached the highest level of development any civilization had seen at the time. While the Europeans were still living in caves, these Black men and women were building pyramids that folks still can't build today! In fact, the three pyramids of Giza are arranged in the exact same orientation as the stars in Orion's belt, and the Great pyramid lies in the exact center of the earth's landmass. The height of the Great pyramid is almost exactly one-billionth of the distance from the earth to the sun. The perimeter of the Great pyramid divided by two times its height equals Pi up to the fourteenth digit. In Europe, Pi was not calculated accurately to the fourth digit until the sixth century A.D. And these ancient Egyptians studied a system of symbolic mathematics as well, so our science is nothing new. These mathematical laws were seen as governing the structure and development of the universe.

"God wrote the universe in the language of mathematics." - Galileo

And who is the author of these mathematical laws? The same ones who'd eventually rediscover them. Us. In the ancient Egyptian "mystery schools," the students were taught that man was God on Earth, and trained in methods to unlock this great potential. In fact, every god, in every ancient religion's scripture, has been described as a great man, and often specifically as a Black man. As it reads in a 1981 issue of the 5% periodical titled *The Black Family*:

God is the highest extent of the mind. And energy and matter is the medium through which he expresses his ideas. And the black physical body of the Original man (the first) is the SUPREME medium. In other words, the amassment of elements…which comprise the physical body of the Original man, is the only vehicle in the universe through which (in all its essence) the great mind in the universe, in any and all ramifications and manifestations, manifested in the character or nature of the Original man.

What is my point in telling you all of this? I want you to look deeper within. Because if you can fathom that there is more to your mind and body than what happens on a conscious level, you can fathom that the same intelligence running your body is also running the planets. That same intelligence, again, is within you.

Get it yet? Think of the mind that designed the universe as an infinite, timeless consciousness. Think of that consciousness as a sea of water. If you take a cup of that water, the water in the cup has all of the properties of that vast sea. Nothing is missing. It's not about quantity. It's about quality. You have all the qualities of that supreme intelligence in your mind. Whether you tap into it is up to you. As I said, most of us function at the lowest level of consciousness for most of our lives. Some of us step up to a higher level. It begins with making the conscious decision to look deeper and see things from a higher plane. Can you get there? (For more like this, check out *The Science of Self*, coming Fall 2011)

Supreme Understanding is a former juvenile delinquent, selfish bastard, and chain-smoking drunk. Supreme received knowledge of self at age 15, after being kicked out of high school. Studying 120 degrees revived Supreme's interest in education. Since then, he obtained a Bachelor's degree in World History, a Master's in Urban Education, several certifications, and - at age 26 - a Doctorate in Education, focusing his research on the benefits of non-formal education (like what occurs among the 5%) with at-risk youth and other disadvantaged populations. Since then, Supreme has given his life for the betterment of original people at home and abroad. Supreme's work has brought him to Ghana, Mexico, the Dominican Republic, India, Japan, Thailand, the Czech Republic, Austria, Germany, England, the Caribbean, and all over the United States. Supreme has presented on a variety of topics with organizations as diverse as the ACLU, the Hip Hop Thinks Leadership Summit, the International Conference on the Social Sciences, the Japanese Ministry of Education, the White Privilege Conference, and the U.S. Social Forum.

LOST IN THE WILDERNESS

Wyking Allah - Morocco (Seattle, WA)

Imagine yourself having been dropped in the middle of a jungle. You are now surrounded by wild animals and poisonous plants…and you're totally ignorant to this environment. What do you think your chances for survival are if you don't know an earthworm from a killer cobra, nor edible fruit from poisonous berries? What do you think your fate will be? Naturally, you are easy prey, as you don't have any means of protecting or preserving your life. Thus, your lack of knowledge is the biggest obstacle to your survival.

This is actually the reality of the world you live in. It's like a jungle and your job is to navigate and survive long enough to find whatever treasure may be found. However, there are hostile conditions, all kinds of predators and prey, plants that nourish and replenish and poisonous plants that take life. Your job is to distinguish one from another and to know who and what you are dealing with at all times.

First you must recognize and control the animal instincts in yourself. You are not an unthinking beast. Second you must know that every person you see with two eyes, two ears, a mouth, is not necessarily a functioning human being. Some ARE unthinking beasts. Your job is to observe the dominant characteristics of those you encounter and deal accordingly. Knowledge, wisdom and understanding are your best defenses. It's survival of the fittest, so you'll need to exercise your mind.

Picture a baby rabbit who hasn't yet been taught by the adult rabbits. What happens when a baby rabbit does not have knowledge of itself to know that it is a rabbit...and it begins to hang out with the wolf? Eventually, when the wolf gets hungry enough, that rabbit becomes breakfast, lunch or dinner. Not because the wolf doesn't "like" the rabbit, but because the nature of the wolf is to eat things like rabbits to survive. The first law of existence is self-preservation.

In order to preserve its own existence or survive, the rabbit must:

◆ Know its kind
◆ Identify threats to its existence
◆ Identify its historical enemy
◆ Avoid things that are destructive to its existence
◆ Avoid its natural enemy

These stories are meant to illustrate the importance of knowledge of self and "knowing the ledge" (awareness of what to do and what NOT to do). How do we learn how to navigate the jungle? How does the story of the rabbit apply to us?

An entrepreneur and educator, Wyking Allah is the founder and Chief Executive of Remix Marketing & Communications, LLC, a multi-service firm specializing in youth and cultural program development, urban marketing and event planning. In addition to his entrepreneurial ventures, Wyking has over 20 years experience in civic involvement, community service and youth development that spans from Seattle to New York. A strong advocate of community involvement and civic service, at age 21, he was runner-up for state representative in his home state of Washington. He has also served in membership, advisory and consultant capacities with a number of organizations and businesses. He is also a Green For All National Fellow. He is a founding director of the African American Heritage Museum and Cultural Center in Seattle, WA, presiding over its Youth Action Committee. For ten years, he has been President/CEO of the UmojaFest African Heritage Festival and Parade, the Pacific Northwest's longest running African-American community festival. In 2002, he founded the Seattle affiliate of Russell Simmons' New York-based Hip-Hop Summit Action Network, which works to educate and empower youth academically, culturally and economically through Hip-Hop. He is

BLACK GOD

Aikuan Allah - Cipherland (Oakland, CA)

The Black Man is God. The methods in which we express this fundamental aspect of our teachings is supported by our ideal of God. Once we have become aware of our true identity it's only natural to strive to be consistent with the best part of our character. On this particular road we adopt certain basic approaches that assist us in staying in tune. Consequently our Supreme Mathematics, and Supreme Alphabets are essential in navigating to the best and most useful part of any endeavor.

"When you know yourself, your "I-ness" vanishes and you know that you and God are one and the same." - Ibn Arabi (d. 1240 CE), also known as As Shayk Al Akbar (The Great Sheikh)

Once enlightened, it becomes more apparent that we have to be accountable, responsible and strive to make our environment more civilized. Also standing firm and not being easily influenced by the segment of the population whose ways and actions are ignorant and manipulative. This involves managing your power effectively and keeping your thoughts and emotions in check. Making excuses should no longer be reasons for lack of accomplishment or falling victim to poor judgment. The enlightened realize that the results we have in our lives are the sum total of the decisions we've made in the past. Therefore our future will be the result of the decisions we make today in the present.

"I am free from spite, arrogance and greed, I am God, I am God, I am God." - Farid-ud-Fin Attar (d. 1220 CE)

In order to travel the right path and get to where you want to be in life your God birth-right has to transcend into action. The realization of God as Self does little without God-Orderly-Direction. One of the ways to determine your God-Orderly-Direction is to determine the pros and cons of the decisions you make before taking action. The "pros" can be looked at as gas stations for your journey, while the "cons" can be seen as roadblocks or detours. The vehicle that is the best equipped will have a better chance to reach its destination, no matter the terrain. Having a positive mental attitude is paramount in having God-Orderly-Direction. I'm not advocating being so self-absorbed that you become detached from reality and not aware of the challenges that persist. What I am saying is find time to reflect on your situation and be proud of your progress. Know that because you're doing what you set out to do your environment is becoming better.

The mind is consistently processing information in a way that moves us in particular directions. Even on the subconscious level, the mind is distorting, deleting, and generalizing. So, before the mind can work efficiently, we must get a clear understanding of what our determined idea will be. When the mind has a defined target, it can focus, direct, refocus, and redirect until it reaches its intended goal. If it doesn't have a defined target, its energy is wasted. It's like a person with the world's greatest voice who has no idea why he/she is in front of a microphone. What would happen if a sculptor changed their mind about what they were sculpting every five minutes? That's what it's like when you try to put your life together without having a determined idea. When you know what the outcome of your determined idea will be, you give your mind a clear picture of which kinds of information being received by the nervous system need high priority. You give your brain the clear messages it needs to be effective. Then you're able to make Knowledge Born!

Grab a sheet of paper and pencil and create your future. Don't even start unless you have allotted some time to do this exercise. Now find or create a place where you can relax and be undisturbed. Set aside at least an hour to do this. You'll agree that your future is worth the time. You're going to learn how to set goals and determined ideas. You're going to make a map of the roads you want to travel in your life. You're going to figure out where you want to go and how you expect to get there. **DO THE KNOWLEDGE:** Do not put any limitations on what's possible. You are the makers of your universe. It's your world! Remember, if you don't design your life your life will be the result of someone else's design without your best interest in mind.

EXERCISE 1

1. Set your determined idea in positive terms. Say what you want to happen. Too often we say what we don't want to happen. For example don't say, "I don't want to be broke anymore. Instead say, "I will do the necessary things to increase my wealth."
2. Be as specific as possible. How does your determined idea look, feel, smell? Become fully associated as if you already have accomplished your goal. The more specific you are the more you will empower your mind to create what you desire. Also be sure to set a completion date or time period.
3. Have an evidence procedure. Know how you will feel, and what you will see and hear after you have achieved your outcome. Once you have accomplished something check it off. Be passionate about it.
4. Be in control. Your determined idea must be initiated and maintained by you. It must not be dependent upon other people having to change themselves for you to be satisfied. Make sure your idea reflects things

you can affect directly. Own up to what goes right and wrong in your cipher. It is you that possess the power to Build or Destroy.

5. Verify that your outcome is ecologically sound. That is, project into the future the consequences of your actual goal. Your outcome must be one that benefits all the human families of the planet Earth.

EXERCISE 2

1. Make an inventory of your dreams, the things you want to have, do, be, and share. Keep your pen moving non-stop for at least 10 minutes. Don't define how you're going to get this outcome now. Just write it down. There are no limits! Abbreviate whenever possible so you can immediately get to the next goal. Let your mind run free. Everything is within your grasp. Knowing your outcome is the first key to reaching it.

2. Go over the list you made, estimating when you expect to reach those outcomes: six months, one year, two years, three, five, twenty. It is helpful to see what sort of time frame you can put on yourself. Some peoples lists are dominated by things they want now and some are dominated by long term goals. If long-term goals dominate your list, then develop steps to put you in the direction you need to go. A 1,000 mile journey begins with one step. Have vision.

3. Now pick your four most important goals for this year. Pick the things you are most committed to, excited about, and things that would give you the most satisfaction. Write down why you absolutely want to achieve each one of them. Be clear, concise, and positive. Remember that if your why is big enough your how will fall in place.

4. Now that you have a list of your four key goals, review them against your determined idea.

5. Next make a list of important resources you already have at your disposal. When you begin a construction project, you need to know what tools you have. To manifest your determined idea you need to do the same thing.

6. Now focus on times when you used some of those resources most skillfully. Come up with three to five times in your life when you were totally successful-in business, sports, building on a high powered degree, relationship etc. Be in that same state of mind.

7. Next, describe the kind of individual you have to be to obtain your goal. Will it take a great deal of discipline or education? Would you have to manage your time better? Write a couple of paragraphs or a page about all the character traits, skills, attitudes, discipline you will need to possess in order to achieve all you desire.

8. Take your four key goals and create your first draft of a step by step plan to achieve them. Ask yourself, "What do I have to do first to accomplish this goal. Or what prevents me from having this now, and what can I do to change this?" Make sure your plans include something

you can do today. Establish your God-Orderly-Direction. It's your world!

Aikuan Allah was Introduced to Supreme Mathematics on December 13, 1989 and became one of the first born in Oakland, California (Cipher Land). Aikuan is a Real Estate Developer, Entrepreneur, Music Producer, Shaolin Temple Kung Fu Student and Teacher, and a Kongo Zen and Qi Gong practitioner. Aikuan is also involved with the upcoming republication of the classic texts, *The Master Key System* and *The Kybalion*.

BLACK IS BEAUTIFUL

Supreme Understanding Allah - Allah's Garden (Atlanta, GA)
Based on an excerpt from *How to Hustle and Win, Part One*

Here's an activity for you. Look at the following pictures and figure out who is Black and who is not. The answers are below. Don't cheat!

ANSWERS

Who's Black? Don't they all *look* Black? In fact, the person who looks the *least* "Black" here is Nicole Richie…and as mixed up as she may be, she is still ethnically a Black person. That's why Paris Hilton called her a nigger you know! So who are these people?

A. South Indian girl	H. Emiliano Zapata, Mexican leader	P. Nicole Richie
B. Popular singer from Bangladesh	I. Filipino man	Q. Carlos Santiago, Puerto Rican Negro Leagues player
C. Moi tribal woman (Vietnam)	J. Brazilian man	
D. Native American man	K. Invisible Man.	R. Geronimo and other Apaches
E. Aeta tribal woman (Phillipines)	L. Andamanese Islanders (South-east Asia)	S. Baseball player from Panama
F. Indian holy man	M. Mexican man	
G. Austrialian Aborigines	N. Australian gang	
	O. Iraqi man	

Just think about this for a moment. Now, this is one of those topics that's dear to me: the global diversity of Blackness. Why? If you didn't already know, my family's from Bangladesh. So I'm technically Bengali, but I usually tell people I'm from India. That's for two reasons: (1) Some people don't know where on Earth Bangladesh is, and (2) Bangladesh was part of India until the British came in and carved it up (along with Nepal, Kashmir, Pakistan, etc.). Anyway, I, like most "first generation" children of immigrants, rejected my parents' culture and did my best to immerse myself in what I thought was "American" culture. Where I lived, that led me to the streets. I didn't know better. In fact, I didn't start researching my heritage until I got knowledge of self. That's when I learned that my family name (*Das*) actually meant "black-skinned slave" and came from the whites who invaded India 4,000 years ago. I started digging deeper after that. The Gods had been telling me that I was Black, or Original, for a minute now, and I'd always thought they'd meant it in a "You're okay with us" kinda way…but that day it all started making sense.

BLACKS IN CHINA?

Sincere Justice Allah - Cipher Land (Oakland, CA)

Growing up as a first generation Chinese male in a traditional Chinese family, I always heard my family and relatives use the term *Heigui*, or "Black Devils/Ghosts," when referring to Black people.

So I know that if you're Chinese and you're reading this, you probably don't identify with being Black to begin with, but that's okay because after you hear what I have to say, your concept of self may begin to change.

"Chinese male" is how I'm usually classified. However, to be exact, I'm an Original Black Man…and I'm God. Let me explain. I'm Original (Black) because the Chinese are direct descendants of the first people on Earth. According to a *Los Angeles Times* article, "Chinese Roots Lie in Africa" by science writer Robert Lee Hotz, an analysis of thirty microsatellite markers across twenty-eight different Chinese population groups (who made up ninety percent of the population) showed that they were "descendants of a single population group that may have migrated into China from the south eons before humans learned to forge metal tools or use a written alphabet…It is now probably safe to conclude that modern humans originating in Africa constitute the majority of the current gene pool in East Asia." So are the Chinese Original? Are the Chinese Black?

If the above research confused you, simply look at the image below. Who's Black? Look at the similar facial features, such as the nose and lips. Who decides who's who? In fact, did you know there are Blacks in China, even to this day? According to M. Dujon Johnson, in his book, *Race and Racism in the Chinas: Chinese Racial Attitudes towards Africans and African Americans* there are indigenous Blacks in present day Guangdong and Macau.

Chinese attitudes towards Blacks weren't always prejudiced or xenophobic. A lot of that is the byproduct of China's interactions with "other" foreigners - namely, Europeans. In fact, the "devil" term was first applied to incoming whites. After enough bad experiences with foreign forces, China became xenophobic. However, with the persistent Western influence (through television and other imports), the Chinese learned how to be racist. However, it wasn't always this way. Ancient historical records

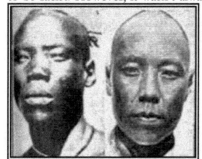

reveal a healthy pattern of trade and cultural exchange between China and East Africa. Some of the ancient respect for Blackness can still be seen in traditional Chinese opera, where "a black face or darker features meant a rough, bold or noble character and a person of courage, righteousness and incorruptibility, or an impartial and selfless personality." Conversely, a white face indicated that the character was "…a powerful villain. The color white is the trait that highlights all that is bad in human nature: cunning, craftiness, deceit and treachery."

Now, this concept might be even harder for you to wrestle with: the Chinese man as God. This too, is our historical legacy. During the *Shang* and *Zhou* dynasties, the veneration or worship of a High God known as *Di* was very popular. In addition, the Shang kings were known as Shang Di, which literally means 'the lord above.' According to Clyde Winters, the first Shang King was called *Xuan Wang*, which meant "Black King" and alternatively as *Xuan Di*, which meant "Black Emperor" or "Black God." The high positions of a king or emperor sure resemble God to me. The connection between you and the king is the same – they're both human. So do you see how the Chinese are Original…and God?

'I was born Black, I live Black, and I'm gonna die Black,
probably because some cracker that knows I'm Black - better than YOU…

The truth is that we have much more in common as Original People (people of color) than we think. Our "divided" mentality comes from years of conditioning and colonization. One of the ways we can find commonality comes from our universal oppression by - and our collective struggles against - the system of White Supremacy, both in our homelands and here in America. Let's just take a look at some of injustices throughout history experienced by our people in the U.S.: the Chinese Exclusion Act, the internment of the Japanese, the terrorism of the Dot Busters against the South Asian community, the Zoot Suit Riots experienced by Mexicans in Los Angeles, the Trail of Tears amongst so-called Native Americans, and the recent Islamophobia experienced by Middle Easterners, just to name a few! Of course, even Whites like the Irish initially experienced discrimination in America in the 1800s. However, as White became a social construct among those of European descent, even the Irish (and other "lower" Europeans) where granted White Privilege, which meant that opportunities for upward mobility that people of color did not have the same access to. Meanwhile, with us beneath them, these formerly despised groups now had someone to pick on with their new allies. Thus, this ideology of White Supremacy served (and continues to serve) to keep the status quo in place. Basically this means rich whites stay rich, while most of us Original People stay poor on a global scale – poorly represented in the media, poor access to food and health care, poor economically, and poor in regards to a culturally relevant education.

In order to realize a better world for all of us, we as, Original People must come together to see an alternative reality to come to life. A few examples of these collective struggles include:

♦ The Black Panthers' alliances with the Young Lords, the Red Guard, and the I Wor Kuen

♦ General Takahashi of Japan's work with The Nation of Islam

♦ Marcus Garvey and Robert F. Williams' alliances with Chinese President Mao Tse Tung and Vietnamese Leader Ho Chi Minh

♦ Che Guevara's revolutionary solidarity with people throughout Latin America and Africa

♦ Hugo Chavez' attempts to unify people of color throughout Latin America, the Middle East, Asia, and Africa

♦ The Nation of Gods and Earth's consolidation of the "Black, Brown, and Yellow seeds" as Original people, reflected in a teaching that empowers people of all ethnic groups.

In order for us to make great changes as a people, we must begin identifying with and acting in the interest of ALL of our people. We must begin restructuring our lives in terms of politics, economics, health, and culture. So will you, as a person of color, continue identifying with the ideology of White Supremacy (the Devil) or will you live in with your people's best interest in mind?

Sincere Justice is a 22-year-old graduate of the University of California, Santa Cruz with a Bachelor of Arts in Community Studies. Professionally, his work is split between working with the Children of Chiapas Foundation and the Asian Prisoners' Support Committee. Since acquiring the knowledge of himself at 19, he has been exposed to an array of world perspectives and has developed a strong interest in understanding the cross-cultural connections between Original People. Sincere is co-author of an upcoming ebook titled *The Black Chinese: Ancient and Modern Connections between Blacks and China*.

SOMOS ORIGINALES
(WE ARE ORIGINAL)
Sha-King Cehum Allah - Power Born (Pittsburgh, PA)

Historically, the merging of the African and Indian is what brought forth the reality of the so-called "Latino." For the two centuries being labeled a 'tri-racial peoples,' a cosmic combination consisting of African, Indian and Spanish (European) blood, the focus has always been put on the 'Spanish' lineage. Due to this cultural conditioning, association with the 'lighter' or that which is seen as closer to 'white,' whilst rejecting 'blackness' as a 'sin' of inferiority. While there are many black and brown 'Latinos' and Native Americans, a large segment of our population is 'yellow.' This has been exploited by our oppressors towards a lack of understanding of who we really are. This acquisition and merger of Native and African culture and people is not solely the result of slavery and stands as a testament to who we are, beyond the Spanish interjection and inference. The Spanish have a role in our history and culture from language to religion, but are not the anchor for our identity. We are the Original people on this part of the planet earth - *Nativos y Africanos*. One people.

Many Native Americans/Latin Americans have the misconception that the mixing of African and Indian was something that was primarily characteristic of the Caribbean, South and Central America, and the U.S. South, as the result of chattel slavery. Archeological and anthropological research from Mexico, the Caribbean and South America reveal Africans were traveling to the Americas, trading and building with the Native peoples prior to Columbus' arrival. This travel also existed in North America, chronicled in centuries old tribal stories, like those of the *Anishnabe/Chippewa* and the tale of *Neganii* and *Abukar.* Upon the advent of chattel slavery, the merging continued with settlements throughout North, Central and South America. These interactions verify the forging together of a new cultural identity prior to slavery. It is the foundation for Elijah Muhammad's use of the term in 'Original Nation' in reference to the collective African-Indian population in America. The assumptive perspective behind this merging as solely political limits our understanding, elevated consciousness and existence. We are literally one people, the Original people.

It was the *conquistadores* of "*Espana*," themselves of questionable ethnic origin, who promoted a 'one drop' theory of whiteness, clearly in sharp contrast to North America's 'one drop' of Black blood making one 'Black.' This mental framework subdued the masses of African and Native people, seizing their identity as they raped and pillaged our women, replacing our self-esteem with obligations to the crown and church. New nationalistic labels of identification were instituted as the countries of the Americas eventually fought for and obtained independence from Spain and other European empires. These new labels forced us to identify with our oppressor and unite under 'his' common cause.

Examination of labels such as *mestizo, mulatto, zambo, pardo,* and *triguena,* etc., initially conceived to divide, would eventually give way to nationalism. The Latin American independence movement, primarily headed by intellectuals and elites, sought independence from Spain, with the rallying cry of common oppression only to take on the same role. The commonality of heritage used to tie those born in '*Las Americas*' and the '*Peninsulares*' (Iberian peninsula- Spain and Portugal) to the 'new land' became known as *Indigenismo.* It utilized the notion of the "Indians" as a novelty for claims of 'heritage' as opposed to ethnic or racial alikeness. It would later develop as a tool against the campaign of '*mestizaje*' or the 'whitening' of society, that took place during the mid to late 1800's and which still persists today. It was also a rallying cry for revolutionary figures as Augustino Cesar Sandino and Emiliano Zapata against the oppression of the ruling class. *Indigenismo* is a wonderful concept that unified the 'Americas,' yet the Euro-elite of the "Enlightenment" period of the 1800's opposed this idea with ferocity. It is they and their descendants, whom have plagued us with the label of being nothing more than a 'mixed raced people,' with no real point of origin. Owing ourselves and our livelihood to that 'Iberian connection,' a perspective which is ultimately termed '*hispanismo*.' And thus, the introduction and usage of the term 'hispanic.'

The terminology eventually manipulated non-European peoples into accepting an identity centered-around conquest. In lands colonized by English-speaking Europeans - Jamaica, Barbados, Antigua, etc., "England" was now their motherland. Today, our people freely refer to themselves as 'Hispanic' or "Spanish." Although we may continue to speak in the tongue of our conquerors, "Castillian" is not our original language. Still, many Spanish-speaking people are adamant about speaking the colonizers language, which allows us to relish in the desire to be other than our own selves. The manner in which someone speaks the language is considered a status of one's social and cultural status, as many countries pride themselves on speaking, what they consider to be, the closest to how it is spoken in Spain. Still, each Latin American country's dialect(s) is unique and is reflective of the Indigenous and African peoples that lived in those areas and very much a mirror of the suppressed identity of the people.

"Inside every mestizo there is either one dead Indian, or an Indian waiting to re-emerge."
- Jose Barreiro, Guajira-Taino Scholar and Editor of 'Indian County'

To 'identify with the oppressor' is the goal of the imperial indoctrination and colonialism yet these empires have been built from our African and Indian blood and the subsequent bondage. Our kindled mentality to maintain their status quo prevents 'us' from reclaiming power over our own destinies. Historians, intellectuals and even government officials have often claimed that the 'Indians' in Latin America were all wiped out, especially in Cuba, Dominican Republic and Puerto Rico. This outrageous claim is far from the truth as history has been recorded by those who have conquered and pillaged.

This truism has fomented mockery on any legitimate reclaiming of Native ancestry, particularly Latin Americans. Making knowledge born (making information known) "we are the Original people." We are "*los indios,*" whether 'full-blood' or *mestizo* or *zambo*. The implications of this truth eventually displace European descendants from our land. The fear of this ensuing revelation can be seen in the reclassifying of race and ethnicity by the U.S. Census Bureau in 2000. By placing "Latinos" and "Hispanics" in the category of 'white,' it boosts their population numbers. This political move will have continued cultural consequences via the constant barrage of Euro-centric propaganda. The deliberate revisions come as whites are about to become the minority in their own country.

The "tricknowledge" of engulfing the minority into the majority has prior precedents. In 1846 after the United States 'stole' the Republic of Texas from Mexico calling it an "annexation." The majority of white settlers in Texas were slave holders and the U.S. government feared that revenge would be taken by the Mexicans and the other Original people who resided there. To prevent an uprising they classified "Mexicans" as "white" (despite their overwhelming Indian bloodline), a label which continued to appear on Texan birth certificates until the 1960's. "*Mexica*" is actually the name of the people we refer to as the 'Aztecs.' The 'Aztec" was conjured up by historians due to their proposed ancient homeland "*Aztlan*"- Southwestern U.S. Regardless to one's actual skin color, there is much more in their bio-chemical make-up that constitutes who they are. Someone may appear 'white,' but they aren't. There are light-skinned "people of color," and their 'blood' and DNA bears witness. As Original people, we range from very dark to very light. However, many remain confused due to how we were/are miseducated with saturated notions of "Spain' and Europe, yearning to be other than our own selves.

The people who descend from the lands of so-called Latin America have a color complex. Many of us still think that "white is right." We continue to link our reality back to a population and culture who are un-alike us, simply because of language, religion, and certain elements of our traditions. Many of us actually believe the lies and think that we are "Spanish," in spite of our latent embrace of '*indigenismo*.' We have been taught that we have Indian in us but we aren't Indian. We have been told that we have African in us but that we aren't African. We end up psychologically 'riding the fence' and making racial selections to suit our needs in society. Still, by the hand of the oppressor, *indigenismo* ended up only being a buffer to keep from being called "black." While it has been documented that 85% of Dominicans have black blood, Carol Amoruso, editor of the *Hispanic American Village*, in her series entitled "Explorations in Black and Tan" noted: "At the same time, a great number of Dominicans still reject their blackness." In an article I wrote for the *Hispanic American Village* in 2002, I interviewed Dominican aestheticians, specialists in hair relaxing, proud of their ability to make black seem white. Observed one:

> We do not say that we are black. We invent a lot of names for our skin, like indio claro, indio lava[d]o or indio canela, but never black. So, the idea is to make you look white if you are black. They teach us that in the Dominican Republic.

Indigenismo has been a double-edged sword. While unifying in many ways, it has been used at the hands of the elites to reshape 'Latin American' society in their particular image and taste. They purported that the average everyday Latino was a '*mestizo*,' a 'mixture' of Spanish, Indian and African. However, this perspective was adopted to create a false sense of 'equality' throughout society and served their purposes as a compliment to nationalism, attempting to erase any evidences or situations that could potentially spark future revolutions and revolts. The 'Indian-ness' of *indigenismo* served to distinguish between being looked at as 'white' and being looked at as 'black,' which was far worse for the intellectual overseers. Once formulated, this concept was then packaged in the form of literature and sent out to penetrate the mindset of the people. Yet all the while, telling the masses of Indian/African people that the majority of Indians died out or had mixed with the Africans so much that no one was actually 'Black' or

'African' or 'Indian' anymore. And thus, Carol Amoruso, also noted in her series about recent immigrants to the United States: "The new Latinos come mostly from the Latin American mainland where the culture is more "indio" and European." Most people from countries such as Mexico, Peru or El Salvador will claim to have "no black in them" when this is far from the truth. Nowadays, biologically speaking, while most people who are so called Puerto Rican, Dominican or Cuban have Indian, African and European blood, so do many other people throughout the Caribbean, Central and South America. The presence of Afro-Indio culture and blood has always been very abundant, even after the decimation of the people, especially population wise. On page 29 of *Black Indians*, author William Loren Katz states: "By 1650 Mexico alone had an African-Indian population (some with white ancestry) of one hundred thousand. A new race was being born."

Many *Mexica* continue the propaganda that Mexicans are not 'Black,' and that only certain towns and neighborhoods have "black blood." Through media, we look over these people as 'Mexicans,' not aware of their unique history. They too, have had considerable amounts of African blood infused into them, although they may contest it. Especially *mi gente* from *Cuscatlan* or as the devil now calls "El Salvador." Descendants of the *Pipil* peoples, who are actually of the *Maya, Salvi's* or *Salvadorenos* have been institutionally and systemically conditioned to think they are different from Africans and have no African blood in them. They have been the victims of a vicious campaign, similar to that which took place in the Dominican Republic under Presidente Rafael Trujillo when he made every effort to 'whiten' society by killing thousands of Haitians and reducing the African presence in the Dominican Republic down to a myth. This is truth, not a conspiracy theory, and far from a mere political ploy to 'unite' the two groups of Original people under false bonds for the benefit of bi-partisan struggle. Many brothers and sisters who are Indigenous and are of the Pan-Indigenous Diaspora actually exist within the African Diaspora as well. With this truth in mind, while someone may choose to embrace one people over the other (usually due to upbringing or life experience), we must strive to embrace both, as both peoples are who we are.

It is very important to understand our relationship to each other and that we are really all one family - we are all of the 'Black family.' We, however, exist within distinct degrees when judged by our melanin expressed through the skin organ, which we call 'shades of black' within the Nation of Gods and Earths, defined as: black, brown and yellow. "Black" is typically seen as just a 'color' and most often associated with 'skin' color, but it isn't a stagnant or fixed idea. It is dynamic. What is "Black" in social standards varies with countries and cultures to be sure, which is the reason why so many so-called Latinos are reluctant to embrace the term. We also must look at the world and universe around us. Do not be blinded by the illusion of the daytime, for even our ancestors knew that the universe and space is black. The illumination of the Sun was born out of the blackness of this space and subsequently everything else in the universe and our solar system. The first organism of our intellectual and social capabilities to manifest presence on our planet, human being, has been recognized in science and anthropology as "black." This does not mean that we're 'as' black as the universe, but a manifestation, in the physical degree, and a supreme embodiment of the sub-atomic intelligence that drives energy through its different forms and brings forth life and matter. The word 'black' has more of a political connotation for us as human beings, especially nowadays, so someone who is referred to as 'Black' isn't literally 'black.' And within the Nation of Gods and Earths we use it to define all people of color, regardless of their shade, as a term of solidarity and reverence for our common origin, whether cosmic or in terms of civilizations. Still, in the mainstream, Puerto Ricans (along with other so-called Latinos) who assert our Blackness are not only outcast by those who identify more so with their Spanish conqueror than their African ancestors, but are also shunned by so-called African Americans who do not see us as 'Black.' Regardless whether someone is Navajo, Quechua, Mandinga, Ghanaian, or even Hmong or Pinoy, they are "Black."

It has been the traditional perspective, of the Nation of Gods and Earths, of Latinos as being 'Native American' and the Original owners of the Americas, but in no way limits us solely to that category. Nor is it to blanket someone's individual history in favor of the collective identity, as some forms of Pan-Africanism often do, attributing any and everything to the greatness of Africa alone. It is a perspective that links us all to an underlying factor, a common point of reference. It is a rallying cry to all my Indigenous brothers and sisters. A rallying cry of unity and solidarity, as expressed through the understanding of Allah and his will to unite 'all the seeds' (shades of the Original man).

The Nation of Gods and Earths embraces all Original people by tearing down the labels of nationalism and tribal identity that create barriers, and bring everyone together for one common cause: education and elevation of our quality of living. It is this perspective that speaks to so-called Latinos, not from a nationalist standpoint, but from a reality that harkens back further than 'Latin Nationalism.' It goes beyond state established boundaries and ties us all into a shared history of ancestral memories. It is not merely the product of intellectuals but a perspective taken on by many Native peoples through the documented history of the Americas. Tecumseh, of the Shawnee, sought to unite all nations and tribes, under one common Pan-Indigenous identity, in attempts to resist and prevent the westward expansion of the 13 American colonies and the genocide against the Original people. He traveled from his home in the Ohio River valley, down south to Cherokee country, amongst the Chickasaw and Seminole, and even westward a bit until he voyaged back north to Prophet's town (the city that he and his brother established as the center of their mission).

It is in this same vein and vision that we need to unite all those of Latin American descent. We need to unify and create solidarity beyond our country borders and ethnic prejudices. It is up to us - the Original people, the black, brown and yellow sons and daughters of the Americas, to re-establish who we are and what belongs to us, especially our birthright. We must be determined in the fight for the freedom to define ourselves in today's society. We must reclaim our place amongst our Black brothers and sisters worldwide, as we are Black men and women. *Somos las personal Originales del Planeta Tierra!*

Sha-King Cehum Allah is a writer/researcher of Native American, Caribbean and Latin American history and culture, as well as a community activist, loving father and dedicated member of the Nation of Gods and Earths. He is working on an upcoming book addressing topics related to the above essay. His blogs can be read at indios.blogspot.com and yellowseed.blogspot.com

FROM HERU TO "HOW YOU DOIN?"
THE DESTRUCTION OF MASCULINE BLACK MEN
Beautiful SeeAsia – New Ark (Newark, NJ)

My favorite Eddie Murphy movie was one of his earliest films, *Beverly Hills Cop*. Eddie didn't put on an Academy Award winning performance (although the film was nominated at the 1985 Golden Globe Awards for best comedy, and grossed over 200 million dollars at the box office), nor was the film Oscar material, but I liked it because he appeared so comfortable in his character. But as I've gotten of age, watching the DVD over and over again, I've noticed what once went over my head: Him having to act like a homosexual throughout the movie. As a matter of fact, Eddie's personality was "femininely-influenced" in several ways, especially in comparison to his masculine mannerisms in earlier films such as *48 Hours* and *Trading Places*. There is an evident distinction between the three films, showing how Eddie changed, not just as an actor but certainly also as a man. An actor is a man first and, in my perception, it takes a change in the man for a change in the actor to take place, at least in terms of the roles he will accept. And do you remember who played a homosexual server giving Eddie a banana to stuff in the "tail" pipe of his fellow police officers in the movie *Beverly Hills Cop*? It was fellow comedian Damon Wayans making his first film debut!

This is no coincidence that two Black men, early on in their careers, were playing homosexuals. Hollywood has been on the afro-homosexual mandate for years when it comes to Black men. And if the old heads can recall, this didn't start with Eddie Murphy's acting career. I am certain that, for as long as there's been film and television, the Black man has had to make an absolute coon of himself by portraying a woman, but in my lifetime this started with actor Antonio Fargas playing a homosexual named "Lindy" in the 1976 film, *Car Wash*. There's even a scene where Antonio gets into a debate with a masculine, militant revolutionary character named Abdul, played by actor/director Bill Bradley.

The laundry list pertaining to the feminization of the Black man in Hollywood is too long to continue. But here's where it saddens me most: When we have started to accept these characters so much that it has been formally labeled a form of comedy. It proves how sick we've become with the acceptance of our men acting as women, to the point where it is forgotten that he, the tranny actor, is actually a man when without the wig, dress and make-up. The seed planted deeper when Martin Lawrence played "ShaNayNay" in the 1990's on his show *Martin*. But in the new millennium, Tyler Perry's character "Madea" has made it obvious that the seed has blossomed into a field of weeds.

The psychological damage started decades ago, with subtle inserts of a Black man with spurts of a swinging hand, growing into an entire movie of a brother in a woman's dress and wig. The subliminal poisons have been pacified into the excuses of comedy and church.

Television is a psychological process of programming. This is why words like "program" and "broadcast" are used within the media industry. Although these words appear to be nouns, in the media world they are actually used as VERBS. "Program" means to set, regulate or modify a specific response or reaction. "Broad" means a large range or a great extent, which refers to the range of the audience it reaches. "Cast" means to form or to cause. All of these words align themselves with a form of manipulation. Therefore, our subconscious has been manipulated with subtle imagery.

Because of this hypnosis, you now have our men - from Hollywood to the high schools - in full feminine swing. Black women now have to compete with Black males for "Best Dressed" in senior yearbooks. And the male that wins is not dressed in masculine attire these days either. Almost anywhere you go now, when you call your local hair salon to book your next hair appointment, you are likely to be answered by a deep voice. It is guaranteed that on every college campus you'll see a Black man in extra tight "skinny jeans," earrings in both ears (and not on some tribal sh*t either), and possibly a little eye liner. I knew we were affected when I went to H&M department store in Manhattan and saw young Black males shopping on the women's side for themselves. It was seriously evident that the feminization seed had been planted deeply in the consciousness of our people.

Slavery has posttraumatic mental illnesses that severely affect us even today, due to the trauma of generation-to-generation torture. Also, the engineering of our foods certainly doesn't help the crisis within us either. Genetically Modified Organisms (GMO) foods, DNA manipulated by scientists (no more farmers), can absolutely destroy the natural character of a human being. Other chemicals (such as BPA, phthalates, and NEPs) also disrupt and alter hormone production. These chemicals have been factually proven to manipulate the hormones of human beings, whether that is D-cup breasts on 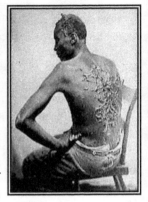 an eleven year old girl or a sixteen year old boy lusting after the star football player.

For the Black man and woman of today, comparing our present conditions to our ancestral lifestyle shows that we are living in a foreign culture that is destroying our bloodline from the greatness of antiquity daily. Our ancestors did not become the legends of yesterday through the bestiality we have been reduced to today. We are all guilty of contributing to this bizarre new world. The Asiatic (African) mind has been broken by all the heinous experiences committed from the Eastern to the Western seas. The acts of molestation and rape of young Black boys was demonstrated in one the realest films about slavery, *Farewell Uncle Tom*, which debuted in 1972.

Cecil Rhodes, father of De Beers' diamond and mining company in Africa, prided himself on predatory practices such as the ravaging of African villages using rape and molestation as a tool of colonialism. And he was gender-specific with the anal and oral torture of young African boys.

The dehumanization of the Black man dates back to his association with the European. The European male-to-male experience in Greece, Rome, Portugal, etc., was enforced on the people they conquered and enslaved. That tradition then seeped into the traditions of the oppressor's religion, and now into the ritual of his forms of communication and media.

The Civil Rights era staged the trick that would ultimately destroy us decades later. The trick was called integration, which taught us to become the defense system for the oppressor and his forms of trick-knowledge, including homosexuality. Our desperation to be accepted and one with our cultural enemies became the knives in the backs of our ancestors, who died for us to be separate from him. Our gratitude to the martyrs of Black Nationalism comes in the form of a man with false eyelashes wearing a fluorescent thong.

Therefore, when the universal justice takes its form in the sword and served with such fury to the necks of the ingrates, I will be one of the few to not fall on the ground in tears but to step over each head and keep it moving.

EM-POWER-U
Mecca Wise Understanding - Allah's Garden (Atlanta, GA)

Tiffany always had a hard time saying "no." When she was just thirteen years old she had her first sexual experience. She tried to say no...all she knows is that she left feeling abused and ashamed. This was her first recollection of being taken advantage of, but certainly not her last. Males and females alike always seemed to have her doing things that she never wanted to do or didn't totally feel comfortable with. She sort of just went with the flow, never really having her own agenda.

She thought back to her many casual sexual experiences, in cars, alleyways, garages, and playgrounds to name a few. All of those interactions were short lived. And remember she never really wanted to. She thought making 'them' happy just might make her happy or at least make them want, accept, or value her. And although those interactions didn't last very long some of their effects did. There were the psychological ones from those two abortions, the emotional ones from the STDs, and the physical ones from the two children that were conceived. The fathers were never heard from again.

She thought about the obsession that she has with food. She had been off and on diets since age ten and had never been secure with her body. She felt her breasts were too small, and her butt was not round or plump enough. She couldn't fathom this was a part of the reason why she let men have their way with her.

She thought going to the club every weekend would satisfy her. She spent most of her paycheck on weave, makeup, and outfits. She just had to find the perfect jeans that would make her ass look more appealing, only to find herself in those similar short lived interactions.

She thought that she had found the right 'one' with Rick. She felt that he completed her. And although he was abusive, insensitive, and had many affairs she felt that she needed him. She didn't know when or how to let go, or who else would ever love her.

Somewhere along the road she picked up a cigarette habit…a weed habit…and an alcohol habit. She even tried stripping at a local adult club…where she nearly picked up a worse drug habit. Many times she felt alone, with no one to talk to, being that she never seemed to get along with other women. Once she even contemplated suicide.

Tiffany couldn't figure out why she always ended up with the same kind of men, in the same situations, with the same kind of drama. She didn't want to accept the fact that it was no one's fault but her own.

Tiffany's story isn't very unique. Does it sound familiar? Ladies, can we accept the fact that some parts of Tiffany belong to us?

♦ Many females suffer from low self esteem which leads to destructive behaviors like unprotected casual sex and drug and alcohol abuse.

♦ Many females are no stranger to unhealthy or abusive relationships/attachments.

♦ Many females are unhappy/ insecure with their body image.

♦ Many females exploit themselves.

♦ Many females feel their value is based on sexual appearance/skills.

♦ Many females are riddled with the guilt, worry, fear, and regret enabling them to move forward in life.

Here are some possible solutions:

Since change starts within us, we must begin to love and appreciate ourselves and our sisters. Many of us have the same struggles and fears. Realize we are powerful and beautiful. Set boundaries in relationships with everyone, whether male or female. If you don't value you, then who will? Realize that we are so much more than sexual beings. Pursue meaningful relationships of longevity based on values and strong foundations. Look at what we want to change about ourselves, whether *mentally or physically*. The changes won't occur overnight, but even small steps will help us reach our goals. Have confidence in ourselves and the courage to overcome our fears. Changing our minds isn't easy but it is the first step to *changing our lives*.

Women, are we willing to break the cycle, change our thoughts, use our brain power vs. our sexual power, learn the beauty of who we really are, start a new journey, and get the knowledge of ourselves? Let us begin.

Mecca Wise Understanding, a proud mother of two, is a native of Pittsburgh, Pennsylvania (Power Born). She is a graduate of the University of Pittsburgh, with a bachelor's in Psychology. She is coauthor of Revolutionary Love, an upcoming book on relationships with Supreme Understanding, Stic.man of Dead Prez and Afya Ibomu. She currently serves as CFO for Supreme Design Publishing. (FYI She's not Tiffany...it's called "fiction")

VANILLA IS BLACK
Faatma Behesht Earth - Divine (Denver, CO)

It's true y'all...Vanilla is BLACK.

Native to Mexico and commonly produced in Tahiti and Madagascar, it was originally called *Tlilxóchitl* by the Aztec peoples, which means BLACK Flower.

Is this an essay about white girls? Definitely not...Yet it may have something to do with my dissatisfaction with the misuse of Vanilla to refer to white women...because why? Because Vanilla is BLACK....It may also be about that misunderstanding of my complexion that leads people to think my lineage is white??? What the f*ck?

Is this an essay about understanding soil (light skinned original women)? Maybe...it could be a conversation about how some understanding soil can (sadly) label themselves as white because they may not know who they are...It's true y'all...Vanilla is BLACK.

Everyone has a story, I know...for those of us immigrant sisters who are light-skinned indigenous peoples, we have one too...usually involving a struggle with traditions old and new and trying to find self while walking the fine line between the ancient and so-called modernity...a lot of experimentation within and without cultures...and at some point rebellion in some form or fashion from old tradition and then the same rebellion from modernity...

My Iranian ass is most definitely displaced...For a long time I just had to tuck the thought away that I was born in the wrong class of people (working class that is) and the wrong culture (so-called Persian). What's interesting is that many so-called Persians who come to this country came as refugees...they were supporters of the Shah or the children of supporters. These families generally have OLD money, and brought it with them, mostly to LA to implant themselves (and get implants) creating what they now call *Tehrangales* (Tehran + Los Angeles = Tehrangales)

That's not how I got here. My lineage is working class. Romeo and Juliet type sh*t brought my parents together and Heroin and its popularity brought my family here...just months before the revolution. Addiction, prison, food stamps, government cheese, canned meat, ghetto public schools, second hand everything and I forgot how to speak Farsi by the time I was 7, even tho' it was my first language.

Vanilla is sooo black…

It wasn't called the black flower for its petals, which are pale yellow (like some of us)…it was instead highly sought after for its pods which become black after they are *properly cultivated*…hmmmmm.

I know many, many immigrant sisters who take the synthetic vanilla road… because they can "pass," they attempt to assimilate into popular white culture, dying their hair blond, getting blue contacts, and starving themselves to fit into the parameters of western European modernity…the result of this is a lifelong façade that ends in exotic bitterness…synthetic vanilla is derived from ethanol…nothing natural about it…and is made to seem other than itself, is cheaper to acquire and the quality is far inferior to the original, which is true of all things extracted from original and all things synthetic that emulate the original.

I did it too in my own rebellious way…well I didn't come up in the suburbs…and when I was comin' up, punk rock kids like me didn't live in the suburbs either (and please don't get punk rock confused with new wave)… tho' many of them did however grow up to be stockbrokers and stay-at-home moms who drive Volvos and take their kids to drama class at the age of 3 (maybe that's how working class white kids rebel against their circumstances).

I was an oddball immigrant, who didn't have a home in my own country (because it became the Islamic republic of blah blah blah) and didn't have one here either (because I apparently represented the Islamic republic of blah blah blah)…and so I felt more at home with the deviants and criminals (who are always more honest about themselves than anyone else)…Punk rock was optimistic depression…social anarchy and socialist theory were such beautiful daydreams….

Well, it ended up being the same exotic bitterness, except now…I know Vanilla is Black, and that pretty much saved my life.

Vanilla is BLACK and let's not get this confused with African, which is also black, yet that's not what I'm buildin' on today…You may get it…you may not…you can ask me to clarify if you need me to…I will explain to the best of my abilities…just know this…Vanilla is Ancient…black, sweet, and essential to after dinner treats…

VANILLICADO PARFAIT
3 Avocados
3 second pour of Raw Agave Nectar
1.5 second pour of organic black vanilla
Puree (I know it's green…but Avocados are really Black, so don't sweat it)
Layers of Pecans or Almonds (or both)
Layer of fruit (I do strawberries, bananas and blueberries)
Eat it. It's good.

Faatma Behesht Earth (aka Faatma Mehrmanesh) has been actively studying with the Nation of Gods and Earths since 1998. She is a mother of three amazing children who are the driving force for how she moves in the world. Faatma is a certified Practical Herbalist, has studied Herbal Therapeutics, Wild Food Identification and Foraging, Food as Medicine, Nutrition, Horticulture and is a Master Community Gardener. She attended the Metropolitan State College of Denver where she pursued a degree in Fine Arts with an emphasis in Ceramics. Faatma co-owned and operated Karma Café, a Vegetarian Cafe in Denver, and is currently a Garden Leader with two community gardens in North East Denver, and is working at Delaney Community Farm. For more information about current projects visit www.solarlivity.com

"MISS INDEPENDENT"

SHATTERING THE ILLUSION
I Medina Peaceful Earth – Power Born (Pittsburgh, PA)

Ladies, sistas, and friends…This is some real talk that may shatter everything that you've been taught about who you are and your relationships to men. Some of you may not like what I'm gonna say, but I'm gonna say it anyway. (And if it really don't apply, let it fly)

Peace. My name is I Medina Peaceful Earth and I am a former "Miss Independent."

I grew up in a home where my mother was EVERYTHING (and to this day we are extremely close). My father was more of a weekend Dad (we'd spend time together on some weekends, he'd attend special events, but he was pretty hands off in terms of raising me). It was more than what a lot of people had but in retrospect, I know I needed more in terms of a father figure. But he could not give me what he did not have. I acknowledge that, have forgiven him, and love him for who he is today, and know that some of my inclinations come from him.

A few years ago, when I asked my mother what she wanted to be when she grew up, I expected a response dealing with a career aspiration. But her response surprised me. She said, "I always just wanted to be a good mother." And she was. She was such a great mother that growing up, I didn't really miss not having a father in the home (they divorced when I was a baby). Quite a few of my friends adopted her as their mother too. She cooked, she cleaned, she went to my games and special events, PTA meetings. She mentored me, encouraged me, scolded me, protected me, listened to me, talked with me. She made sure I was taken care of and educated so I would grow up to be a great woman.

A lot of who I am today comes from the environment my mother created and for that I say praises due. But there's also another side. There are challenges. I came up with a "do it yourself mentality," or as the Pussycat Dolls say in one of their songs, "I don't need a man to make it happen!" Of course I had relationships with brothers, and due to how my mother raised me, I hadn't gone through too much drama because I developed a pretty keen insight on "how to pick em." I could see trouble, drama and all kinds of warning signs right away and I avoided those brothers like the plague (no offense fellas). I protected myself. I did not rely on a man to do anything for me and because of that I became...

Miss Independent.

Now some of you may be saying, "Well what the hell is wrong with that?!" You turned out pretty good right?

And I have. But in reality, I did not do it alone.

The term "independence" in regards to this subject matter is an illusion and dare I say unnatural. Why?

Because the nature of the universe is not independence. It's interdependence.

The universe is a system and within that system, all living things depend upon something else to survive and thrive. We need each other. We rely upon the trees for oxygen. We rely upon the environment for food. We depend upon the sun to nurture our planet and without water there would be no life...a perfect combination. We pay taxes so that the government can put together $700 billion bailout plans (go figure!). Men cannot produce life without women and women cannot produce life without men...period! Even entertaining the idea of artificial insemination, you still need the sperm!

Many of us raised in female headed households have struggles with "listening to a man" or taking leadership from a man. Why? Because we haven't had to do it! It's something foreign to us. It's like throwing a cold pail of water in our faces. It's shocking. It sounds crazy. It's unfamiliar. It's like ploppin' somebody in the middle of Russia who does not speak the language. It's disorienting. It's a struggle. It feels unnatural.

Why? Many of us have never seen it up close and personal in real life. We are not used to it. It does not resonate within the fiber of our being because we have been taught and trained that a man may not be there (whether these words were spoken or not...we heard it or saw it played out in day-to-day life) so you gotta what...DO YOU! We were not raised with direct examples of brothers providing strength and a level of leadership in the home.

Many of us have been doing it ourselves to survive. We have been "superwoman" because we have had to hold our families together through the devastation of our brothers falling victim to various societal plagues (racism, slavery, violence, drugs, the "baby boy" syndrome, the prison industrial complex, etc). We should be celebrated for our strength and endurance, but to me, this is not the family model to strive for because so many of our families are falling apart. And for the sisters who raised babies that turned out great without a man in the home, praises due. I know there are success stories. I just see the other side of the game every day.

Being an "independent woman" is not something I advocate because some of the joy or love, peace and happiness within that is an illusion. Some of us are fakin' it until we make it. Oftentimes, some of us are straight up frontin'!

NOW PLEASE DON'T GET MY WORDS OR INTENTIONS TWISTED! I repeat...PLEASE DON'T GET MY WORDS OR INTENTIONS TWISTED!

In my eyes, there's nothing wrong with a sister having her own job, car, resources, etc. I don't advocate being so dependent on everyone else that you don't have the ability to think and do for yourself. It ain't ever cool to "bloodsuck" somebody, not even the person you say you love. That is one of the ways of the 10%. In my way of life, the Earth rotates on her own axis as well as revolves around the Sun. To build alongside a king, you must be a Queen, and the more you develop yourself, the more you can bring to the table. You must have the ability to be self-sufficient. If you wanna be with a boss, you gotta be able to be "boss lady."

But beneath all of the strength of doin' it ourselves, many of us know deep down that ain't necessarily how we want things to be and that isn't the best thing for our children. We just deal with what IS and keep it movin'. No time for drowning in sorrow or feeling sorry for ourselves. As great of a job that we sisters have been doing, holdin' it down in the absence of our brothers, many of our communities are in disarray. Our conditioning, life experiences and egos mask our pain. And some of us are too busy making things work to retreat within oneself and figure this sh*t out. Some of us are still little girls who miss our fathers and pile on accomplishment after accomplishment as a royal shield and wear it proudly.

I DID THIS WITHOUT YOU! I MADE IT WITHOUT YOU!

And what can this manifest into when we are lookin' at the brother we're with or a potential prospect? I DON'T NEED YOU TO DO THIS! I CAN MAKE IT WITHOUT YOU!

Sometimes we say it plainly, and sometimes it's an underlying thought that comes out through smart-ass comments delivered in a mist that most can hardly detect. It can come out as sarcasm or nitpicking.

We are like onions with lots of layers. Some of us are on the verge of imploding. We hold it all inside because we don't want anyone to think we are weak. We have to "be strong" to keep going on.

When many of us "independent" women get into relationships, there's sometimes less cooperation and more competition. How in the world are we supposed to have healthy relationships when we are always competing with each other, trying to out do each other? How will the Black family survive?

Now don't get me wrong, we are not the only ones responsible here. Frankly, for many of us, the source of our pain is a brother who somewhere in our lives, in childhood, adolescence or adulthood, did not deliver, whether it be our fathers or our mates.

When I came into the knowledge of myself and got into the relationship I am currently in, I respected who the brother is because HE IS WHO HE SAYS HE IS. He does what he says he will do. I am intelligent and bring a lot to the table AND I also am able to respect his leadership because he knows more than me, has experienced more than me, and I trust and am secure with the bond we have based on knowledge, growth and development. It's based on logic. And through the knowledge and wisdom came the love, the highest form of understanding. If he did not live up to who he says he is, a woman like me would not have been able to go from independence to interdependence.

I have come to know that the Black man is God (not what is typically thought of as a God in the sky with magical powers, but the original man who is the embodiment of knowledge, responsibility and many other qualities)...not because I have been brainwashed (and I know at least a few of you may think that...hey you're entitled to your own perspective. You don't live my life so it may be hard for you to see). Not because I am under some "Deebo mind control." Not because I was forced. It's because I saw the idea manifested. The knowledge dominates with equality, not control. Brothers, with all that we are and all that many sisters have gone through in life, you simply cannot separate theory and practice here. I am a very practical person, and if it doesn't make sense, if there's no practical application, an idea is difficult for me to entertain. I need proof. And honestly, so do a lot of women.

So brothers, you must know that if you want us to build with you, if you want us to trust your ability to be responsible, if you want us to listen to you, if you want us to learn from you, you must lead by example. You must give all that you have and all within your power to be who you say you are.

Whether it's "strong Black man," "educated Black man," "king," "God," "boss," "maker," "owner" you must BE THAT. And yes, when you think about it, that is a tall order. You've got big shoes to fill. We know that this is your nature, but that nature must be nurtured so that the world can truly see the reality of who the Black man is. If she is trying to be all that she can be, and you are not, you will have problems. You won't achieve the natural level of equality, balance and homeostasis for a healthy interaction. You will have power struggles and it won't be good. It will be a royal headache for the both of you.

Some of us have 87 requirements for what we want in a man and end up "losing time searching for that which does not exist." Our "ideal" man becomes an idea that never materializes - a "mystery" man. I ain't sayin' 'don't have standards,' but we gotta be reasonable too.

I see your magnificence and know that you have it in you. And I know that as much work that sisters have to do within ourselves, brothers have also got their fair share of work to do to destroy the negative and build upon the positive. Easier said than done. There are obstacles. This wilderness of North America has dealt many of us a hell of a hand. But I know you can do this. We have to do this for our future.

So I will say this to the brothers on behalf of all of the sisters who are not ready…On behalf of all of the "independent women" who haven't yet peeled their layers to the source of their pain…the sisters who are trying to work on themselves, preparing themselves for a healthy relationship and haven't yet found the answer…the sisters who are trying to love you but are going through hell building that things will turn out right…the sisters who are moving up the social and economic ladder achieving "success" but are having a hard time getting and keeping a man (some of you may say you don't want or need one now, but as you grow older, most of you will)…the little girls who become teenagers who become women trying to replace the father they never had with men they are in relationships with…the sisters who are not ready to face their trauma…the sisters who have buried their trauma so deep, they don't have a clue it exists…all the sisters in straight up denial…On behalf of all the sisters lookin' for love in all the wrong places…

We need you.

WE NEED YOU.

And you know what?

You need us too.

Interdependence…it's simply the nature of life itself. I never said it would be easy. It may be one of the hardest transitions you may have to make in your life. But if you can master this part of yourself, you'll reap the rewards. Love, Peace and Happiness.

I Medina is an emcee, poet, and author who writes about what she sees and experiences. Her community work is what inspires her artistic expression, and it is through this work that she feels most validated as an artist, by bringing the words on the page to life through her daily work with youth, families, and our community. She moved from Berkeley, California to Pittsburgh in 2001 to earn her Master's in Social Work. She is a proud citizen of the Nation of Gods and Earths who has had knowledge of self since 2004.

She is currently the Program Manager at Community Empowerment Association's Asante Nation Safe Passage Initiative, an afterschool program which works to empower at-risk youth. She also works with CEA's Saturday Academy and the Urban Renaissance Arts Movement, a city-wide arts and culture initiative for Pittsburgh youth. Under her artist name, Angel Eye, she'll soon be releasing her first mixtape *Eyewitness*, and a book of poetry and perspective, *Affirmations of a Brown Suga from Berkeley*. She is also developing a lifestyle company, "Refined and Fly," advocating modesty and magnificence for women and girls. You can find her at www.myspace.com/angeleyecali or on her blog at imedinapeaceful.blogspot.com

RIGHTEOUSNESS AND RESPONSIBILITIES
Sha-King Cehum Allah - Power Born (Pittsburgh, PA)

Peace! Paz! Las matematicas de hoy son "Comprendimiento y Cifra." Today's mathematics is "Understanding Cipher."

Understanding is the ability to see things for what they are, and not for what they 'appear' to be. This means that ones understanding or comprehension of a cipher (being a person, place or thing) is not superficial, as in an 'opinion,' but rather it permeates the cipher's entire being, looking not just into it but rather 'through' it. Understanding is growth and development because once achieved (not everyone can 'get' an understanding) it stimulates and warrants the elevation of a person mentally, intellectually, morally, etc., as they forge themselves towards becoming a more complete human being.

It was this understanding or 'clarity' of the bio-chemical dimensions of man, the Original man, that lead a scientist (by the name of 'Yakub') to ultimately bring about a change in world history. This was done through the creation of the 'white man.' Whether or not you subscribe to the theory of Yakub as revealed by the Honorable Elijah Muhammad, there are stories from many different Original cultures that describe the 'white man' as "unoriginal," meaning 'not from the beginning,' and have remarkable similarities and interconnectedness. Modern western science has revealed (reluctantly) that "whiteness" is a mutation (as scientist Keith Cheng of Penn State College of Medicine verified and revealed back in 2005), which occurred in the Near East a little over 6,000 years ago (http://genetics.suite101.com/article.cfm/when_caucasians_turned_white), along with the trait for blue eyes (www.msnbc.msn.com/id/22934464) and other traits that comprise "whiteness."

The question is as to whether or not the mutation (genetic alteration) was instigated through nature (as in 'evolution') or the result of human determinates and scientific observation and application, being born through selective breeding, as the story of Yakub illustrates. There are those of us who are more likely to accept evolution, as in man gradually becoming lighter due to environmental factors. However, there are many examples, one of which being the *Inuit, Buryat* and *Chukchi* people of the Artic who retain a considerable amount of melanin and defy such theories. Otherwise they would have 'evolved' into 'white people' from being surrounded by snow and ice. Paul Lawrence Guthrie states in his book, *The Making of the Whiteman*, of evolutionist Charles Darwin:

> When Charles Darwin discussed the origins of race he too expressed the opinion that selection, over the course of many generations, had to have been used in bringing about what he called "the characteristic differences between the races of man." He even went on to conclude that without some form of selective breeding, such racial differences simply "could not be accounted for in a satisfactory manner.

So in reality, whether or not an "individual" named Yakub pulled this off (the selective breeding and creation of white people) is less important in contrast to the actuality of them being born through a selective process. It is the principle behind the story which is the most important and relative. Another important question would be "why?" which is something to be discussed in another article. However, today's degree in our lessons focuses on the fundamentals of the process and states:

30) Q. Tell us, what and how the Devil was made?
Ans: The Devil was made from the Original people by grafting and separating the germs. In the Black man's body there exists two germs: a black germ and a brown germ. Yakub, with his law on birth control, separated the black germ from the brown germ and grafted it into white, by destroying the black germ. After following this process of 600 years, the germ became white and was no longer original. Also, by thinning the blood, the germ became weak and wicked and was no longer the same.

Thus, this is how Yakub made devil.

As we see, it was the understanding of the cipher (the Original man's bio-chemical structure) which allowed Yakub to employ a policy of 'separation,' in order to fashion a being outside and away from the bounds of the nature in which humanity was conceived. This shouldn't be a surprise considering Europeans track record around the planet with people of color (Original people). A policy of 'divide' (separate) and conquer, as well as their fascination with genetics and cloning (after all they were "made in our image and likeness").

It was through the primary principle of 'division' that Yakub had achieved his means. For as Europeans traversed the globe they set out to both divide up peoples,' families, etc., and as well separate man from nature in their pursuit for material happiness. Interestingly enough, the later goal seemed to be an 'ancestral memory' of sorts, lodged deep in their DNA, since they in fact are 'made' and not 'natural,' that is 'occurring within nature.' Our peoples were shocked to see a people whose skin color couldn't be found to resemble any soil they had seen. Our mercifulness and humanity accepted them as part of the human families, even after 514 years of conquest. Yet they continued to and 'continue' to divide the Original people - the black from the brown, the brown from the yellow. However, their reality was conceived in thought by an Original man - Yakub. This means that the devilishment that they have committed was a reflection of the mental reality being exhibited by Original people prior to their existence. They, being the material or physical manifestation of the same mindset. For we had long been warring with each other at points in history, tribe against tribe, kingdom against kingdom, exhibiting little understanding in the cipher for and of each other.

It wasn't until our Father, Allah, the founder of the Nation of Gods and Earths (the 5%ers), brings a supreme understanding into the world (cipher). It was Allah's intention (will) to end religion, raise up the children and unite the seeds - black, brown and yellow ("red" being a variation or shade of brown) as one. As well as unite the human families- the Original peoples with the Colored (meaning distorted from its original state) or 'white' people, through a bond of education, love (the highest form of understanding) and righteousness, by bringing us out of "hell" with the teachings of Supreme Mathematics.

Black, Brown, Yellow, White...

Knowledge, Wisdom, Understanding, Culture...1, 2, 3, 4...

1+2+3+4=10 (there are 10 digits in our number system, 1-9 plus 0. The number "10" is just "1+0" which equals "1.") Thus "all" becomes "one."

"Oneness" is unification and Allah is "one." Allah advocated unification in a time where it was very unpopular, considering the number of so-called Black "militants" seeking separation from "white society." He was called an "Uncle Tom" because of his work with the city government of New York and the Mayor aide Barry Gottehrer. He vocalized the idea and need for "Black and whites" to unite and be "civilized." After all, we understood them to be a part of the human families regards to the atrocities of history and the then current state of society. Allah said that all things must "change or die." He focused on the "change" over the "die."

We desire to reach and teach our white brothers and sisters of the human families. As long as they desire harmony and righteousness. For acceptance of our way of life means certain responsibilities become incumbent upon them. We have long allowed them to learn and do like the Original man, coming amongst us. Two films I recently had the chance to see illustrate such. The first was a more contemporary film entitled *Pathfinder*. It is about a young Viking/Norse boy who is abandoned during an early Viking expedition in North America, 600 years before Columbus. The Vikings sought to settle the new land but not before killing and enslaving the Indigenous people. The boy is abandoned because he refuses to participate and is left to die, only to be saved by a Wampanoag woman who takes the boy amongst her people to live and be raised. As time passes the boy soon has to confront "himself" and take a stand against the returning murderous Viking expedition. The second film was an older one from 1957 entitled "Pawnee." Similarly, a white boy, this time a 'settler,' was reared amongst the Pawnee people, only later to confront his 'own people' as droves of white settlers attempted to steal "Indian" lands on their migration westward. Both themes echo *Dances with Wolves*, a movie starring actor Kevin Costner, which came out in the early 1990's. However, the story behind *Dances with Wolves* focused on an adult Union Army officer (Costner) and his experiences living amongst the Lakota Nation. The officer is given a Lakota name which meant "Dances with Wolves" and soon found himself defending the Lakota against the encroaching "white" army.

The underlying principle behind each movie was the responsibility given and choice they had to make when confronted by 'their own.' Allowed to come and live amongst us, respected and loved as one of 'our own,' their responsibility was then to uphold the way of living that gave them life. Each had to make difficult decisions in defending that honor in the face of their own people (biologically), and succeeded.

Something very similar occurs in our present society, when white people empathize with Original people. Growing up, my peers and I often used to comment on how some white people may want to listen to Hip-Hop music, wear baggy clothes, adopt and utilize some of our mannerisms, and "be like us" per se, but don't want to accept being harassed, oppressed, and jailed like us. Many may empathize with "struggle" as there are many poor white families who experience the same conditions as us. Yet, the melody of the music changes when it comes to defending righteousness and revolution. It's often easier to bond together with the realms of negativity and crime. It's easier to parallel one's self with the destruction of others if you are destroying yourself or are being destroyed. It's more difficult for those white people who may have assisted the Black Panthers, actively supported the Civil Rights Movement or any Black "cause." Especially, those who willingly accept the teachings of Allah and his Five Percenters. Many are attracted to the principles of self-mastery and internal development, refutation of religion and a way of life predicated on being in harmony with the mathematical order of the universe. However, one can not accept the positive without a willingness to accept the negative. Throughout periods in history we have been viewed very favorably in the eyes of the masses and the government authorities, been considered a gang even and slandered with conservative media accusations of being linked with Al-Qaeda. The perspective about us will change with the audience. So to walk this path is not easy and is a sacrifice, one that is expected, in exchange for the life-giving teachings bestowed upon those who become Five Percenters. Especially "white Five Percenters," like the First Born Caucasian 5%er, Azreal, taught directly by Allah. White Five Percenters or white people in general, who align with Black struggle become quite unpopular in white social circles and in many cases become what Chicago Black Panther Fred Hampton referred to as "class suicide." They ultimately risk forfeiting all of the luxuries and benefits of accepting and perpetuating Euro-centrism in this country. They fail to uphold the status quo of white supremacy.

The films I mentioned show a clear parallel for our current situation. As the Nation continues to grow from its 1964 Harlem roots, more and more people across the world, from every one of the human families will be exposed and many will want to add on. It is integral for a European or European descendant to strive for an understanding of the cipher. Both of themselves and their role in the struggle and the Nation of Gods and Earths and a clear perspective of what it means to uphold the teachings of Allah and his Suns and Daughters.

MURDERING FOUR DEVILS
Supreme Understanding Allah – Allah's Garden (Atlanta, GA)

In the 120 Lessons of the Nation of Gods and Earths, there is a lesson that brings up the murder of four devils. What Allah taught his young Five Percenters was that these four devils weren't necessarily people, but they symbolized the vices of man. Gods and Earths don't teach that the devil himself is within the Black man, only that the weaknesses that produce a devil are in us. Allowed to grow and mature to the point of permanence, we become (mentally) like the devil himself.

Some of us are addicted to a pill, a powder, or a plant, and we can't admit it. Some of us are chasing money like it can buy happiness (but we stay miserable). Some of us are extremely insecure or full of hatred for others (really ourselves). Some of us have bad tempers and anger management issues. Some of us really, really, really, like sex…to the point where we'll f*ck anything with a hole in it…if we're desperate enough.

And sometimes, we can't reconcile with these weaknesses, so we justify them. We talk about our bad habits like they're cool and not really a problem…knowing in our hearts that we're killing ourselves. Most of us glorify our sexual exploits, ignoring how many bad experiences we've had…or how sex has never really made us happy for more than a few minutes. We call our emotional displays of anger "how a real man reacts" when that is rarely the case. Most of us will spend our lives struggling with our inner demons, and some of us never win.

The simple fact of life is that everybody has weaknesses. We all have internal vices. We each have our own dogs to walk. And your issues aren't the same as your best friend's, so this is a war you've got to wage on your own…you can find support, but you'll never find anyone to fight this fight for you.

"The man who can not get angry is a fool. The man who will not is wise." - Seneca

What can we do? The first step is to identify your weaknesses. Name your devils, the most significant vices you have (right now). Seriously. I'll give you a minute.

The lesson I mentioned above compares the devil to a snake, saying "if allowed to live, he would only sting someone else." The issues you just named are the ones that come up again and again in your life, and you may not even be *aware* of them. That's the nature of a snake. But if you allow a snake to live, it may hurt others…but it's also very likely to keep hurting you. And the first law of nature is self-preservation, so why keep up a habit that's gonna sting you again and again, and will probably end up killing you because you *let it*?

So cut the grass low and the snake's heads will show. Ask people what your vices are and be ready to hear some things you may not like. For some of us, they're pretty obvious issues like our addictions and dependencies.

But even those kinds of issues have layers, as we've learned. Sure, you might chase a lot of pussy. But why? What creates that need in you, to a greater extent than it does in other people? Sometimes you can't kill the snake because you think you're cutting off its head, but you're just whacking at its tail.

No, you kill it, and leave nothing left. Until the day that happens, you live every day with the intent in mind to kill that snake/devil every time it tries to rear its ugly head. You've got to go past when Jesus said, "Get thee behind me, Satan!" and kill that motherf*cker.

Ways to kill a snake	Ways to kill a vice
Suffocate it	Never allow it to breathe/develop
Overfeed it	Indulge it until you've had too much to want anymore
Poison it	Allow a bad experience to turn you off from it
Cut off its head	Work actively to eliminate it
Burn the field and replant	Start everything about yourself anew
Kill the babies	Eliminate related thoughts and behaviors

The greatest struggle is within. Eliminating your bad habits may be the hardest thing you do, but it is certainly one of the most important.

The above essay is based on an excerpt from Supreme Understanding's book *How to Hustle and Win: A Survival Guide for the Ghetto, Part One*, available at www.HustleAndWin.com or www.SupremeDesignOnline.com

❧ 2 ☙
THOUGHT
MANIFESTED

THE MIND IS THE MASTER KEY
...WHICH OPENS ALL LOCKS
Almighty God Dawud Allah - Savior Cee (Columbia, SC)

"How wonderful then the plane of the mind is!
The mind is its question, and is itself its answer." – Hazrat Inayat Khan

A Master Key is an instrument, which opens many locks, and a Master means the Sole Controller. Mind made matter. Mind is present in matter and is conditioned by matter, until Mind rises superior to matter and controls the matter it is in through right education; meaning Knowledge of Self. Educate means bring forth, draw out of, to lead, also to cultivate with truth. Because every mental thought is attracted to a vibration and this produces Mind Over Matter by the Law of attraction. So the number one question on a person's mind should be, 'what am I thinking?' Remember what the Bible says, "As a man thinketh, so is he." The Divine Living Mind thinks, which causes a condition producing an effect. The completion of the Mind's thoughts causes conditions and the effects depends on the mechanism to which it is attached. The capacity or size of the brain stem, also the cleanliness of the brain (meaning a small brain or an unclean brain will not understand the highest thoughts) will affects one's ways and actions.

Our Consciousness rising from our sense creates our environment because thoughts concentrated on positive or negative purposes become positive or negative power. See, there is only one Power, One Mind, but it can be used for good or bad. Man's conscious and subconscious thinking are the masters of the Sun Center (the solar plexus) of the Body where all life and energy flows. So by the quality of our thoughts we think and entertain determines the quality of the thoughts our Sun Center radiates which determines the quality of our ways and actions.

There are five stages to the Mind: (1) the conscious Mind; (2) the subconscious Mind; (3) the super conscious Mind; (4) the magnetic Mind; and (5) the Infinite Mind. The Mind is a magnetic Force of Energy, which activates on two or more objects one positive, one negative and its function is to solve problems and overcome obstacles. The Divine Living Mind has the Supreme Force and Power to Perceive its essence thus controlling the universe with Supreme thought and Power by acting on and interacting with Atoms. Thoughts are electrical currents of energy from the magnetic field of the mind. Now electricity is energy in motion and its effect depends on the mechanism to which it is attached, man or woman, positive or negative, good or evil. So when we change our Minds, our bodies will follow. There is an Old African saying: "Open your Mind and your wings will grow and then you can fly." The energy of Life travels in a circle in perfect balance. Until we find our center, we will never be whole Blackmen and Women. Our center is the Knowledge of Self. Because of the Lack of Knowledge of self, we develop coping mechanisms, which are very unhealthy and keep us unhappy. It's not the crust that makes the pie, it's the filling which is inside the pie (the Mind).

The Black Dot (our real center in the heart of our Mind) is the seed of

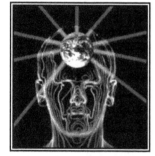

life, which is a hidden doorway in our mind to hook up with our ancient knowledge of self (genetically), i.e. the door way to our ancestral memory bank. This Black Dot is known to modern science as the Pineal Gland (known to the ancients as the "third eye" or "Mind's eye"). The Pineal Gland produces neuromelanin (brain melanin). Dr. Richard King says the Black Dot is "the Black room of the Kings' chamber of the Great Pyramid, the black stone of the Kaa'ba in Mecca, the capstone of the pyramids, the black dot in the all–seeing eye of Horus." The Black Dot (hidden memory bank) is a doorway out to the infinite conscious mind which is the ALLAH in us, the Fifth stage of the Divine Conscious Mind in the Blackman.

'Our true Self is all-knowing by its nature.
It is the source of infinite knowledge within us." - Swâmi Abhedânanda

The Conscious Mind is the Watchman at the gate for our five stages of the divine living Mind; it keeps guard over us, to protect us from infiltration and thieves. The Most Important tool it has is light, the ability (meaning the power of the mind to do anything) of consciousness, radiant health, strength and harmony which will bring us into a realization that nothing is "impossible" (a word only used in the dictionary of fools), once one understands the Supreme power within.

"Truth" refers to correct reasoning power. Thought Power coming from the Divine Living Mind controls the forces of energy, where all motion, light, heat and color have their origin. The Mind is the Master Key, which opens all locks by producing thoughts. Our conditions are but the outward manifestations as our thoughts change. All outward or material conditions must change in order to be in harmony with their creators, which are thoughts, but thoughts must be clear-cut, steady, fixed, and unchangeable. We cannot take one step up and two steps back and expect good results. When we want Peaceful and harmonious conditions in our lives, we must develop a harmonious mental attitude because it's our mindset that determines our thinking, our thinking determines our attitude, and our attitude determines our behavior patterns. Our behavior patterns determine our ways and actions, and our ways and actions determine whether we are righteous or unrighteous.

"Peace is not the absence of war; it is a virtue; a state of mind; a disposition for benevolence; confidence; and justice." - Spinoza

In closing, the subconscious Mind perceives by Intuition (urges from inborn impulses) that is really a process of rapid thinking. It does not wait for the slow method of conscious reason. Thus, our conscious mind ought to be on duty every waking hour, because when the Watchman at the gate of our mind is not on guard, its judgment is suspended, and the subconscious is unguarded and left open to suggestion from without or within. The true and living God is not constantly influenced like the 85%, because he is the Sole Controller. The Blackman is Allah. Peace!

"Man is the sum of all of his thoughts." – James Allen

Almighty God Dawud Allah is a Nation elder, historian, and prolific author. He was born and raised in South Carolina before getting the knowledge of himself in the Bronx in 1977. His books normally address topics relevant to the teachings of the Five Percent. His published works include *Be Ye Perfect, In the Beginning that Never Began, The Secret Society of Freemasons Revealed, the Babies are the Greatest,* and *The Seven Master Key Lessons of the Divine Master Builder,* from which the above essay is taken. Dawud's books are available in most Black bookstores, or directly through Afrikan World Books.

THE PRINCIPLES OF LEARNING
First Born Prince Allah - Mecca (Harlem, NY)

6 PRINCIPLES OF LEARNING
1. SILENCE
2. LISTENING
3. REMEMBERING
4. UNDERSTANDING
5. JUDGMENT
6. ACTION

7 CHARACTERSITICS OF A WISE PERSON

1. One does not speak on things one does not know.
2. One admits when one does not know something.
3. One does not interrupt.
4. One is not hostile to question or answer.
5. One deals with first things first and last things last.
6. One is not quick to answer.
7. One always acknowledges the truth.

4 QUALITIES TO DEVELOP IN YOURSELF

1. LISTENING – paying attention with your eyes and ears.
2. CONCENTRATION – Being able to focus intensely with your mind's eye on what is being said, done or studied without distraction.
3. REMEMBERING – Developing the ability to recall and/or recite all important details of discussions, speeches, lessons, pictures, etc.
4. MEMORIZING – Developing the ability to retain, organize and present in order, all facts, information, knowledge, etc. when questioned.

First Born Prince Allah was third of the First Nine Born that Allah taught and chose in 1964 to continue educating the youth. Prior to meeting The Father he was one of the feared Blood Brothers that were cleaning the Harlem streets of drug dealers, pimps and profiteering Caucasians. Initially he was known as Al-Jabbar until he changed his name when The Father told his students to utilize names that would distinguish them from other nations. Prince applied his life to educating the youth who were seeking direction, and was a regular fixture at The Allah School of Mecca up until he was killed in October 2001. The above plus lessons were distributed by Prince to those who he taught or mentored, a number which may reach into the hundreds, and - if one is to count the students of those students - possibly into the thousands.

IDEAS AND REALITY
I Majestic Allah - Power Born (Pittsburgh, PA)

On the Knowledge Born day (the 19th), I had an insightful exchange with I Medina Peaceful Earth regarding the relationship between ideas and reality. I Medina, being the pragmatist that she is, questioned the worth of an idea if it can't be manifested into something real and tangible (Knowledge being made Born). I countered that there are many reasons ideas don't come to fruition (i.e. timing, quality of work, process, etc). However, that may have nothing to do with the worth or relevance of that idea.

First, there are some ideas that need other ideas or realities to make them work. For example, the idea that we need Black businesses in our communities is as relevant today as it was 30 years ago, b.u.t. the "ideas" of unity and trust are preconditions for *that* idea to be able to be manifested into reality.

In the context of understanding the mentality of our current population, the following dynamics exist: (A) The 5 percent (those who know and willingly share), and the 10 percent (those who know and manipulate such for gain), live based upon ideas. (B) Meanwhile, the 85 percent (those masses who do not know and are prey to those who know) live based upon the reality that they see.

The power of an idea is that it allows one to see beyond their particular situation and environment. All the great men and women of time immemorial were propelled by an IDEA.

However, when looking at the idea/reality relationship, it is important to have balance and understanding. People who live based on ideas alone can find themselves disconnected from reality. Meanwhile, those who live based only on their supposed "reality" often find themselves stuck in the doldrums of their environment, never seeing beyond their particular situation. It is imperative that we find the space where we are not only living in reality, b.u.t. creating our own reality. So let's now see where we want to go, and create an action plan to manifest our ideas.

I Majestic Allah has been a devoted member of the Nation Of Gods & Earths for 18 years. I Majestic is a noted organizer, writer & speaker whose writings have been featured on various blogs, websites & magazines such as *Stress Magazine*. A tireless youth advocate, he has been involved in youth development for over 10 years. Currently, he works as a program manager for the Dropout Prevention/Truancy Intervention program of a grassroots community organization in Pittsburgh, Pennsylvania.

IS BEAUTY ONLY SKIN DEEP?
I Medina Peaceful Earth – Power Born (Pittsburgh, PA)

"Read not to contradict and confute, nor to believe and take for granted, but to weigh and consider." -- Francis Bacon, Sr.

Women all over the world have been dressing modestly for centuries and continue to do so today. It is absolutely nothing new. A woman's appearance and specifically her style of dress is an indicator of how she feels about herself, her thought process, her experiences, exposure and her values. When we get up in the morning and select what we will wear for the day, we are consciously and subconsciously sending a message to all those we encounter saying, "This is who I am!" So what message are you trying to project? What first impression are you trying to make?

When a woman puts on a power suit or business casual clothing, she is projecting the message that she is striving to look and be professional. When you see her you may think she may be going to work or to a conference or an important meeting. When a woman wears a long silky dress with a shawl and heels, you know that she is probably going to a somewhat classy formal event. When a woman wears a police uniform, you assume she's a cop...unless it's Halloween. When a woman wears "African" garb, she projects the message that she probably has somewhat of an African centered view on life or she has a different cultural perspective.

When a woman wears a crotch length mini-skirt, a tube top, and some hooker boots, where if you bend over or sit without your legs crossed, your goodies are exposed for the world to see, what message is she conveying? Many of us are never asked, nor do we ask ourselves that question, and if we do, here are a couple typical responses:

1. "I wear what's in style"

Ans. Okay, so that means that your style is predicated upon the creative whims of fashion designers, many of whom are unalike yourself (many are gay white men) who place gaunt unhealthy looking women onto the runways to model their clothing (many of whom have boyish size 2 figures...hmmm), and the clothes go into specialty boutiques, into department stores, and on to your local mall retailers. And, scantily clad clothing is not the only style that is trendy. Besides, some designers get ideas from the street or from the styles of original people, but do we ever get credit for it?

2. "I wear it cuz it's cute" (that used to be my favorite one to use)

Ans. Something being "cute" is relative. That is not a universal term. There is no absolute meaning to the word "cute." You think something is cute due to the context of your life and what you have been exposed to, by which you develop responses, and as you get older, that combination of responses turns into "your style." What you think is cute, someone else may think is unattractive and vice versa.

3. "What I wear has nothing to do with who I am" (my old second favorite)

Ans. Um, yes it does. We usually say this when we are getting defensive or have not gone through the recesses of our thoughts to get to the point of origin of why we dress this way. Your clothes are ABSOLUTELY, EMPHATICALLY an indicator of who you are, it's just not the only indicator. Doesn't how you eat, how you speak, and the music you listen to give others a glimpse of who you are and your way of life? Well, the same logic applies regarding your wardrobe choices. We oftentimes say the above when we are challenged about our way of dress and are resistant to self-analysis and change. If you wear it because you wanna "use what ya got to get what you want" - though that's usually a saying prostitutes use, and is now a dysfunctional phrase passed on from woman to woman (often times from an uncivilized mother to her unaware daughter) - at least you're being honest.

We have to stop deluding ourselves. When we intentionally wear cleavage exposing shirts, it's because we want someone to look at the ta-tas.

When we wear those little crotch length denim skirts (I mean doesn't the name itself sound foul?), it's because we want someone to look at our legs and the hill back there. These thoughts may all be subconscious and we may not think it when we put the clothes on, but after really thinking about it and being honest with ourselves, you tell me what you come up with. When you intentionally put that sexy sh*t or that freakum dress on, when a man sees you, he is giving you the attention you are asking for. When he looks at you, he doesn't think of how intelligent you may be…he thinks of (surprise) SEX! So if a brotha is salivating over you while tryin' to hold a conversation, or staring down ya shirt while you're supposed to be talking "business," don't get mad at him cuz he's not looking into your eyes…check yourself first cuz he's gonna look if you put it out there!

4. "Some women in other countries walk around topless, so what's wrong with what I wear?"

Ans. We are not in those countries. Different countries produce different cultures, different standards of beauty, and different perspectives on how a woman's body is viewed. In the United States, a woman's body is a commodity that is objectified through the process of long-standing sexism. Women are socialized to be sex objects and men are socialized to chase it, so when ya put it out there like that, you're like a walking advertisement for some of the sexual pleasures he may get once he pulls you. In this country, it's just too much to ask for a man who hasn't yet deconstructed his own thoughts and life experiences yet, socialized as he has been, to not think that way when he sees a woman walking around half naked. Remember, he's constantly exposed to the same images as you, and he is socialized to desire a woman who looks like that.

As a woman who has only been consciously dressing modestly for about four years now, thinking back to when I first decided to embark on the journey of getting the knowledge of self and striving to be a productive citizen in the Nation of Gods and Earths, I had to conduct an analysis of every part of myself, and a large aspect of that was getting to the root of my dress code. Women of my society who are called Earths, usually wear what is called "3/4ths," because 3/4ths of the planet Earth's surface is covered by water and as self-respecting women and Queens, we dress modestly and cover our hair to show the world a different paradigm of womanhood and a positive standard of beauty… that you can be beautiful, intelligent, smell good, and have ambitions without all your goodies hangin' out.

Coming to this conclusion and accepting modesty as a part of my way of life was very difficult, but very rewarding in the end. It was difficult because I had to study myself, and through a logical process of being asked and asking myself questions, I came to the conclusion that I used to wear revealing clothes to boost my self-esteem and attract attention, because I was not as confident as I should have been with my other attracting powers. I knew I was fairly intelligent but I also knew that I had it goin' on physically and coupled with media images and popular standards of beauty in the wilderness of North America, music videos, movies, Miss America Pageants, magazines, you name it, I thought that this was how I had to dress to get the attention I wanted. Showin' skin was in baby! It was deep, and I realized that my thoughts and feelings about this went back as far as the third grade (be careful of what your little girls are exposed to! They are picking up messages that are integrated into their subconscious that will shape how they consciously express themselves.).

I fought this concept and thought that my mental did not have to match my physical…that I could still be smart, nice, community minded and active, love and build with the babies, and wear what I wanted. Back then, I didn't really understand the importance of consistency and discipline. Due to the barrage of distractions that we are exposed to and integrate on a daily basis, consistency is a challenge in the United States nowadays. I suppose you could say I was tryin' to be 'revolutionary but sexy.' Looking back, I now realize how much of a contradiction that was. Real revolutionaries had other things on their mind beyond striving to appear to be sexy all the time. Not to say that a woman can't feel sensual or comfortable with her sexuality, however, there is a time and place for everything, and having "sexy" as one of the dominant themes of my existence didn't really make sense. As my God says, "Civilized people do things inside." So "sexy" was not the legacy I wanted to leave behind.

Another dilemma I had was that I thought there was only one way to look modest and rock 3/4ths. Later on, as I grew and developed, saw different examples and looked within myself, I found that that was totally untrue. Me changing my wardrobe forced me to have to be more original. This is not to say that I couldn't wear some of the styles that I considered fashionable, trendy, attractive, or designer clothing, because I can, but I simply wear them in a different way…

There are lots of different options, but you, as the original woman, with her own level of beauty and uniqueness, have to be creative enough to put it together, and if you do it right, you'll start setting trends! Where do you think the "earthy" look came from? People will start asking you how you put your outfits together, where did you get that head wrap from, lovin' your accessories and matching purses, and complimenting your shoe game…Give it a shot and you will see where your creativity takes you and just how refined and fly you can be!

DID I DO THAT?
HELL YEAH, YOU DID!
Allah Universal - Starksville, MS

Today's Supreme Mathematics is Knowledge (1) Understanding (3). The 13th degree of the 1-40 states:

Q: But brings rain, hail, snow and earthquakes?
A: They continue daily to teach the 85% that all that they see such as rain, hail, snow and earthquakes is caused by that so-called mystery-god, that no one will be able to see until he dies, and this is believed by the 85%, while the 10% knows that when a man dies, he will never be able to come back and tell the living whether he lied or not...

WHAT YOU KNOW (1),
BECOMES WHAT YOU SEE (3)

In the above degrees, we can interpret the "rain, hail, snow and earthquakes" as the various circumstances of your life. Where do they come from? A mystery god (something outside of yourself)...or you?

This lesson of Life, shows and proves how one is NEVER a victim, and is actually THE cause of all situations in their life, like it or not. We are all Masters of Self, knowingly, or unknowingly. Knowing and Understanding it is the difference between Living/Freedom, and just going through the motions.

Everything that you know has been acquired not only by the 5 senses, but also by genetic inheritance, osmosis, subliminal influence, inductive and deductive reasoning, and just plain old intuition (aka the 6th sense), along with other processes not mentioned here. The five senses in the average person, makes up about 10% of their mental powers, which is the conscious mind, not much at all really. There is still another 90% of our mental activity that is still right there, ready to be used by those who Know and Understand how to access it.

Ever hear the saying "believe none of what you hear, and only some of what you saw"? Well, there is a lot of truth to that. Let's say that the windows on your car had 90% tint, and you could only see 10% of whatever light is coming into those windows. would you drive across your state or country behind that tint, and expect to make it safely? Probably not, unless you know the roads by heart.

Yet, "they" advocate daily that your five senses are the only tools you have to know and see the world. Bullsh*t! Your subconscious mind is MUCH more powerful. It, unlike the conscious mind, is always in operation, always processing the data that your five senses takes in, keeping you breathing and your heart beating, digesting your food, cleaning out toxins, fighting diseases in the body, reflecting on your past, planning your future, asking you what you think about the person next to you in the passenger seat, telling you how you feel emotionally, AND commanding your body on how to drive that car without thinking about it! If you fall asleep behind the wheel, it produces the dreams that you experience, and runs the internal alarm clock that wakes you up (and then tells you to watch the f*cking road!). F*ck a computer, the subconscious mind is THE Ultimate Multi-Tasker!!! Basically, anything that you do without having to think about it is being done by the subconscious mind.

The Honorable Elijah Muhammad said that he never saw Master Fard Muhammad sleep. Well, for those that Understand, he was only referring to his subconscious mind.

The conscious mind uses the brain and spinal cord as its main tools (cerebro-spinal nervous system), and the subconscious mind uses what's known as the sympathetic nervous system, which is ruled by the solar plexus (your 2nd brain mass, under your diaphragm). And the SOLAR plexus is the literal SUN OF MAN (Refer to 8° in the 1-40; and John 1:9). You know those hearty laughs that some people have, that seem to light up a room and get everybody else laughing? Well, that's the Solar Plexus at work. That's where your mind literally shines its light on the world! It, along with the cerebro-spinal system, is what transmits and receives every thought that you've ever had, and will have, as well as the ones you are having now. and let's not forget about the thoughts of those around you (watch the company you keep). They together produce your aura, or "magnetic," and that's what ultimately attracts EVERYTHING that EVER comes to you in LIFE! The good, the bad, and the ugly of it ALL!

There is NO mystery to this! I'm sure by now, a lot of you have heard of "The Secret," and/or the "Law of Attraction." For starters, it is not a "secret" (21°, 1-40), hasn't been for quite some time, all of the prophets and great teachers taught it in one way or another. As a man thinketh, so is he. "And the Word was made Flesh." (John 1:14). As above, so below. What things so ever ye desire, when ye pray, believe that ye receive them, and ye shall have them." (Mark 11:24). And the list goes on...

A SIMPLE EXAMPLE OF HOW IT WORKS...

I see an attractive woman, and the thought, "Oh sh*t! I gotta have that!" comes up. That's my conscious mind at work, one of my senses (sight) sparked a desire, for what my subconscious mind already knows that it likes. My subconscious mind, as a reaction, begins to feed to me ideas on what I should say to her, and then tells my conscious mind to move my legs and walk over to her. "Hey, how you doing? I don't know you, but um, I got the feeling that I'm about to know you real well" (and no, I don't use this line all the time, only when it'll work. It's what follows that line that does the work. Women HATE for a man to say something stupid, and vice versa, but anyway). She laughs, another sense (hearing) tells my conscious mind how cute her voice is, while my subconscious mind starts feeding me thoughts of how her voice would sound moaning and hitting that high note. I start breathing a little bit harder, now I can smell her perfume. More desire. Subconscious mind working harder to come up with questions to interview her, see where her head is at, etc...All the while, I'm keeping a smile on her face, stimulating HER conscious and subconscious mind, drawing her in more and more, so now we're both lighting up the room, yada yada yada, I see her later that day, she comes up to me to spark convo. She has now been officially "attracted." We end up exchanging phone numbers, and then I'm back to what I was doing before I saw her. The desire has been sparked, the seed has been planted; now I leave it alone and let my subconscious mind do the rest. She calls a couple of days later, more mind to mind contact, etc. and you know where the rest of this goes if you play your cards right.

How many times have you gone through this scenario, without thinking about what caused all of this to happen? (9°, 1-40)

The point of it is. The subconscious mind, is the most POWERFUL FORCE IN YOUR LIFE! What you go through in your everyday life, starts with in your mind, and ends up becoming your physical reality! The subconscious mind is what moved and controlled you until you were about 6 years old (22°, 1-40). Your conscious mind is hired about that time as the security guard of the subconscious mind, saying what thoughts go in and get stored away, to be attracted later in life. It literally creates the circumstances to bring that about, and that has been happening ALL OF YOUR LIFE! Whether you notice it or not, it is a Universal Law, whatever is in your subconscious mind, good or bad, is brought to you, one way or another. That being the case, how can you EVER have the AUDACITY to blame ANYONE else for YOUR situations that YOU CREATED?!

So, the question to be asked is, how do you control/MASTER it (13°, Supreme Alphabet)? Answer: Get to KNOW and UNDERSTAND (MASTER) yourself!

There are many thoughts in your subconscious mind that may not be your own; they were planted there (8°, 1-36) when you were a baby and didn't know better. As an Adult (and I'm presuming that anyone reading this is an adult, or will be soon), you have to know what the f*ck is in that subconscious mind, so that some bullsh*t don't creep out of it! Mental death, or mental illness, is simply the result of a subconscious mind full of garbage that isn't being regulated by a clearly thinking conscious mind. The conscious mind is the filter, and needs to be vigilant in order to keep all of the nonsense that surrounds you out. Those grafted thoughts, if allowed to GERMinate, WILL come to life, and this is how "devil" is made (30°-33°, 1-40) The REAL devil, that f*cks up your life, is one that YOU allowed to grow from YOUR thoughts! The REAL meaning of taking the devil off the planet is mental house cleaning (34°, 1-40). Religion cannot do it for you; it takes REAL work that can only be done by you! All anyone else can do is tell you what needs to be done, and advise you on how to do it, but the work is yours alone to do. Once again, ain't no mystery to it.

"All of the above is caused by the Sun of Man." 8°, 1-40. Only doubt and fear can keep you from creating what you want and desire to be present in your life. Hell, that doubt and fear might not even be yours; it is not your natural state of mind! A lot of it comes from our parents, and what they put into our subconscious before we could think for ourselves. These are what Scientology calls engrams, or the "pins in the babies' heads" that Gods and Earths refer to (28°, 1-40). In plain English, it's bullsh*t thoughts and beliefs. If you don't pull these weeds up out of your mental garden, they will just multiply and make that land worthless, and spread to others, especially THE BABIES! Just as with a computer, if you put Garbage In, it can only spit Garbage Out (GIGO). It works the other way too, however: Good In, Good Out.

Get to Know yourself, so that you will Understand clearly how to take control of your life, and not be controlled...Get Wealthy, Stay Healthy.

"Sun know you are Allah! Never deny yourself of being Allah, even if the whole world denies you, never deny yourself because it's your own doubt that can stop you from being Allah!" – The Father Allah

Allah Universal, born physically and mentally in Beautiful Cream City (Milwaukee, WI), was conceived and is currently living in Master Self (Mississippi), fathering civilization one mind at a time. Allah Universal has pointed thousands of people in life's right direction in a short 30 years on Earth, and is currently a supervisor for two Fortune 500 companies. He also maintains a blog at http://universallanguage007.blogspot.com

WHAT DO YOU FEAR?
Precise Infinite Peace Allah - Supreme Culture (Syracuse, NY)

What is fear? FEAR, by definition, is a feeling of anxiety, distress or being afraid. The feeling may be based on current observation or a memory of some past observation or experience. This feeling may be based in actual fact or it can be totally imaginary. Whether the feeling is factually based or completely imaginary the result is the same. Left unchecked, FEAR has the ability to incapacitate. Fear is so powerful, even when it is unconscious, that it can deprive you of the ability to think and function properly...even without you knowing what you are afraid of.

The thing about fear is that it's a learned response. I remember as a child in grade school going to the gym to get a shot. I remember as I waited in line there were kids leaving the gym that were screaming and crying. I could sense their fear and because of this I too became afraid. I don't remember getting a shot before this experience so I didn't know what to expect. I asked my classmate what all the fuss was about and my friend told me shots hurt. Then the story of shots went from hurting to your arm falling off, swelling to the size of your thigh, pain that can make you go to the hospital, etc., etc. The mental imagery was so intense that at that point I was just as afraid as the kids I saw leaving the gym. Was my fear based in actual fact? Was I even aware of this fear until I started observing people with both my eyes and ears? The answer is NO!

In many cases FEAR is a feeling we learn (planted in us) when we're young, either mentally, physically or both. Then this feeling is reinforced over time so that when we're older we still suffer from its effects.

I commonly refer a treatment for fear as "getting out of your own way." The problem is that people don't embrace fear. When a person becomes fearful there are two ways they can handle it. They can either run or fight. Many people do not know how to use both of these natural responses effectively. You have those who always run and you have others who always fight. The key is to utilize both of these responses when it's proper.

To begin making such a determination you have to look, listen and observe with all your senses. In the culture of I-God we call it "doing the Knowledge." This could even mean researching or studying what it is we fear. How many things are we afraid of that we haven't even bothered to study? The more we learn about something the less mysterious and frightening something, someone or some place becomes. All you need is the courage to do it

If there's something that really frightens you, do the Knowledge to it. Whatever your fear is, whether it be spiders, witches, spirits, demons, dogs, change, snakes, or whatever, study it and learn about it. You might find that after you've investigated a person, place or thing, it's not what you thought it was. You might find it's not as frightening as you originally perceived and even if it is something you'll continue to fear, at least you may discover ways of dealing with it. Don't yield to fear just because other people do. Do the knowledge and learn how to deal with fear.

> Precise Infinite Peace Allah is a trained mediator with both a Bachelor of Arts in Non-violent Conflict Resolution and knowledge of 120 Degrees. Precise is also an author, computer builder, disc jockey, and accomplished singer/vocalist.

WISDOM IS THE WAY
Wyking Allah - Morocco (Seattle, WA)

"He who has extensive knowledge is not a wise man." - Lao-tzu, Tao te Ching

Making the wise choice includes putting knowledge and facts before action. Facts are gained through objective observation, study, research and analysis. Wisdom is knowledge in motion or activation, whether through words and actions. Everything begins as a thought or idea, but for an idea to be able to be born onto the physical plane that we call reality, there must be way, method, means, medium, vehicle, etc. Even when you know where you want to go, you need a mode of transportation. Every idea needs a field of operation, just as a seed needs fertile ground and conditions to grow.

Wisdom is the way a thing must go in order to get from one place or state of existence to another. There are usually many different ways in which we can pursue an objective or goal. Every way has its own set of factors, circumstances and conditions that must be taken into consideration. Some paths of travel are smoother than others. Some have more twists and turns. Some have more hills and valleys. As a wise person you must study the travels of those before you and survey the land to calculate the most efficient path of travel to reach your destination.

ARE YOU A RELUCTANT MESSIAH?

Supreme Understanding Allah - Allah's Garden (Atlanta, GA)

Did you know that Dr. Martin Luther King, Jr. didn't WANT to be a leader? He was actually PUSHED into the forefront of the Civil Rights Movement by the elders who were too scared to do it themselves. As a young minister with a passion for social justice, they saw him as the perfect fit. But he didn't. He tried to decline, but they didn't relent. The rest, as you know, is history.

Jesus too, was not always excited about his job. Many times, he is quoted asking "Why?" he's been given such a difficult task. Even at his crucifixion, he still doesn't seem to fully understand what's going on ("My lord, why hast thou forsaken me?").

Let me be clear, I'm not encouraging you to believe in invisible spiritual forces that decide our fate. However, when you understand the larger scope of the Blackman as God, you will see that we were here before there was ever a physical Arm, Leg, Leg, Arm, Head. In fact, we designed the physical body AND the Arabic language...and wrote a historical sequence in advance that would one day bring the two together, only for us one day - trapped in the wilderness of North America, still recovering from slavery - to realize what Allah truly means.

What kind of a mind manufactured this world? It's ours. And it's still at work. Psychoanalysts like Carl Jung have tried to describe the collective consciousness of humanity that we describe as the superconscious mind. Jung called it the unconscious mind, because for white people, it is. Just as the pineal gland (the "third eye") is 85% calcified in whites, and mostly clear among us! This mind goes much deeper, and is much more expansive in scope and the magnetic conscious (the mind we fully share) and the infinite conscious (the mind that extends beyond space and time, and designed this universe). For us, these advanced stages of consciousness are the reason why Original People throughout the world have come up with similar inventions and ideas without any evidence of cultural contact or exchange! They are also what allow us to sense what each other is thinking. And returning to the topic of Dr. King and Jesus, this mind is the force that produces great leaders among us. Every time period and civilization has its messiahs, and this Blackmind is the source of all their inspiration. Should you be able to fully tap into it, you may be one yourself. But are you ready for it?

The Bible tells us about Moses, who had killed a man in anger, fled for his life, and lived with self-doubt. His stuttering made him so self-conscious that when the Lord called on him to lead, he attempted to decline. The Lord promised that he would empower Moses to do whatever was needed, and a reluctant Messiah was born. There are several reluctant figures in the Bible who channel the divine energy described as God to accomplish great things. This list includes men like Jeremiah, who most certainly didn't want the job of Prophet, but later explained, "If I say I will not mention him or speak any more in his name, there is in my heart as it were a burning fire shut up in my bones and I am not able to hold it in." (Jeremiah 10:9). When you have tapped into your true calling, it takes a LOT to turn it down.

What does this have to do with you? Everything.

When I would wonder how an uneducated (schoolwise, at least) brother from Danville, Virginia...who kept company with tons of shady characters...who had troubles of his own...and who'd never met any prophet from the East...could come to such an incredible realization that he would eventually produce a culture that would effectively change the consciousness of the world...I am in awe. How did Allah come to realize the mathematical principles that govern the universe...and then give them to us in a way that would not only survive, but spread? How did Allah design this culture in such a way that we didn't die off or get destroyed like almost EVERY other Black organization of that era? How did this man know in 1968 that he would be gone the next year (that's recorded in his FBI files)...and understand how to prepare us to survive?

Simple. He tapped into what was naturally his. And ours. That infinite consciousness that wrote the programming for this entire universe, mapped out its history in advance, and produced Messiahs from ordinary men for hundreds of thousands of years. Allah was another Christ, and if the Christ in the Bible wasn't a real historical person, then Allah was THE Christ. After all, FBI COINTELPRO files from Allah's time also make it clear that they were intensely fearful of the rise of a "Black Messiah," who could galvanize the Black community to make a TRUE change. Marches and protests were no problem for them. What the white power structure was worried about (and still is) is a change in our consciousness. And that is why this culture is a natural progression from all the other movements that preceded us. Garvey made us proud to be Black. Noble Drew Ali introduced us to Islam. The Black Panthers gave us political consciousness, but no concept of God. The Nation of Islam avoided political consciousness, but used Islam to teach us that we were Gods, though they taught that within the context of religious belief and a hierarchical leadership of "big Gs" and "little Gs." And then the Five Percent emerged.

Allah produced the culmination of Black consciousness in America. An awareness of our true divine nature, a commitment to social transformation, and NO RELIGION. Allah did that! A dude don't just come up with this stuff in his basement eating Cheetos.

And there's work to be done. We have the consciousness, but the political action has to take place. Community reform has to take place. Social transformation is the only step to come. There's no further consciousness needed than what you find right here, among us. To spend more time on that would be a WASTE of energy we should be using to change the world, as Allah said we'd do.

So this is where you come in. Are you a reluctant Messiah? Do you have a sense of what your true calling could be, but you're reluctant to embrace it? Or are you so full of self-doubt that you haven't even allowed yourself to see what you're really here to do? Trust me, if you're reading this book, you're probably not meant to work a desk job until you retire one day into oblivion. No, you are one of those who will be in a history book one day. But what side of history will you be on? Allah taught us that we should find ourselves in the Qur'an or Bible, because our history may already have been written! I know my calling. Do you?

GOD HAS NO RELIGION
Transcript of an Interview with Allah the Father

Protect the child. Show him [that] if he doesn't do right he is going to go to jail, just like the Muslims [teach]. I'm not against anyone, but they are really teaching their children not to smoke, drink or do anything to require other people to follow their standards. Now, I don't teach the child not to smoke. I teach him to get the understanding of it! Because I don't have no religion, because that doesn't do anything for him. Now if you taught the child under religion like the Muslims, they say no smoking. And if you do smoke, they send you out. They can force - what? Religion!

You can't win nothing by force. If you give the child something to fight for, then show him what he is fighting for, he'll win this war. And you've got to have the manpower to do it...So you got to keep the children together and you got to kill all religion. Other than that you are going to lose all fighting in them...And the Five

Percenters, I'm teaching them that they can't go on religion because religion has never did anything for them. Like my mother, she said, "Jesus, Jesus, Jesus." I know he's over there in Jerusalem, dead in the earth, because he hasn't showed me nothing!...

Now I was in the Army. I don't teach them not to go in the Army. I went and I came back. I saw action. I got the Bronze Star. I got all these medals. Now I came back home. I didn't benefit from it [in terms of] luxury, but I did benefit by knowing how to teach a man. They teach a man to make a boy a man. This is what I did. I don't teach them not to drink. I teach them to keep their mouth what? Shut! And listen and learn. Because I might tell them to drink...to get to that man I want to get to. Just like the United States teach the FBI...

All my people are against me because they thought that I was supposed to have came out, when I came from Matteawan, and joined them - and I haven't joined any of them yet and I'm not going to join them because I'm civilized. We don't talk about nobody on religion, politics, war and protest in the United States...Because religious people fight against one another. You can't tell me they don't because they do!

They'll tell me that, "Why should you tell the child not to eat swine?" I say, "Why? It's in your Bible, in Leviticus and Deuteronomy." I'll show them where they are not even good religious people...In the Bible it teaches that Jesus had many disciples but they only had knowledge and wisdom. Jesus was the thirteenth. He had knowledge and understanding. He was the only one that they had to kill. Because why? He had knowledge and what? Understanding! Where the other ones had the knowledge and wisdom, they had to go and get Jesus. He was the only healer. You understand that?

Now this is the way it is. You can't do the wisdom until you have the knowledge, right? When you go to school you got to have the knowledge before you could come out and put that into practice. And they don't know you got it until you go out and put it into practice. This is why I teach the child to go and get the knowledge, come back and put it into practice, then the people will get the what? Understanding! Then they'll know your Culture. No one taught me this. And I'm telling you the knowledge now because this is the 11th month, which means Knowledge - what? Knowledge!...

And this is what you better do because I'm telling you...To hold any nation together - I read in a book what a white man said one time and I take all book knowledge and use it to benefit myself. I don't care who I heard it from. He said the wealth of a country is the children. Not the money. Once upon a time there was no money. The wealth of any country is the children. And if you don't keep the young people strong, how you going to win?...[Interviewer: How do you make them strong? In what way do you get the young people strong?] Feed them the right foods. Don't teach religion...I can tell [religious people] all about them but they can't tell me nothing about me because I'm a new breed that they don't know about. Now what are they going to tell about me when I can tell them all about themselves?...

I can show a religious man that he never led anyone to God. Not the Pope or anyone. They all died and all the people in the Bible died. Now where are they? Where are they? The only way you will find God is if you keep on reproducing until he make himself known. And the Pope, he's supposed to be a successor to God. Where did they show the people [the proof]? Have they? Elijah says W. D. Fard is God. Where is he? They make me sick...

They didn't force me to go to church in Matteawan. They said "Allah we don't have your service here." I said "If you did have Muslim service, that is not my service." Because I don't have no religion. And they didn't force me to go. They put on my paper "very religious man" and I said, "No, I don't have no religion." They put on my paper that I was a leader and I said, "No, I'm not a leader."

The record above is pulled from the transcript of Allah's discussion with officials at the Otisville Training Institute for Boys, a juvenile correctional facility where some of Allah's Five Percenters had been placed. Shortly after his release from Matteawan, Allah came to Otisville to clarify what he taught and what he wanted for his youth. This interview was conducted November 15, 1967, and is the only surviving audio record of Allah speaking. In recent years, some have attempted to portray Allah and the Five Percent as an "extension" of the Nation of Islam, using questionable sources as authorities while ignoring others. However, the existing historical record reveals that Allah was clear on his ideology and intentions.

BELIEVE IN JESUS AND LOSE YOUR MIND
Almighty Supreme Scientist – Born Mecca (Baltimore, MD)

"A casual stroll through a lunatic asylum shows that faith does not prove anything." - Friedrich Wilhelm Nietzsche

When someone asserts that they "believe in god," I interpret that they are simply warning me that they are a very, very crazy person. They have, in effect, lost their mind!

"Worship God. It's easier than thinking."- Chapman Cohen

Let me explain...Religion unabashedly asserts that we are entirely incapable of successfully thinking for ourselves. The theology of Christianity, for instance, implies that, if we do not allow the mystery god, Jesus, or holy ghost to make up our minds for us, we are bound to fail and/or be punished in everything we do. We are not capable of making the right choices in life and we must depend on the mystery god to think for us at all times. So, we are encouraged to "pray to god" constantly, adopt certain

71

customs and traditions, and immerse ourselves in a particular lifestyle to remain on the 'right path.'

"Religion is now the first obstacle to women's advancement. Religion pulls human beings backwards, it goes against science and progressiveness. Religion engulfs people with a fear of the supernatural. It bars people from learning and never allows people to exercise their choice." - Taslima Nasrin

This belief creates the impression that our own intelligence is actually an obstacle, rather than an asset. It implies that mental consideration and investigation is a tremendous waste of one's time, energy and effort. Consequently, thinking itself soon becomes a hazard and our brain becomes our worst enemy. Thus, it should be clearly understood that theists are offering that there is absolutely no opportunity for us to be victorious without having the mystery god program our brains. In fact, in the event that we even attempt to think for ourselves, we will be punished with a severe punishment. This is because a 'true', or 'good' theist, believes without question. There can be no doubt that holding this belief is self-destructive and dangerous. Interesting enough, however, is the fact that theists spend a tremendous amount of time and effort attempting to make an argument that their way of life is supreme. Simply by asking us to consider submitting to the mystery god, theists are calling on us to utilize the very instrument they assert is faulty and unreliable: **our intelligence**. They are asking us to make a 'life saving' decision.

"When we blindly adopt a religion, a political system, a literary dogma, we become automatons. We cease to grow." – Anais Nun

How can one 'decide' that a particular doctrine is the 'true religion' or that there is a so-called god without some degree of mental deliberation? For example, how does a Christian theist come to believe that there exists a "Jesus Christ?" Did he use his intellect or was it through some other means? Was he compelled to accept this idea by threats of force, ignorance, haste, or was there a sound, rational line of information to lead him to the said conclusion? **THIS IS IMPORTANT TO CONSIDER** because the common theist will behave as if his beliefs, or faith, simply fell into his head unknowingly. The theist will happily confide that he "just has faith" and that you should "just have faith" and "accept your lord and savior Jesus Christ," as well. Why? Because "just having faith" breaks the natural decision making process. It, essentially, asks you to make a decision **NOT** to make a decision!

With all of the so-called arguments made by religious people, isn't the religious community attempting to appeal to our intelligence? If we are capable of making a rational and right choice about accepting Jesus, what does this reveal about our decision-making ability? For one, it proves that theists know very well that man is fully capable of making intelligent decisions on his or her own.

Advocates of religion seek hope we never notice the contradiction. Critical thinking and free thought are formidable opponents to anyone wanting to make a person docile and submissive, mentally and/or physically. To counter our natural tendency to want to think things through, weigh our options and make the best decision, religion introduces the thought-interrupting mechanisms of belief and faith. Therefore, I offer, once more, that anyone who adopts, defends and celebrates these kinds of psychologically destructive practices is dangerous both in principle and in practice.

> *"I have found Christian dogma unintelligible.*
> *Early in life I absented myself from Christian assemblies." - Benjamin Franklin*

OOH, YOU GON' GET A WHUPPIN'

It doesn't matter if a person is civilized and does right in all his undertakings. If he is unwilling to accept the so-called 'god' as his maker and owner, then he will be punished with a severe punishment. It is this line of emotional 'reasoning' that they save for people smart enough to recognize and question the weak foundation of religious beliefs. Intimidation is mental coercion. Make no mistake, when the theist asks us to believe in his religious teachings, he is ultimately demanding us to believe or suffer the consequences. What a choice. When the theist offers that they are obeying god because faith is an outstanding practice or 'god said so', it's not the whole truth. Instead, their ultimate motivation is the psychological promise of sanction from punishment, the possibility of reward.

Offering that we will be punished or destroyed is only poor substitution for concise explanation and sound argumentation. Threats do not compel mentally grown people into action. We have to break the rope of arbitrary, irrational and emotional action. If theology declares that something is right, wrong, evil, or immoral, then we demand a more thorough explanation than because 'god says so' or the 'bible tells me so.'

> *"No amount of belief makes something a fact." - James Randi*

The theist trains himself to believe that it is wrong to question the so-called 'authority' of their 'god', religious book, or any leader of their religious institution. This actually tricks the theist into blindly accepting whatever a person tells them they must believe. Thus, they expect to be punished for independent thought and investigation. They are programmed to feel guilty if they do not habitually involve themselves in religious customs. And they believe they rightly deserve hard times and headaches for the very thought of leaving the hold of their mystery god. This internal guilt and lack of self-confidence combined with a promise of eternal reprimand and punishment, keeps the theist 'in his place.' Consciously or subconsciously, religion attempts to chisel away at man's confidence in himself until he becomes docile, timid and doubtful of his own self-control.

Decisions are generally based on one or more of four basic elements: (1) Knowledge, (2) Emotion, (3) Ignorance and (4) Urgency. As discussed elsewhere in this book, knowledge is always the most reliable factor for determining a course of action. Emotions, ignorance and haste are all unsound bridges to successful decision making. While we are constantly being compelled to utilize factors 2, 3, 4, rarely are we exposed to factor 1 (Knowledge) as a viable avenue to action. We are given everything but a strong foundation to make decisions and thus structure our lives.

DIE, DIE, DIE...YOU DOUBTING THOMAS!

"A man is accepted into a church for what he believes, and he is turned out for what he knows." - Mark Twain

Theology requires that we must believe without question or be tagged as evil, immoral, amoral or damned to hell. Extreme as it may seem, in the religious paradigm, to 'doubt' literally means to die. Perhaps not doubting was a simple matter in the days before easy access to scientific thinking. Unfortunately, events like blood turning into wine, rods turning into snakes, men walking on water, angels, demons and monsters are just not a visible part of man's existence nowadays. (As if they ever were)

The act of making a decision itself involves identifying and evaluating all alternatives and choosing the most rational option from a given selection. Theology often attempts to disrupt the natural process of decision making by setting up unnecessary emotional time constraints on its believers. For instance, it is the position of the Christian community that the so-called "Jesus" is en route from behind the clouds in the sky (coming to 'get' all of us non-believers) and we must choose now to submit or we will be punished upon his arrival. Perhaps a few Christians actually believe "Jesus" really IS coming to save or destroy those who do not believe their theology and this is their reason for insisting that making a decision to submit is such an urgent matter? However, what is this so-called urgency founded on? Why is a man told that he must choose as soon as possible, often that same moment? Is it because the Bible, written Quran, "Jesus," or the so-called mystery god said so? Wouldn't it be a risky to rush this kind of decision? If it's such an important matter, then a detailed, thorough investigation and evaluation, regardless of the "impending danger," is warranted, is it not?

In fact, delaying making a decision can be an important and necessary aspect of being successful in our undertakings. However, delaying the decision-making process and not automatically believing in the teachings of Christianity allows us to search for additional information, wait for more suitable alternatives to arise, or even to change our minds. This means that it would be a disadvantage for Christians to encourage us to be careful, investigate all we can, and, in our own good time, decide to 'accept Jesus.' Instead, the Christian community sabotages our ability to make sound decisions by inducing fear in the weak and rushing them to believe, as well as by establishing social institutions and practices which insulate its believers and further reinforces the idea of embracing ignorance.

"Let the human mind loose. It must be loose. It will be loose. Superstition and dogmatism cannot confine it." - John Adams, letter to his son, John Quincy Adams, November 13, 1816

Indeed, there will be numerous occasions when we will be required to act without complete certainty of the outcome. However, this does not mean that we should put our feet in the "circle of belief" and "eenie meenie minie mo" our decisions in life. We still are obliged to make a decision based on our knowledge and understanding of the best available evidence. Unfortunately for theists, the best avenue available to us now-a-days is not within the confines of the Bible, written Quran, or any religious leader or doctrine. It is a scientific method which allows us to make corrections, try new possible solutions, and discard the course of action that is not all-wise and right and exact. All things which are not compatible with the rigid, dogmatic doctrine of "have faith or else!"

QUESTIONS:

1. On what grounds should we consider forfeiting our evident self-control to become directed by the not-so-evident mystery god of religion?
2. Where is the evidence to show that we are incompetent and a threat to ourselves in the absence of that mystery god's direction and guidance?
3. Where is the proof that the theist is receiving any success in life that is outside of the grasps of the nonreligious individual?

Unfortunately, I can assure you that no theist will sincerely address, or consider, the above questions as long as they remain satisfied with 'just believing.'

The constant insistence of there being a mystery god who is superior to us, but unseen, only works to produce a weak, slave minded people. What if religious people directed as much time and energy trying to discover and learn about themselves as they do their mystery god? What would happen if each theist would simply make a more earnest effort to improve their decision-making process, instead of devaluing themselves and their abilities by surrendering to their beliefs? It should be clear that theology tries to 'convince' us that we are unable to guide ourselves, protect our families, and control our environment (i.e. homes, neighborhood, etc.) without tagging the problem-solving palm of the invisible "Jesus" in the sky.

I don't fault religion for being the product of superstitious and unaware minds. I also do not hate theists for holding the beliefs that they do. However, I am very skeptical of the man or woman who will continue to rely on religion as his or her guide and measure in life after they have been exposed to scientific and mathematical evidence that contradicts their belief system. Why would I expect someone to deal equally with me in any other area of life, if they have already expressed a bias in favor of belief and mysteries? If someone proposes that myths and assumptions about themselves and the universe hold a greater importance and authority than their own observation, experience and logic, then such a person is a certified weak link in the chain of civilization.

Any rule, command or law must be understood before one acts. We are not absent-minded children. Unfortunately, because the Nation of Gods and Earths demand evidence of the mystery god and the reason for 'his' religious rules before we comply, we are cited as being negative, evil, rebellious, and oppositional or wicked. It is for this reason, the members of the Nation of Gods and Earths are so often portrayed as being pitted against morals and ethics. I would ask the theist who holds this position, "Does the so-called mystery god submit to the rules and commandments of your religion?" The fact is, the mystery god cannot submit to himself. Therefore, what do they imagine is keeping that so-called mystery god civilized, moral and upright? Obviously, the same thing that keeps Supreme Scientist righteous: **his intelligence.** But, of course, not too many people can understand this because they have LOST THEIR MIND!!!

"The inhabitants of the earth are of two sorts: Those with brains, but no religion, and those with religion, but no brains." - Abu'l-`Ala' al-Ma`arri, poet of Ma`arra

---

Almighty Supreme Scientist was born in Cream City (Milwaukee, WI) in 1977, and received a B.A. in Sociology with a minor in Psychology from the University of Wisconsin, Milwaukee in 2000. Scientist is currently the Vice President of American Utility Choice and CEO of Black Nutrition Productions in Born Mecca (Baltimore, MD). As an educator and mentor, he has worked closely with the children and families of Cream City, Born Mecca, and its surrounding communities towards helping children become strong servant leaders.

PRAY AND IT WON'T COME
Supreme Understanding Allah - Allah's Garden (Atlanta, GA)

"The sailor does not pray for wind, he learns to sail" - Gustaf Lindborg

One of the primary characteristics of our self-realization as God is the fundamental understanding of cause and effect. E. Franklin Frazier, in his classic research into man's spiritual and religious culture, described "magic" as an individual's belief that some sort of formula could be used to achieve real effects. That is, a magical object, incantation, or belief, could decide what would happen in physical reality.

Those who believe in magic would, for example, recite a prayer for rain. If it did rain, the belief in the power of the prayer and the gods/belief systems with which it was associated would be affirmed and reinforced. If it did not rain, fault would be attributed to the practitioner who would find some flaw in either his recitation, himself, other unforeseen circumstances, or the stronger magic or will of evil spirits plotting against the needs of the practitioner. To cite a modern example, think about bowling. When a bowler rolls the ball, he prays or says his "lucky words," hoping for a strike.

If he gets a strike, he feels his prayer works.

If he doesn't, he blames it on his roll, the ball, or other factors.

But he never figures out that his prayer didn't change anything. So…how far have we come?

As they say in the film *What the Bleep Do We Know?*, people today, with all of our scientific advances and technical knowledge, still retain a "backwater" concept of God and spirituality. Prayers are nothing more than the magic tribal people subscribe to. They have no real effect. There is no mystery God. As Min. Farrakhan has said, rain is real. How can you attribute a real effect to such unreal causes (Mystery God)? Anyone who is aware of the water cycle should have abandoned the theory of God "making" it rain. However, I have heard grown people describing fog over a cemetery as "spirits," loud thunder as "God's anger," and disasters like Hurricane Katrina as "God's will." This is not to mention the childlike beliefs that praying for prosperity (or tithing for prosperity) will somehow relieve the poor of their financial conditions, or that elderly people are really cured of their ailments in those mega-churches with the charismatic white evangelists.

"I prayed for freedom twenty years, but received no answer until I prayed with my legs." - Frederick Douglass

Don't get me wrong, our MINDS do have power. We CAN affect reality with our thoughts, especially our own health. Studies have shown that people who are able to focus their minds can channel their thoughts to heal themselves and improve their own lives. But studies have NOT shown that religious people can call on an unseen God to help them out in real affairs with any degree of success. Even the Bible says, "God helps those who help themselves."

"Stop the mindless wishing that things would be different.
Rather than wasting time and emotional and spiritual energy in explaining why we don't have what we want,
we can start to pursue other ways to get it." - Greg Anderson

So rather than pray for my desired results, I introduce causative stimuli or action to produce the inevitable effects. In simple English, I put in the work needed to make it happen.

The above essay is based on an excerpt from Supreme Understanding's book, *How to Hustle and Win: A Survival Guide for the Ghetto, Part One*, available at most Black bookstores and online at www.HustleAndWin.com or www.SupremeDesignOnline.com

THE BEAUTY OF KNOWLEDGE
Knowledge Infinite Supreme Allah – Interior Cipher

This build pertains to the very first degree given in Supreme Mathematics, Knowledge (1). Knowledge is the foundation upon which we stand. Knowledge is the beginning of one's mental resurrection. It is the 1st stage of Light that shines within the Mind.

The Messenger of Allah, The Hon. Elijah Muhammad, said this of knowledge:

One of the attributes of Allah, the All-Wise God, Who is the Supreme Being, is knowledge. Knowledge is the result of learning and is a force or energy that makes its bearer accomplish or overcome obstacles, barriers and resistance.

Knowledge is superior to belief! This is an actual fact. Belief is defined as a state or habit of mind in which trust or confidence is placed in some person or thing. So to believe in something is to trust that it is true, but we still do not know it to be true. Belief is uncertainty which is not a firm foundation upon which one can stand in full confidence. Therefore, belief can never surpass knowledge.

Some brothers believe in God. Some brothers acknowledge the reality of themselves as God. Many people's incorrect beliefs exist simply due to a lack of the knowledge of self. Self is composed of the element's that make up one's whole identity. There is a duality of self expressed as the Higher Self and the lower self. The lower self is rooted in the earthly plane. It is the seat of man's carnal desires, bodily instincts and sensual nature. The Higher Self is rooted in the heavenly plane. It is the seat of man's higher mental and spiritual faculties and his divine nature. It is our true essence.

The Knowledge (1st) degree in the Supreme Alphabet is "Allah." Allah is the foundation of all things in existence. Allah is The One. Allah manifests Himself in all of His creation, in every particle, yet there is only one vehicle which Allah, the Infinite Living Mind, created to serve as the truest living manifestation of Himself, and that vehicle is the Black body of the Original man.

We are dealing with Knowledge. So let's review the Knowledge degree in the Student Enrollment:

1. Who is the Original man?
Ans. The Original man is the Asiatic Blackman, the maker, the owner, the cream of the planet Earth, father of civilization, God of the Universe.

You see, Knowledge is symbolic to the Original man. Just as Knowledge is 1st in the Supreme Mathematics, the Original man is 1st in Allah's World Manifest. He is the 1st man to walk upon the Earth.

When we say that the Original man is God and that we come in the name of Allah, some Muslims who follow the Arabs' understanding say that it is blasphemy, b.u.t. this is the blast for them if they can see - The Holy Qur'an, Surah 2, Ayat 30 states: "Behold, thy Lord said to the angels: 'I will create a vicegerent on Earth.'"

Now let's break it down. "Vicegerent" is composed of "vice," which means "in the place of," and "gerent," which derives from a Latin root meaning "to carry or carry on." So a vicegerent is one who carries on in place of someone or something. In place of what? In the place of a righteous but unseen being, the Original man's physical composition is Allah's vehicle to carry on as God on the physical plane.

Again, the Holy Qur'an, Sura 15, Ayat 28-30 states:
And when thy Lord said to the angels I am going to create a mortal of sound clay, of black mud fashioned into shape.
So when I have made him complete and breathed into him of My spirit, fall down making obeisance to him.
So the angels made obeisance [prostrated themselves], all of them together.

Here, we have Allah breathing His Spirit into the Original man. This goes back to the Higher Self, the Original man's true essence, which is Allah. Also, the angels bowing down in obeisance to the Original man demonstrates His divinity and symbolically conveys the fact that the Original man is God.

Do the Knowledge! Peace.

KNOWLEDGE VERSUS BELIEF
WHICH SIDE ARE YOU ON?
Almighty Supreme Scientist - Born Mecca (Baltimore, MD)

"The belief you have is without knowing, whether you believe rightly or not. When a man believes a thing and doesn't have nothing but belief, whether it's right or wrong, and has no proof, he just believes." - Elijah Muhammad

A brief investigation of the devil's civilization will reveal a wide variety of distortions and falsehoods. To the inquisitive individual who is in search of an answer to any one of life's common equations, there are many so-called 'solutions' floating around. Around every corner, someone is professing to possess the right and exact method of action. Whether it is a 'new and improved' remedy or a 'well-known, ancient' ritual, there is no shortage of ideas. What is the most reliable source for discovering the truth? How can we distinguish fact from fantasy? These are some of the most significant questions we can ask ourselves in becoming critical thinkers.

To the average person, there is no difference between the concepts of belief and knowledge. Belief is the acceptance of something as true in the absence of, or in spite of, proof. Knowledge is the result of using the five senses of sight, touch, taste, hearing and smell to observe. However, to the average person, "believe" and "know" mean the same thing: to be sure about something.

"I do not believe in belief." - Edward M. Forster (1878-1970)

For those of us who understand and value science, we understand that the above concepts are not interchangeable and that a lack of understanding of these two concepts has been the very foundation of Original People being used as tools and slaves. It is common among the unknowing masses of the population to practice belief as the basis of their lives. In fact, our orientation into a belief system begins even before we have developed the necessary skills for distinguishing between fact and fiction. During childhood, we were predisposed by our active imaginations to accept various pretend notions about life. As we developed in age and maturity, we began to adopt a more critical standard of qualifying and disqualifying our concepts about the world around us. No longer could we simply believe in a myth that was contradictory to, or out of the perimeters of, our senses. As a result, we were carefully weaned from one fictional expression of life to the next. The latter differs only by being slightly more complimentary to our growing logic and understanding of the real world around us.

We begin our enrollment into deception being exposed to talking animals, to storybook and television characters, to the Easter bunny, to the Tooth Fairy, to Santa Claus, and ultimately 'graduating' into accepting a Mystery God that no one can see until he dies (supposedly!). While we tend to suffocate our youth in fanciful ideas and stories early on in life, Proper Education must Always Correct Errors before they are big men and women. Why is this so? Because we know very well that, if they are to survive and be successful as adults, they must be able to know life in actuality from what exists in their imagination. A child with an imaginary friend seems acceptable; an adult with an imaginary friend is pathetic. A child who believes in talking animals seems cute; an adult who does is disturbed. Do you feel comfortable around adults who hear voices? Or does it depend on who the voices (supposedly) belong to? This is why - as the child matures - we must reduce, if not eliminate, the reliance on myths, legends and beliefs.

> *"He can't be stopped with knowledge. Knowledge and belief are different.*
> *I can believe that there's an airplane out there on the door steps, but that may be just a belief.*
> *There is no airplane out there." - Elijah Muhammad, The Theology of Time*

The likelihood of adult success increases as such proper education increases. We can even identify the growth of civilization by the number of individuals graduating from primitive belief systems to educational and scientific systems. Having agreed that - at best - assumptions about life (also known as beliefs) only contribute to psychological comfort and, oftentimes, actually hinder clear perception of reality, we realize the importance of an education that facilitates the skills needed to discover truth and reject falsehood. This is the form of education advocated and practiced by The Nation of Gods and Earths.

There are basically two schools of thought within the 5%: the religious and the scientific. Muslims are characteristic of the former and The Nation of Gods and Earths the latter. It is important to note the differences in the methods each group utilizes to discover truth and also their individual rites, rituals, and behaviors. While many are interested in the "Knowledge" of the 5%, one must be careful of religious ideology presented as science. Oftentimes, when a person comes in the name "Five Percent" it is only a shield to cause the listener or reader to lower their defenses. The problem with this is that the term "Five Percent" is not specific enough, because individuals (or groups of people) often seek to associate themselves with our wisdom and understanding without going through the labor mandated by our culture.

The Nation of Gods and Earths (who are categorically affiliated with "Civilized People" and not "Muslims and Muslim Sons" of the 5%)

discover, learn and live the Science of Life, not the religion of Islam. You may ask, "What is the difference?" The principal distinction begins with our awareness of the criteria for determining what is, and is not, a fact. Science is based on one's observation, involves experimentation, and requires evaluation of all evidence before qualifying or disqualifying a hypothesis and arriving at a conclusion. In contrast, religion - which is a system of integrated beliefs - begins with the conclusions, and, at best, only allows the believer to "work backwards" and "prove" their beliefs through a biased collection of "supporting data." Religious people can share the same body of knowledge studied by the Gods and Earths, but they do not study this information in the same way. We critically examine, while others do not. The foundation of our way of life is knowledge. This is the difference between us and nearly everyone else. This is the significance of what Allah established in 1964.

"A true idea has no need of any faith." - Ken Harding

The advocates of belief offer that there is something 'beyond' the realms of our sensory organs (sight, smell, taste, hearing and touch). This is their 'reason' for asking us figuratively, and occasionally literally, to close our eyes and cover our ears to find some sort of 'hidden truth.' It would seem most logical to the wise and intelligent that, if one were looking for something 'hidden,' abandoning one's sensory agents would only complicate the matter. However, according to religious people, belief is required as the first, and most important, step to finding truth. In fact, religious people are actually 'rewarded' for "believing the hardest" given the least evidence.

"Believe nothing, O monks, merely because you have been told it...or because it is traditional, or because you yourselves have imagined it. Do not believe what your teacher tells you merely out of respect for the teacher. But whatsoever, after due examination and analysis, you find to be conducive to the good, the benefit, the welfare of all beings – that doctrine believe and cling to, and take it as your guide." - Gautama Buddha

Because the principle of "belief" is the foundation of any belief system, once we remove reliance on belief, the entire system falls into pieces. This is dangerous to the people who manufacture the beliefs and belief systems (for very specific reasons). And this is why the best defense for advocates of belief is to attack Knowledge as the foundation.

"The word 'belief' is a difficult thing for me. I don't believe. I must have a reason for a certain hypothesis. Either I know a thing, and then I know it – I don't need to believe it." - Dr. Carl Jung, psycoanalyst

Why? Because the birth of scientific thinking commemorates the death of potential religious thoughts and tendencies. So it is not entirely the fault of the blind, deaf and dumb that they hate and fear science and mathematics. This is especially evident when witnessing the manner in which science is advertised to the masses as a labor rather than a luxury. Not to mention the fact that too many people (the 85%) automatically assume that science is synonymous with the white man! Indeed, what a tragedy. This ignorance even extends to the area of children's television shows and movies where scientists are depicted as being crazy and eccentric villains, often costumed in long white jackets. In fact, it is these kinds of mental images that infiltrate the minds of the youth and condition them to hold negative opinions about science, even as they grow into big men and women.

The religious community, and the powers that benefit from it, must undermine scientific thinking in any way it can. This is most necessary for any belief system, if it is to preserve its appeal. If ever the blind, deaf and dumb were to discover that scientific thinking is the only shown and proven route to truth, religion would no longer be needed. If ever the illiterate thought that they could solve their problems in life by understanding the processes of the natural world, they would have no need to appeal to the 'super' natural elements of their belief system, in the process impoverishing themselves, while providing for the increased prosperity of the ones who propagate the beliefs.

However, it is not always easy to detect where people (and groups) stand when it comes to "Knowledge as the foundation." This is because many people appear to deal in Knowledge (or Science), but only to the extent that it supports their pre-existing contentions (Much as some members of "other" nations only "pretend" to use Supreme Mathematics and Supreme Alphabets when it is advantageous to their appeal). Oftentimes, this is achieved by skirting religious ideas with the language of science. However, after careful examination, many of these people later reveal that they are not interested in a scientific examination of their "ideas." And we are soon bombarded with the beliefs they would like for us to adopt.

"A Word to the Wise! Beware of False Knowledge; It is more dangerous than ignorance!"
- Universal Shaamgaud Allah

THE POWER OF THE MIND
Lord Jamar - Brand Nubian

I'd been wanting to get into the acting field for some time, but part of me felt like, "Okay, I'll get into this music thing, then someone's going to see me, like, 'Oh I need you to be in a movie.'" That was something that was always in my head but I never verbalized it, so it never happened.

I used to watch the show *Oz* like, "Damn, I love this show, but I need to be on this show. They really need me. They need some Gods up in here! They have a show about jail, and we're damn sure represented in the penal system, especially in New York, so I was like they need to have some Gods on here. And if they're going to have a God on here it needs to be me, you know what I mean?

I don't know nobody at HBO - nobody, nothing, I'm just meditating like, "I need to be on here." Watching it every week, "I need to be on here," and I vocalized it. I finally said it out loud to my manager at the time.

I'm like listen man, get me in a movie, something. The best he could do was send us to a premiere. It was the HBO premiere for *The Sopranos* when it was first coming out. So we went to that, and boom, a bunch of people from *Oz* were there, supporting HBO. We end up meeting with some of the people that work on the show, and it turns out a lot of them – white and Black - were fans of Brand Nubian. So I ended up exchanging numbers with Dean Winters, the white guy who played O'Reilly on the show. Through him, I met the creator of the show. One day, Winters called me like, "Would you ever want to be on the show?" Of course I responded, "Yeah I want to be on the show!"

Next thing I know, Tom Montana, the creator of the show, says he wants to have a meeting with me. So I go down to the meeting, and Montana starts talking to me like I'm already on the show. I didn't do nothing, I didn't read nothing! I could've been illiterate for all they knew! But he was just talking to me like, "We want you on the show but we don't know in what capacity," and he's asking what I would do. So I told him, "Listen, I'm not doing any homosexual stuff and, honestly, I don't want to play no cop." So they were like, "Well, we've just got to figure out a character for you and then figure out a crime that got you in there."

So I said, "Have you ever heard of the Gods and Earths?" He hadn't. I gave him a basic synopsis of the Gods and Earths, how we represent in the penal system and all that. And I let him know that we teach that the Black man is God. He looks at me and says, "So if the Black man is God, does that mean the white man is the devil?" I looked this man – the white creator of the show - right in his eye and said, "Yes it does."

At first, it was silence.

Then, he responds, "I like it, I like that." He liked it. That was the defining moment, because anybody else who wasn't sure of themselves, or sure of what they're dealing with, or just plain nervous, thinking, "Damn, if I say the white man is the devil that means he's not going to give me the job." Not me. I looked the top dude in his eye because he's no bigger than me. Not physically, but as a person. I'm God so there's no higher than God. Just because you're the creator of the show doesn't make you more supreme than me. I said, "Yes, it does mean that the white man is the devil." He says, "I like it."

He put me in as Supreme Allah, a name I suggested in homage to a brother I used to run with, who's currently incarcerated. He wrote the part and then wrote everything else for my character based on my input. I felt it was important that the Gods be represented, because I hadn't seen the Gods on film since this movie called *Short Eyes* back in the day with Chris Mayfield. That was a movie that had me excited when I first saw it because they talked about Yacub and had the Gods in there building for real! I was like, "Wow, this is great!"

But since then, I hadn't seen nothing featuring the Gods, as far as a movie or a TV show. So I was like, now I have a chance to bring the Gods to a more global stage and a different life than just music. I did Oz longer than any other rapper they had on there. I did a season and a half before my character got killed. And that opened up a lot of doors for me. I ended up doing *Law and Order*, *Third Watch*, *The Sopranos*, and I've done a few different independent films. I've also been doing voice-over work with ESPN. A lot of people don't know that, for the past few years, I've been the voice of the Winter and Summer X Games. Doing *Oz* opened the door for me, but it was really the power of the mind, it was me focusing and meditating on something that physically brought me to that place. Do you understand what I'm saying?

Lord Jamar is a prolific emcee and actor. He is a member of the hip-hop group Brand Nubian, which formed in 1989. As an actor, he is best known for his role of Supreme Allah on the TV series *Oz*. He has appeared on *Law & Order: Special Victims Unit*, *Third Watch*, and *The Sopranos*. He has done production work for artists such as Dead Prez, Buckshot, Shaka Amazulu The 7th and Tom Browne. He released his debut solo album *The 5% Album* (an album dedicated to the Nation of Gods and Earths) on June 27, 2006. He is currently working on several projects, including a biopic film on the life of Allah the Father.

DROPPING SCIENCE
C'BS ALife Allah – New Heaven (New Haven, CT)

According to everyone I've spoken to who knew Allah, he had a unique cadence, or style of speaking. This was due, in part, to the fact that his family was from down South. Combine this with the unique way that Allah interpreted the degrees and you had a specific vernacular that he passed down to his sons. It was this "self-styled" wisdom that helped make the Nation of Gods and Earths what we are today. That's because this vernacular was attractive to the youth AND it was attractive to those people whose lives depended on the 'streets.' This is part of the heritage that we inherited from Allah. Thus, we are able to communicate with the common man with a common touch. It's important to come to the people as the people so as not to alienate the people.

With Supreme Mathematics, we received a universal language. With the Supreme Alphabet, we received a glossary. With 120 degrees, we received a map that we can use to navigate through life. Our collective vernacular is oftentimes referred to as "Building" or "Dropping Science." Some 'scholars' have called it "sciencing." Man, I just talk so people can understand. We use uncommon words llike tricknology, interorientation and devilishment. We make them relevant to the people. One of the aspects of 'sciencing' is reverse acronyms (backronyms). You can find this among the Nation when we break down various words utilizing our Supreme

Alphabet such as I Self Lord And Master (I.S.L.A.M.) or God Cipher Divine (G.O.D.).

Another aspect of our vernacular is breaking down words into the component syllables and seeing what words resonate with those syllables. Some groups refer to this as lexigraming. You hear this when the Gods and Earths break down words like Knowledge as "know the ledge" or Wisdom as "Wise the Dumb."

Even with the lingo, it's still all about HOW you display it. The Nation has had schools in various cities since the late 60's yet the spreading of this knowledge was never limited to a building like it is with many religious organizations (churches, mosques, etc). This is probably due to the fact that Allah left Mosque #7 of the Nation of Islam in order to bring this message to youth on the streets. And our Nation didn't even have a school until some years after we came on the scene in 1964. So what you had were a whole bunch of youth who didn't have a place to teach. So they took it to the streets. By the time the Nation did get a school, the ethic of street teaching was already in place. Our "schools" were already on every corner. We only acquired buildings to add on to what we were already doing. Thus the first school, now known as Allah Youth Center in Mecca, commonly known as the "Allah School," was originally known as the Allah Street Academy.

In fact, the "cipher" in hip hop culture came directly from the Gods building in ciphers. Instead of having one person on one side speaking to the audience, the Gods put the speaker in the center so that he was an equal distance from everybody. And the Gods were basically required to have big mouths. What I mean is that the Gods were instructed by Allah to build where they were at. They were told to engage the people when walking the streets. Even when building amongst ourselves in public we were taught to speak loud enough so that passerby can catch an earful of what we are building about. This draws people into the conversation. This is the power of magnetic. And this is what makes people want to learn about something they previously knew nothing about.

All of the above are verbal techniques that appeal to the conditions of our people in the wilderness of North America. It propels people to think in new ways. So when the Gods and Earths are building, do the knowledge – you may hear something that sparks your mental, and gets you "thinking outside of the box" from inside of the cipher.

❧ 3 ❧
THE BIRTHRIGHT

WHY IS THE BLACK MAN GOD?
Supreme Understanding Allah - Allah's Garden (Atlanta, GA)

INTRODUCTION

The following essay is a brief attempt to present and explain the godhood of the Black man for contemporary readers. I have made significant effort to limit the technical vocabulary, so as to ease the pace of reading, and to avoid clogging the passages with overly technical details and footnotes. The following arguments are summaries, and not meant to cover the immense body of knowledge and wisdom available on these topics. Although some references are provided, the reader is encouraged to seek further information on their own. Good questions produce good answers. To be fair, I have also included a few of the common counter-arguments I have heard, as well as brief responses. The reader is encouraged, above all, to read with an open mind.

THE ORIGINAL MAN

It is important that we first establish that the Black man is the first man, or the original man. Several major anthropological studies have documented this widely accepted fact. All peoples descend from him, either naturally or unnaturally. Europeans have even created fake fossils like the Piltdown man to try to discredit and distort the origins of humanity and place the first man in Europe. The earliest fossils of man have been found in South Africa and East Africa. Further information can be found in *The African Origin of Civilization* by Cheikh Anta Diop. *Forbidden Archaeology: The Hidden History of the Human Race* by Michael Cremo contains a wealth of evidence detailing the earliest existence of highly-advanced humans throughout the world, far predating even the earliest accepted date of three million years ago.

Original means the origin of all that follows. In stating that the Black man is the original man, many of the references that appear in the following pages, referring to "man," can be understood to refer to the archetype of man himself, the Black man. Some authors have advocated that the true human is the hue-man, or man of color, and that mankind refers to the "kind of man" that followed.

THE FATHER OF CIVILIZATION

Blacks developed the first civilizations. Throughout the ancient and prehistoric world, Blacks have been the founders of all known civilizations. Examples include: (a) the first dynasties of ancient China, (b) the pre-Hellenic Minoan and Mycenean civilizations which birthed ancient Greece and Rome, (c) the ancient Egyptians of course, (d) the pre-Semitic Chaldeans, Babylonians, Sumerians, and their other middle Eastern neighbors, (e) the Kushites and other obviously Black civilizations in the continent known as Africa, (f) the Olmecs, the early Mayans and other Black pre-Columbian civilizations of the Americas (including the Black Indians Columbus met upon his initial voyages here), (g) the ancient Black civilizations of the Indus river valley in India, (h) and the Black civilizations of ancient Europe. Evidence of these claims can be found in *African Presence in Early Asia* edited by Runoko Rashidi, *African Presence in Early Europe*, *African Presence in Early America*, and *They Came Before Columbus* by Ivan Van Sertima, and *The African Origin of Civilization* by Cheikh Anta Diop. Further evidence can be found on numerous articles, available on the internet, authored by Clyde Ahmad Winters, Runoko Rashidi, and dozens of others. Much of this information, and more, should also be available online at the *Global African Presence* website. (www.cwo.com/~lucumi/runoko.html)

THE SOURCE OF THE WORLD'S LEARNING

Until the contemporary attempts by Europeans to discredit the capabilities of Blacks, the Black man has been regarded as surpassing all people and nations in his wisdom and intellect. Visitors from far-off lands studied among the Black teachers of Ancient Egypt in the Mystery Schools. Socrates and other Greeks regarded as the fathers of European philosophy were trained at these schools by Blacks. Plato, Socrates' student, challenged the Greek concept of God, which was in fact a Europeanized version of the Black gods of Egypt. Plato, not having met the true and living Gods himself, appeared disgruntled with the human flaws of the otherwise supreme Greek gods.

"Through philosophical thinking the Greeks came to the point of subordinating, distrusting, and even minimizing anything physical. Anything that possessed flesh was always underminded in Greek thought. And so in order to receive inspiration from Jesus the Greeks had to apotheosize him...The birth of Jesus is quite similar to the birth of the sons of Zeus. It was believed in Greek thought that an extraordinary person could only be explained by saying that he had a father who was more than human. It is probable that this Greek idea influenced Christian thought." - Dr. Martin Luther King Jr., critiquing the myth of Christ

The Greeks were, until the era of Plato, still praising and worshipping the Black men of Egypt. These facts are documented in George G. M. James' *Stolen Legacy* and Martin Bernal's *Black Athena*. Examples include Zeus and Hercules, who were modeled after Osiris and Horus, and the Black god Imhotep, who is revered in the primary creed of medicine, the Hippocratic Oath. These Black individuals were not mythical figures, but historical men of note. After Plato, the idea of a transcendent, immaterial deity became popular. This is known as Neo-Platonic thought. Most of the religious traditions of this region (Judaism, Christianity, and Islam) were influenced heavily by this way of thinking.

Other examples of the Black man's reputation as the source for the wisdom of sages are the famed Library of Alexandria in Egypt (burned by Europeans), and the Universities of Timbuktu. Also important is the learning of the Black Moors, who ruled Spain for 700 years (711-1492 AD) and taught the Europeans much of what they know now. It was in fact the Moors who brought Europe out of its Dark Ages, much as it was Blacks who brought Europeans out of the caves to teach and civilize them some four thousand years ago. Books on these topics include Ivan Van Sertima's *Golden Age of the Moor* and Paul Lawrence Guthrie's *Making of the Whiteman*.

THE SUPREME BEING

All living matter is subservient to the Black man's rule. Given the premise of Darwin's theories regarding the survival of species, it is evident that all life until this point has culminated in the development of the supreme Black man, beginning with the simplest one-celled organism. All living things are bound to the universal laws of mathematics, the language in which God, as the creator, wrote the universe, and in which God, as man, speaks and lives.

THE BLACK MAN IS DOMINANT

The Black gene is dominant. Most (unbiased) human biology textbooks will explain this assertion in detail. The Black man's genetic legacy, even after generations of imposed race-mixed, have consistently proven him physically superior. Any observer of contemporary sports can testify to that fact. God upon designing a home for himself (the universe, and specifically the Earth), chose a supreme vehicle in which to inhabit it. Although flesh, the Black man's physical body was designed to be the original and greatest form possible. This is where the phrase "the physique of a Greek God" came from. Keep in mind that the true Greek gods were Black men from Egypt.

GOD IS REAL, NOT UNREAL

The term "Supreme Being" suggests two things, one that God is Supreme, and the other, that He is actually a being that exists. In terms of beings that we can actually validate and verify, the Black man has never heard, seen, felt, tasted, or smelled anything greater than HIMSELF. While, there are things that exist that are unseen, they can be verified, even measured. We cannot see the temperature, or the wind, but there are scientific instruments we can use to document their actual existence. On the other hand, an unreal God is ascribed as the cause of very real circumstances. This defies the laws of cause and effect.

People credit God for natural disasters, but investigations can be done to determine the actual physical or natural causes. An invisible God does not make it rain; rain is produced from a well-known process known as the water cycle. In essence, nothing can be proven to be supreme over the Black man. While believers will claim that their feeling is proof enough, people's feelings have never proven anything. People have felt the presence of ghosts, aliens, witches, warlocks, mermaids, imaginary friends, and Santa Claus. Many of these people have been very adamant, even forceful, about having others believe what they believe in. Does that prove that it is real?

THE GOD OF SCRIPTURE

The God of all religious traditions has been a Black man. The authors of the scriptures have recorded numerous instances where God is described either as a man (Genesis 2: 8, 18:1-3, Exodus 15:3, 24:9-11, 33:11,), as Black (Daniel 7:9, Revelation 1:15), a group of men (Genesis 3:22, 11:7), or the nature of man himself (Psalms 82:6, John 10:34). One of the words used for God in the Old Testament is Elohim, which means "Gods" in Hebrew. Actually Elohim is the plural of Eloh, a popular name for the God of the Old Testament. El (from Eloh), is merely a botched transliteration of the original Hebrew name. The vowel points were added later, changing the "A" (or Aleph) to "E" and thus turning Al or Allah into El or Eloh. This was the work of the Jewish Masoretic scribes who were given the task of rewriting (and editing) the Pentateuch by hand around the sixth century AD. This can be found in several texts on the history of the Bible. And the god El, by whatever name you call him, was definitely first regarded as a man (pictured in a gold statue above).

The word Allahim (or Elohim), is also used to refer to the group of men who were regarded as the leaders of the Hebrew people, the Judges. The other popular term for God in the Old Testament is YHWH. YHWH is not meant to be pronounced as "Jehovah." YHWH, when written in Hebrew from top to bottom, represents the form of a man. This is why the tetragrammaton YHWH was referred to as the "Ineffable Name" which means it could not be said. Even today, orthodox Jews refuse to utter this name. It is because these letters do not represent a phonetic word, but pictorially represent the reality of a man, as in a hieroglyphic.

Similarly, the name Allah, which has made it from its origins among the Black Arabs of Mecca to the pre-Columbian Blacks of America AND the first Black slaves and finally to the mainstream of Blacks in America is a name best understood in the present context of Arm-Leg-Leg-Arm-Head. The name Allah was also used as the word for "man" amongst the Black people of ancient Harappan civilization in India.

The New Testament's message is clear. Jesus, a Black man (Revelation 1:15), attempts to redeliver a message of righteousness to the people. One can see, upon thorough reading of the Bible, that his message is not about praising and worshipping him (John 14:12), but about manifesting the God within and improving their lives. Jesus explains to his followers that they are Gods also (John 10:34), but to no avail. The people insist on following him and making him their God. Several solid articles on Christianity and the Black Christ can be found online as well (for example, http://melanet.com/clegg_series/wasjesusblack.html) The fact that the God of the Bible is Black has also been well documented by Dr. Wesley Muhammad and others.

In the Qur'an, Allah is described as having a face that believers will see in the last days (presumably after death). The Qur'an makes mentions of Allah's "hands" being tied down, but otherwise, the Neo-Platonic influence on Islam is strong. Still, Allah makes Adam out of Black mud to be His Khalifa, or vicegerent, on Earth. A vicegerent is a successor responsible for handling the duties of his predecessor. The concept of Allah as man in early Islam has been thoroughly addressed in a doctoral dissertation on the subject by Dr. Wesley Muhammad.

Nearly all religious and spiritual traditions teach the doctrine of God as man and man as God. This paradigm, however, is usually reserved for the esoteric (hidden) side of the teaching. For example, there is mainstream Christianity, and then there is Gnostic Christianity, which teaches of man as God and God as man. Islam has Sufism, Judaism has the Kaballah, Buddhism has the Hinayana school, and Hinduism has the tradition found in the Upanishads. All of these are considered the lesser-known aspect of these major traditions, and all teach that the Black man is God. Even in African religions, there is a tradition regarding the transcendent God that is removed from human affairs, and the immanent God, who is physically present, but people are not allowed to personally see him. Of course, the earlier traditions were very explicit that all of their Gods came in the form of men. Godfrey Higgins' *Anacalypsis* is an old, rare work with several references to the Black Christ, the Black Krishna (of Hinduism), the Black Buddha, the Black gods of Egypt, and other Black gods throughout the world.

Christianity, the most popular religion among American Blacks, was given to Blacks before slavery by European missionaries employed to soften up the native people's defenses. Thus the South African saying, "First they had the Bible and we had the land. Now we have the Bible and they have the land." Small conflicts were then magnified into fullscale wars while guns were poured into these countries. Prisoners of war and other kidnapped Blacks then became slaves for white landowners. These white landowners noticed that the Muslim slaves were always fighting back and leading rebellions. They began systematically stripping Blacks of their old culture, language, history and traditions and supplanting these with European ideals and programmed fear. Along with this, they taught their slaves Christianity to keep them pacified in hopes of one day attaining heaven after death. The slaves were told of a white Jesus, son of a white God, and the white chosen people of God. They were taught to be obedient and serve as slaves and take their beatings. If they rebelled, they'd go to hell, but if they'd submit to what was in effect hell on earth, they'd have heaven after death. Today our people practice the same kind of religion, on the same premise. Though white pictures of Jesus are not as popular among American Blacks as they are in Africa (where they are the norm), the Christianity practiced is still a slave religion designed to keep the suffering and enslaved from questioning, challenging, or changing their conditions on earth.

THE MAKER AND OWNER OF THE UNIVERSE

The world's learned initiates have always regarded Blackness as the source or origin of all people and all things. Dr. Richard King's *The Black Dot* explains this phenomenon. Melanin, which gives Original People their skin complexion, is discussed elsewhere in this book. It should be noted that white skin is an unnatural anomaly, produced by selective breeding, not nature. More information on melanin in the Black man's body can be found in *Melanin: The Chemical Key to Black Greatness* or *Melanin: A Key to Freedom*.

Before the creation of the physical universe, Allah was present as the creative intelligence that spawned itself and began developing all life and matter from an initial atom. This first ATOM, imbibed with the innate intelligence of God, was Allah The Original Man. The Sun replaced this atom as the representation of the Black man until ultimately God himself could take dominion over the earth in the flesh. Intelligence still exists on a subatomic level, as is evident from experiments conducted on light particles which were able to consciously change their course. Man's sperm is consciously able to determine which direction to travel to reach the egg, without a brain. This universal, infinite intelligence is active in its highest form in the individual mind of the Black man. The Black man is the primary conduit for the intelligence that once created the universe, as he is the Creator himself. Elijah Muhammad has written about this self-creation process in depth in *The Theology of Time*. A fair approach to the issue of the universe's birth can be found in *The Left Hand of Creation* and a number of other texts on the topic.

THE MODERN CONTEXT

Considering the ubiquitous and inhuman attempts by Europeans to systematically destroy the Black man, it is evident that there is more to the true nature of the Black man than an ex-slave whose services are no longer needed. While Europeans have no qualms with promoting education and healthy habits among college-bound Black women, Black men have been pushed increasingly towards jails and early death. The white-led media perpetuates and promotes images of criminality and ignorance among Black youth. Black men are consistently targeted and discriminated against in nearly every American institution, from law enforcement to education to employment. Black men are characterized as overly aggressive, mentally inferior, prone to criminal behavior and wanton violence, devoid of any moral character, and incapable of alleviating their negative circumstances. Throughout the world, the situation is the same for Black males. In regions where Blacks are the dominant population group, the whole region is usually being ravaged and decimated by war, famine, or AIDS. When these factors are still not enough to keep the Black population from growing, as was the case in Black India, birth control and forced sterilization has been implemented. The global agenda for world white supremacy is clear. The Black man, God, has been and still is the only impediment to that mission.

IS IT CLEAR YET?

COUNTER-ARGUMENTS
There is only one God, not many.

As polytheistic as it sounds to say that Black men are Gods, the statement is anything but. There is only one God, and that God is THE Black man. The Black man is a unified whole, much as the water on the earth is in reality one connected body that is split into different regions, or containers. We share a mind at its highest level. This mind is the one that designed the universe in the language of mathematics, and set the processes by which all natural systems would continue to operate. While, at our conscious level, many of us are focused on eating and talking, there is a higher level to our consciousness that functions on the wavelength of intelligent design.

It sounds racist to say the Black man is God.

God is the Original Man. The primordial man, the first physical vehicle for God's immanent presence on Earth, was a Black body. Throughout the universe, Blackness prevails as the origin of all things. Black body radiation, Black holes, and the presence of melanin in space tell us a great deal. The first humans, of course, were Black. Today, the Black man is found throughout the Earth in a variety of shades and hues. Many of them are natural descendants of the original Black genotype, while others are admixtures resulting from miscegenation with whites. Who are whites then? Paul Lawrence Guthrie, in *Making of the Whiteman*, documents the creation and exile of the white race, who would forever change the course of human and social development on this planet. Numerous theories abound as to the origins of the white race, none of them entirely plausible. The vast differences between white people and Black people could only result from selective breeding, as Darwin noted, not from any evolutionary process. And certainly not simply due to cold weather, as African Presence in Early

Europe by Ivan Van Sertima documents the presence of Blacks having lived in arctic regions for thousands of years without their skin lightening. At any rate, the statement of Black Godhood is a positive statement and one of affirmation, not of condemnation of other people.

It sounds chauvinist to say the Black man is God.

Just as the Sun and Moon occupy important places and roles in the solar system, so do Man and Woman. An immense body of scientific research details the significant physical, mental, emotional, and social differences between males and females. Stating that the Black man is God is not meant to degrade or debase the Black woman, but to affirm HIS role, and not take anything away from hers. God represents the creative force in the universe. In all scriptural and mythological accounts, God somehow "impregnates" either the Earth, the celestial void, or the blackness of space, to produce life and/or the universe. The planting of the seed would be futile without the fertile soil in which to plant it. Early mythology related the woman to the Earth, the receiver and bearer of life. Many of these ancient societies eventually abandoned the worship of the Black God, the Father God, as He was described as distant and unconcerned with human affairs. Instead, the focus shifted to the Earth Mother, who was celebrated and praised for her fertility and the sustenance she provided. Today, we refer to the Black woman as a Queen, as the Mother of Civilization, and as the Earth.

There is no God.

Several authors have addressed the debate between intelligent design and the possibility that this universe, this Earth, and humanity, were the products of chance and coincidence. The likelihood of just one atom simply phasing into existence by chance is so remote that it can't be calculated fairly. The evidence for intelligent design is great. However, it doesn't point to the immaterial, invisible God of the Creationists, but to the culmination of God on Earth, the Black man,  as its source. Much as a computer program can be written to repeat in cycles, or concentric spirals, of activity, history has followed a natural set of laws and patterns to produce this exact stage of development. The original writer for this program, or history, was the infinite (since the beginning) Black mind, present in the ultimate (final) Black man. An examination of history will lead one to question the probability of coincidental events, the aligning of real events and prophecy, the cyclical or spiral nature of all development, and why on earth is the same spiral that one can find in the formation of the universe's galaxies and the currents of the Earth's waters, present in our own fingertips?

The Black man can't be God or the Black man wouldn't be living in such depraved conditions.

This argument appears to make a great deal of sense. Why on earth would GOD be dancing around on BET like a clown, flashing guns and money amidst a bunch of gyrating scantily-clad women? Or why would GOD be trapped in the slums in abject poverty, with the highest incarceration rates in the country, failing to educate himself or uplift his people, and instead choosing to smoke, drink, and fornicate his life away?

Well, for beginners, this deplorable image of the Black man is, in great part, more of a construction of the media, than an accurate representation of the GLOBAL Black man. The Black man is a unified whole, comprised of peoples of color from all over the world, representing a multitude of different behaviors, attitudes and lifestyles. One thing these peoples have in common is their oppression by white supremacy (also known as European imperialism, British colonization, American capitalism, manifest destiny, the Crusades, Christian conversion, etc.).

"If the soul is left in darkness, sins will be committed.
The guilty one is not he who creates the sin, but he who creates the darkness." - Victor Hugo

The results of this system in America have been especially tragic. Black people, kidnapped from peaceful and prosperous homelands, were sold in the Americas, stripped of their language, ideologies, and culture, and brainwashed. The brainwashing never ceased. In fact, examination of the Willie Lynch letters shows us that further brainwashing was instrumental in continuing the oppression of the Black male beyond his physical bondage.

In the Bible it states that "the last shall be first and the first shall be last." During the time the Egyptians were building pyramids, Europeans were creating large mounds of waste in Europe. The garbage piles these cavemen created were often so large, they have evolved into modern-day hillsides. Today, the reverse seems true. But there is a sleeping giant awaiting awakening. Even in the worst of conditions, in jails and ghettos throughout the U.S., Black men continue to awaken to the knowledge of themselves and begin the journey back to their true nature. For every individual walking in darkness and chasing the American dream of money and sex, there is another individual walking up out of that sleep and seeing God in the mirror.

"The 500 years of resistance have not been in vain.
From 500 years of resistance we pass to another 500 years in power." - Evo Morales

THE CULTURE OF I-GOD
Sha-King Cehum Allah – Power Born (Pittsburgh, PA)

The Blackman is the total embodiment of life itself. He is Supreme Mathematics. He applies and projects his mind onto and into his Earth, to manifest his reality on that planet. Nature is the feminine expression of mathematics. Nature exists within the realm of equality (6) as we understand it (nature) on the Earth. Nature is a system based in mathematics yet slightly different (in principle and application) from the process that brought it forth in the blackness of space. For example, light travels at the rate of 186,000 miles per second or 300,000 kilometers per second. However, the estimation of light's speed is a definition based on how fast light travels in a vacuum (like "space"). The speed of light depends on the material it moves through as each planet has a different density and atmospheric composition, the speed of light will change. Mathematics is manifested differently through "6" and "7," the Blackwoman and the Blackman. So within the Nation of Gods and Earths, as the Blackman is resurrected and elevated back to his birthright, being the foundation, he can then heal the woman and educate the child- 1,2,3. So a lot of emphasis is placed on the Blackman's divinity. Because as father of civilization and God of the universe he is responsible for the entire human family, yet it starts with him. The world will never change if the Blackman doesn't change. All things start with "one" and come back to "one" (1-9, then 10 which when simplified, 1+0=1). Look at the big bang theory, from one particle to a solar system. Look at your life, one thought, one decision and then a world created from it, which all falls back on your original intention or thought. All things must return to their origin in this world. This is the culture of Allah.

THE SURE REALITY
Truth Allah - Interior Cipher (Pennsylvania)

"My forehead is worn out doing the sujdah. Whoever has achieved Him has achieved Him from within. Nobody has ever found Him from outside or elsewhere and nobody will ever find Him from anywhere except from within."
- Bulleh Shah, Sufi poet-saint of Pakistan

The Qur'an teaches us that Allah is the Truth; the Sure Reality; the Supreme Reality. REALITY means: the quality or state of being actual or true; one that is real; or the total of all existing things (the All in All). REAL means not pretend; not imaginary. SURE means certain; impossible to doubt.

How does one detect reality or what's real?

ANSWER: By touch, taste, hearing, smell, and/or sight.

What you can't detect with your 5 senses, you have to imagine. Therefore, it's not REAL. Allah is the Sure Reality, meaning impossible to doubt. B.u.t. you can always doubt that which you can't touch, taste, hear, smell, or see. Therefore, to say that Allah is unseen (a mystery/unknown), b.u.t. is a sure reality is not intelligent. How can you acquaint someone with the Supreme Reality (existence/ being) if neither of you can detect him with your 5 senses? You can't!

How can the Supreme Being be "Supreme" if he can only be imagined (or exist only in the "unseen world")? B.u.t. these same individuals will tell you that the devil can exist in the unseen world and the seen (physical) world. That's not intelligent. Many religious people say they acknowledge the devil in people (hence exorcisms, baptisms, etc.), b.u.t. most of them will never acknowledge GOD (the Greatest Good) in people. Therefore, such a "God" is not unlimited, as he does not exist everywhere (omnipresent), is not all powerful (omnipotent), and is not all knowing (omniscient).

There is not one thing that anyone can name that a "mystery" God can do for man, that a man or woman can't do for him/herself. Some say: "If you are God, then walk through that wall" or "If you are God, then levitate over that wall," which is also not intelligent, because they have never seen their "God" walk through a wall or levitate over one. So it still would not "prove" that I am a Supreme Being (or Sure Reality) according to their standards, because they have never seen their "Supreme Being" accomplish such amazing feats.

Although you can show and prove it through the Bible and Qur'an, it is not necessary for us to use them as a "point of reference" in justifying or explaining how the Black man is the Supreme Reality. We were the Supreme Reality before there ever was a Bible or Qur'an, because the Black man is Supreme Being (God) by nature.

WHAT GOD IS AND WHAT GOD IS NOT
Kuahmel Allah - Love Allah (Los Angeles, CA)

God does first things first.
God is responsible and handles business.
God doesn't procrastinate.
God is a man of action, who welcomes a challenge.
God is reliable, not disingenuous, trifling, or funny-style.
God is a mover and shaker.
God is a team player.
God knows his role and is helpful.
God knows when to step up.
God fights the good fight.
God is an authority, not an authoritarian.

God is pragmatic and reasonable, not a blowhard ideologue.

God is a thoughtful policymaker.

God covers all the bases and is thorough.

God listens.

God is informed and in tune, not speaking what he doesn't know.

God is a student of life who learns from mistakes, not let them consume him.

God is the best learner, one people want to learn from.

God strives to shine in all he does.

God is not vulgar, rowdy or disruptive.

God is humble.

God is not an extreme cynic.

God thinks positive and makes the best of all situations.

God is creative and sees endless possibilities.

God is talented, skilled, inspired and inspiring.

God is productive, not wasteful.

God is a contributor, not a user.

God is progressive.

God is assertive, not passive-aggressive.

God is not an emotional basketcase or paranoid maniac.

God is the rock, sturdy and sure.

God doesn't constantly second-guess himself.

God is confident, and strong-willed even when others around him aren't.

God owns his issues and screw-ups, and doesn't do excuses or cover-ups.

God is righteous, not immoral or unethical.

God doesn't abuse or batter.

God is not a troublemaker, thief, thug, or murderer.

God is no criminal of any kind, but a law-abiding citizen.

God is the law personified.

God has empathy and is considerate of others.

God is tolerant and open-minded.

God is not racist, sexist, or oppressive to the unalike.

God doesn't practice hate or discrimination.

God is about the people, all people.

God is both a leader and a good soldier.

God does not try to dominate because he's naturally dominant.

God is in charge and in control.

God is head of the household and the family.

God does what it takes to keep the house in order.

God is merciful but not weak.

God is no loser, never pathetic or mediocre

God can destroy but isn't destructive.

God is not a predator but a protector.

God is one others can relate to.

God is a good brother, cool without trying too hard.

God knows when to be serious and when to lighten up.

God is not anti-social, but the life of the party.

God is a renaissance man.

God is not holier-than-thou.

God is not religious, not a blind follower or idolater.

God is not a mysterious, magical fairy tale.

God is living mathematics in thought and action.

God is intelligent, the highest intelligence in the universe.

God is not pretentious or unrealistic. God is real.

Who is this God talked about so emphatically?

You. In the flesh.

Peace. God!

Kuahmel Allah is a native of Southern California, emerging from the Love Allah (Los Angeles) cipher, where he began studying in 1993. Though known mostly for his creative efforts, Kuahmel is known by many among the 5% for his pragmatic, holistic, and progressive approach to Nation teachings and related issues. For many years, he has been the person to call or email for many across America wishing to begin or renew their studies, and point them in the right direction.

THE TRUE AND LIVING GOD
Manifest Supreme Knowledge God Allah – Interior Cipher (Minnesota)

"God was manifested in the flesh, justified in the spirit, seen by the angels." - Timothy 3:16

First things first, before one can understand why the Blackman is God, they have to understand "Black," its omnipotence and its ubiquity. Black is the universal foundation of all things in existence and the one reality from which all life evolved. Black is life's essence and has neither a beginning nor an ending. All throughout the East from KMT (Egypt), Iraq, India, Greece, to Mexico, South America, etc., God has always been depicted as not only being Black, b.u.t. a Black Man. They depicted God as Black because they knew their God(s) derived from the cosmos which existed in complete blackness, and from that state God created the physical man with an Arm, Leg, Leg, Arm, and Head (A.L.L.A.H), and clothed him in blackness.

They depicted their God as a physical man because, after searching for trillions of years and not being able to find this mystery god that white people invented for their own earthly salvation, they came into agreement that the only God was/is the Son of Man. So being the Supreme Gods that they were created to be, they lost no time in searching for that which does not exist. So they made God after their likeness and identified Him as "He."

In the book *Early Christian Belief in a Corporeal Deity* by D.L. Paulsen, he asserts:

> The view that God is without a body or parts...in the beginning it was not so...the Christians for at least the first three centuries of the current era believed God to be corporeal.

Islamic Scholar Muqalat Bi Sulayman, in his book *Al Ash' Ari, Maqalat al-Islamiyyin* asserts:

> God was flesh and blood in a human body. God is in the form of man, with flesh, blood, hair, bones, hand, foot, head, eyes, etc.

Martin Bernal (*Black Athena*), George G.M. James (*Stolen Legacy*), and many others assert that the Greek (white) God was based on the Black God of the East, the same God who they got all their knowledge from. I think it's safe to say that the Nation of Gods and Earths (NGE) presents the Original God of the old, not the grafted Greek god of the new! The Blackman is honored as God on every corner of the earth as well the heavens above.

I opened this build in the Supreme Sign of Peace, and I'm closing it in the same: The P.owerful E.ye (3rd eye) of A.llah C.ees E.verything!

Manifest Supreme was educated by I Sure Supreme Being God-Allah, who along with Divine Savior (who is now a doctor in a Minneapolis Hospital), Shaheem and Sincere, became Minnesota's First Born, after Ali Quan of Philly brought the knowledge there in 1989, renaming it Master Now. Manifest Supreme can be reached at: Malachi Kilgore, #205781, 970 Pickett St. North, Bayport, MN 55003-1490.

C.R.I.P.
COMMUNITY REVOLUTION IN PROGRESS
Knowledge Allah - Interior Cipher (California)

I would like to greet the readers with PEACE. My name is Knowledge. When I say peace I not only wish you peace in life but I also want you to recognize that Proper Education Always Creates Elevation, which is vital to all human life. Without it, we couldn't become self sufficient as a people.

However, I'm a 22 year old Black man who's currently serving a 10 year sentence in prison due to the LACK of peace in my life. This is my first time being incarcerated as an adult, and I've been locked down since the age of 18.

For the first 18 years of my life, I lived in the Imperial Courts Projects in Watts, California. During my youth, I heard plenty of different stories about life in prison as a Project Crip. From a young ghetto child's point of view, it was glorifying. It was something that I and others my age wanted to do; to gain a reputation as being hard, a straight gangster, go to prison, get on swoll [buff], and come home as a locster who's done time, survived it, and was back in the bricks, hood rich, with a name that commands fear and respect.

"If we don't stand for something, we may fall for anything." - Malcolm X

So I sought all of the above. I couldn't wait to kill someone so I could go to the pen, get blasted up [tattoos], get into some riots with the Blacks and other races, get big, and come home looking and feeling like a legend.

Now, I'm experiencing the reality of it…first hand…
STUCK…with 10 years of my life GONE.
WAS IT WORTH IT? NO!

See, when I was told about the pen, I wasn't told that I would basically be dead to my homies on the streets. I wasn't told about them not sending me any money, letters, or pictures. I wasn't told that my homies would be out there nailing my woman as she began to turn her back on me, along with the great possibility that the rest of my family would turn their backs on me as well. I wasn't told that I would be lonely and lost as a ghetto child in a man's body, searching for a sense of direction that I ultimately could find nowhere else but within myself.

As a young Black man in prison, all the odds are against me. I could lose my life at the blink of an eye, behind the color of my skin, or the area I grew up in. Not to mention that we live in bathrooms! Think about it! We eat like savages and are controlled like children. We are told when to eat, when and where to sleep, when to go outside as well as when to lock up, and when to SPEAK.

All of these control issues can easily ruin a man and his consciousness if you don't have the mental strength to face your opposition head on and turn a negative into a positive. But you must know what's negative and what's not, and what's your real opposition and what's not, because our minds can easily lead us wrong when we lack proper understanding of our position in life. So one must know thy self. I mean, really take the time to look inside of your soul to find out who you are as a person, and not the image you made for yourself. In my case that image was MOE CORLEONE, PEE JAY WATTS CRIP. Now I wasn't born with that name nor the mentality. That's something that was put into me because of my desire to live the Mafia life, as well as the people I looked up to as role models.

Some may fool themselves into believing that they were born to live life on the edge, not even living to see the age of 25 because of the colors they wear or the street that they grew up on. We Black men are constantly dying behind something that we DO NOT OWN! Because if the white man wants to bring down what ever block he pleases, he will bring in his troops and do so.

I recognized this need for growth among us, and I saw that life is bigger than red and blue. I realized that if I made that right turn down a positive road, there was a great possibility that I'd live to see the age of 65 instead of 25.

"It is better to die on your feet than to live on your knees." - Mikhail Bakunin

I really begin to realize what CRIP used to be about and that's in its name: COMMUNITY REVOLUTION IN PROGRESS. A fight for change in our community! Why not? Improving our conditions… instead of only making the streets unsafe for our children and elders by shooting at each other, burning down blocks, and allowing no one to visit the area if they're not from the neighborhood. They are just blatantly stealing our children's youth, giving them only 3 options: death, jail, or lost on drugs. But I'm going to start with self, and then help my community by living like a real CRIP of COMMUNITY REVOLUTION IN PROGRESS, fighting to change myself and my surroundings.

To do so, I had to look outside of my immediate homies and expand my closed mind. I had to do a lot of reading and contemplating, so I could grow mentally and reinvent myself as a young Black male who'd grown up in poverty, lived the struggle, and walked on thin ice, faced with those 3 options: death, jail, or strung out on drugs. But this young Black male will keep a strong mind and make it OUT.

As you can see, prison was my destiny, but I do have a second chance at life. So after giving the streets and negativity 18 years of my life, I chose to give the positive the rest of my life...however long that may be.

I came into the teachings of the 5% NATION OF GODS AND EARTHS. It completely changed my life. I've been exposed to knowledge that I wouldn't have thought twice about before, because I was too trapped in the streets, searching for the wrong type of guidance.

I also met many great men in this HIDDEN UNIVERSITY - men who are helping mold me into a powerful, refined Black man. I went from wanting to be known as a Mafia Don, a hardcore gangster who's only for himself, for whom life is not really an issue...to being called by the name KNOWLEDGE, recognized as a strong Black man of influence. A true warrior who never stopped fighting his struggles - only now against the real opposition - and is helping bring his people together, instead of tearing them apart.

> Pay no mind to those who talk behind your back, it simply means that you are two steps ahead

It hasn't been easy. My first year of trying to transform myself, it was hard to find acceptance from a few of my childhood associates. They weren't used to seeing me like this, striving to be positive and do what's right for myself and my people. They rejected every part of my change, basically saying, "MAN, DON'T LIVE LIFE TO THE FULLEST - KILL OR BE KILLED! THAT S ALL WE KNOW AND LIVE FOR."

WOW! I couldn't live like that. I couldn't be stupid. Why choose those same 3 options when I now see millions more?

Whoever feels they want to die early or spend the rest of their lives in prison behind this madness...must be insane! I've had many fights and arguments behind my change. Those who choose the 3 options look at my transformation as "soft" because they are still BLIND, DEAF, AND DRIVEN by stupidity.

But out of 100% of the people who know me, 98% of them say "Knowledge, continue on your road to success. I'm glad that you woke up at an early age instead of at an old age. We Black people need more people like yourself."

So the 2% of people that want to see me stay BLIND, DEAF, AND DRIVEN by stupidity - they mean nothing to me, and their opinion holds no weight!

And when you are ready to change yourself, you have to be ready to go through the same thing. If you find yourself in a situation where someone is trying to hold you back from succeeding in life, keep holding on and march with your heads to the sky and your eyes on the prize: SUCCESS! Let no one stop your destiny, and always remain aware of the real opposition against you. Continue to grow and educate yourself so you can become a self-sufficient, positive person of influence. And together, we can create true COMMUNITY REVOLUTION IN PROGRESS

> Knowledge is currently in the belly of the beast (incarcerated) in California. Because certain prisons do not allow in literature containing the location of prisoners, he can be contacted at the address provided at www.knowledgeofself.us

FROM INMATE TO GOD
Born Knowledge Allah – New Jerusalem (New Jersey)

"If we were to cast aside every man who had made a mistake once, useful men could probably not be come by. A man who makes a mistake once will be considerably more prudent and useful because of his repentance.

I feel that he should be promoted."

"Will you guarantee him?" "Of course I will"

"By what can you guarantee him?"

"I can guarantee him by the fact that he is a man who has erred once. A man who has never once erred is dangerous."

– Hagakure, The Book of the Samurai

I am often invited to speak at prisons, and it always amazes me to see such a great number of original men. Then I think of where they might have been if they'd had the true knowledge of who they are. They certainly would not be part of the fastest growing, most recession-proof industry in AmeriKKKa. Yes, the prison industry is a sure bet for those who profit from it.

These original people were somehow fooled into believing that poverty, crime and ultimately prison were somehow their fate. While others choose to pursue the AmeriKKKan dream, they have chosen to waste the opportunities that others risk their lives for, just to get to this country. Many of them have fallen for myths that have been given to them by a mass media machine that profits from their poor choices. This machine teaches acquisition, not achievement. Thus they allow the media to sell them a lifestyle that does not include education, clean living and family values. Being in an incarcerated condition, he has left the defense, education and leadership of his family in question. In many cases, women have been left as heads of households with the responsibility of raising boys. Even though many of these women are well intentioned, they are ill-equipped to teach boys to be men.

The bright side of this situation is that a man's personal history will change as soon as he accepts the fact that he is the true and living God of this planet. Being God is a huge responsibility. God must acquire the knowledge needed to become the intellectual, economic and cultural head of his family. Before he is released from prison, the Blackman with knowledge of himself must prepare for his challenge by educating himself. If there are any available educational or employment preparation programs, he should take advantage of them. If not, he should associate with others who have positive experiences to learn from. He should leave prison with the determination to raise himself up from someone being used for the betterment of others, to a builder of a nation. This is the transformation that should occur through the acquisition of knowledge of self. As man transitions from the prison of physical and mental slavery into the world of physical freedom, his mind too must be free. This is the significance of Black men gaining the full knowledge of themselves at their earliest opportunity while incarcerated. Without proper knowledge of self, and the wisdom of proper follow-through, that man is more likely than not to return to incarceration, possibly never to reemerge.

"Every saint has a past and every sinner has a future." - Oscar Wilde

---

Born Knowledge Allah is a Senior Instructor in the Continuing Education Department of a New Jersey community college. He specializes in professional and personal development with special emphasis on life skills and job readiness training. Born has over 20 years of corporate and educational experience which he uses to help people improve the quality of their lives. An author and lecturer, Born is the author of the books, *From Jail to a Job* and *The Teenager's Guide to Getting a Job* (both available at www.jailtojob.com). He has addressed, among others, the Congressional Black Caucus and the Charles Hamilton Institute for Race and Justice of the Harvard School of Law. He is an active member of Omega Psi Phi Fraternity and a youth mentor spending his life committed to community empowerment. His primary message is "Independence through Self-Reliance."

EARTH BY NATURE

RIGHTEOUS BY CHOICE

Sci-Honor Devotion - Born Power Truth (Bridgeport, CT)

Earth is the title that the righteous Black woman of the Nation of Gods and Earths carries with pride. She is the Mother of Civilization and Queen of the Universe. The planet Earth is the 3rd planet from the sun and is 93 (9=Born and 3=Understanding) million miles away from that energy source. Here, she is able to born understanding, or give birth to the best part mentally  and physically. She is secure in her position and it is through her perfect position that she sees her greatness and understands the divinity of her proper placement in the universe. The planet weighs 6 sextillion tons. The number 6 is significant in that it is considered in mathematics to be a perfect number. This means that when all of its factors are added up (1+2+3), you get the number you started with, which in this case is 6. So when you put the knowledge (1), Wisdom (2) and Understanding (3) together, you get equality (6). Also, the number 6 is half the sum of all of its divisors. 1+2+3+6 = 12 / 2 = 6. Therefore, it is balanced. The number 6 (Equality) is significant to life and plays an important role in the carbon atoms existence on the periodic table. Its atomic number is 6, meaning that there are 6 protons in its nucleus. Carbon is the basis for all organic life, down to the shape of the honey comb cell and even the smallest snowflake with each 6 sided figure having a unique pattern of its own. 6 is a number that represents balance. The Earth is balanced as everything that exists has a duality. She too is balanced and is in tune with and honors her feminine attributes and qualities. The Earth is not composed of just dirt, but is blessed with rich, fertile soil which with proper nourishment can produce great mental and physical seeds. She is not walked on, but carries and supports life. When the Black woman saw herself as being Divine, her thoughts changed, and her behavior followed.

The planet Earth is covered approximately 3/4th (3 = understanding and 4 = culture/freedom) under water. The refined Black woman covers herself approximately 3/4th of the way, which will often if not always include her head being covered with a crown because she understands her culture and is free to be refined in it. By doing so, she keeps her best part which she considers to be her precious jewels preserved for those and only those who deserve it. Those precious jewels are her mind and womb, which both have the ability to bring forth life. She is not interested in sharing or giving up her goods so easily. Her goal is to remain refined and respected. She is not striving to be looked at in a lustful way by men. She knows her worth and knows that being Sexy or being a Diva are not what she aspires to be. She is capable of being so much more. She walks with dignity and self respect, has high Self Esteem, and embraces her natural self.

She is the 1st teacher and leads by example. Those who are around her see her wisdom through the example that she sets. She is an example of Refined Womanhood and does not "lose" herself when in the company of uncivilized people. She holds true to her culture always. She also sets the standards by which her daughters want to aspire and her son's would want their wives to be. She is a person that she herself would admire, respect, and keep close as a friend / sister.

The Earth has a Wise Dome and applies wise words, ways, and actions, respectfully. She is a P.O.E.T. This means that she applies P.roper O.rder while E.xecuting the T.ruth using Supreme Mathematics as her guide. She is loyal, dedicated and devoted to righteousness. She has positive thoughts and ideas and communicates them clearly and refined when articulating and adding Wisdom to the Cipher (20) and stands on that square which is 360 degrees of completion, The Truth. She is not swayed negatively with emotion, yet uses her emotion to

continue to propel her toward truth. The Earth is humble yet firm, flexible but not weak, and confident but not cocky. She is a student and a teacher, thus will do the knowledge first before ever manifesting a thought. She is constantly aspiring to gain wisdom, so, she learns through trial and error by taking the best part of every situation and placing value on the jewels that she has received. She is capable of studying many sciences and remaining grounded in her Supreme Mathematics, while taking the best part of the science. When she is in need of information, advice or assistance, she will not hesitate to seek it, humbly.

The Earth is e-motion-al. Her Energy is Always in Motion. She is in tune with these emotions and brings clarity to them through peaceful evaluation of the situation at hand. The Moon - which has an effect on the Earth's waters (or wisdom) - revolves around the Earth. The Earth remains centered and never allows her emotions to get out of hand by acting like a lunatic. She is always in control of her emotions. She allows herself to be creative in order to let these emotions show and uses them to express her feelings, and knowledge. Her emotions are a motivation to her. They prompt her to be motivated in doing what needs to be done.

There are 4 devils specifically that she rebukes. They are Hate, Lust, Greed and Jealousy. Hate being a strong emotion of animosity or dislike for someone or something will eat away at her. She learns to agree to disagree and take the best part of everything, therefore, she does not hate. Lust is an intense and unrestrained emotion usually pertaining to sex. The Earth is not obsessed with sex, nor does she use any sexual powers or prowess to manipulate, or trick a man into being in her control. The Earth is not greedy and holds fast to the principle of Equality. Greed is a selfish desire to obtain more than what is needed, excess material goods, social positions or power. The Earth does not misinterpret material wealth or status for true happiness. She is however, a "Poor Righteous Teacher" yet, not taking this term to the extreme by being "broke" but instead being rich mentally and sharing her riches with others. Her goals are to obtain the 12 Jewels, which are, Knowledge, Wisdom, Understanding, Freedom, Justice, Equality, Food, Clothing, Shelter, Love, Peace, and Happiness. Lastly, she is not jealous and wants for her brothers and sisters what she would want for herself. She is secure in her perfect position in the universe and strives for greatness regardless to whom or what. The Earth is also not vindictive or vengeful as she understands the principle of justice. Also, if she sees something that she desires, that desire inspires her to work towards attaining that which she seeks.

"To no form of religion is woman indebted for one impulse of freedom." - Susan B. Anthony

The Earth knows God. The 17th letter is Q (1=Knowledge 7=God). She is a Queen. She stands by the side of God who is the Supreme, Being, Blackman. She is very careful when choosing a mate, her king, her God. She knows that she is a valuable jewel and whoever should have her will be worthy. The Earth has respect for her relationship with God. Her dealings with her God and their Universe are sacred. Knowing that, she honors him and what they have together. She knows the value and importance of the family structure; man, woman and child, never getting it twisted with monetary value, Therefore, she never has an "I don't need no man" mentality. She needs him just as he needs her for life to go on.

Her womb is the receiver and bearer of life. It is a vessel of nourishment and even when she gives birth, she continues to be a source of nourishment through her breast, which are the way in which the child receives liquid gold to prepare him or her to become strong enough to stand on its own. The Earth knows that being the carrier of God's seed is a blessing and she respects herself, her body her baby, and her Blackman accordingly. She strives to provide the best possible environment for her baby while in and out of her womb. She is not just responsible for her physical children but for all human families.

Her home is a reflection of herself, therefore, it is clean, unpolluted and sanitary. She sees her home as a sacred space and will respect it as such. There is nothing wrong with liking material things. However, the Earth knows where true value lies and is mindful when prioritizing the needs of her home. She has a clear understanding of the difference between needs and wants. She has many tasks, needs and wants and prioritizes her responsibilities so that things get done and are attained in order of importance. The babies are the greatest and therefore, stay at the top of her list of priorities.

The Earth is health conscious, valuing her health because she knows that she must be healthy, strong and in a good position to contribute to society. She knows that living foods result in life and dead foods result in death. She is a C.H.E.F. which means that she C.hooses H.ealthy E.nriching F.oods to serve her family. She maintains a righteous diet so that she will not be toxic and polluted. Bad soil cannot produce great fruit. She respects the planet Earth and uses it to maintain and heal her family by learning about herbs and other beneficial jewels that the planet has to offer. In addition to being a physical healer, she is a mental healer and has the ability to bring peace to wherever Dis-Ease exists. She is radiant and Peace emanates from her.

Not only is she knowledgeable about food preparation and mental healing, but she is also skilled in other areas of focus such as business, education, trades such as sewing, crocheting and other money making skills, survival and life skills in general. She is motivated to learn as much as she can and shares her knowledge with others.

The Earth is a sister to all. She knows how to exist at home and abroad, thus, she is able to maintain relationships with people who grow to know her, trust her and love her. The Earth is compassionate, open minded, can give advice without criticizing and does not get caught up in gossip as it is a nonproductive parasite, eating away at the seams of universal family. She keeps her word and should be valued as a true sister.

The Earth strives for and expects greatness. She produces greatness. She will not compromise her standards out of desperation but is able to be compromised with and will do so for the benefit of the whole. She keeps positive thoughts, ideas and goals. The Earth strives toward the 12 Jewels. She is ever proud of her history and desires to leave an unforgettable legacy and impact on humanity. She is a motivator and she herself is motivated. She will not wait on any mysteries, but will take the initiative to get the things done that must be done.

The Earth is productive. She is in constant rotation and builds diligently and consistently in Allah World Manifest. She never comes empty handed and always has something to bring to the table, even if it is simply a helping hand. She has sincere motives and is genuinely looking to add on for the benefit of herself, and her family, near and far. She adds on to at least one or more of the Nation of Gods and Earths' Growth and Development areas of focus, which are Security, Health, Public Relations, Economics, Communication, and Education. This she practices within and outside of the nation. She is respected in her community and has built or is in the process of building a positive reputation so that she has some sort of influence on the youth and all human families in the area.

So, as you can see, with all of her positive attributes and duties of greatness, the Earth definitely has a role and position not only within the Nation of Gods and Earths, but within all that exists. The Earth holds this title which is her birthright, but she is righteous by choice. She is respected, protected and loved.

Sci-Honor Devotion, CD, CCCE, CPD is a certified Labor Doula, certified Postpartum Doula, certified Childbirth Educator and Homebirth Midwife Assistant. She is a homeschooling mother of two children. Originally from the Desert (Queens, NY), she and her vegan family now rest in Bridgeport, Connecticut. She is a co-founder of the Uhuru Homeschool Hut in Pelan, where parents who have decided not to send their children to institutionalized schools can come together for a common cause. She is the founder of Earth's Natural Touch Birthing Services, providing labor support, postpartum support, childbirth education, prenatal yoga, holistic maternal retreats, sacred seminars for women and girls and more. She is member of the International Center for Traditional Childbearing, Doulas of North America, the Childbirth and Postpartum Professional Association, and a board member for Sistahs for Better Birthing, a local chapter of The International Center for Traditional Childbearing.

Sci-Honor is co-editor of *Even Without the Village*, an upcoming book on urban parenting. She also writes for OriginalThoughtMag.com's "Understanding" section, which focuses on children. She can be contacted at (212) NY-MOM-01

AN EARTH'S JOURNEY

A MATHEMATICAL HISTORICAL NARRATIVE

Earth Izayaa Allat - Mecca (Harlem, NY)

1) Knowledge: An initial awareness, an idea, thought:

I was now 16 years old. My parents are Dominican immigrants who arrived

here in 1990, and like most recent arrivals into a foreign country, a house or big apartment were not accommodations we could have access to. As I sat there, as I did on most nights, I thought about the many questions of life and continued my Astronomy research. I was one of seven "minority" students chosen to work two years with a mentor from the scientific community. Growing up in the Washington Heights ghetto, the largest Dominican enclave outside the island yet raised to traditional *campesino* parents, was an experience that allowed me to seclude myself from the streets and immerse myself in my studies. While most kids were out smoking weed or cutting class, I was at home writing in my journal. During this particular night of 1999, I wrote: "This world is only a speck in the Universe. It's like a snowflake in the middle of the North Pole. Humans don't realize this. They don't think that anything they do affects Earth." Furthermore, "I always ask myself, how does mathematical application and explanation relate to our world? It seems stupid because I do know how it relates. All distances, movements could be explained in numbers. I just wish I can better explain the world in a mathematical way." It was at this point in my life that I started to gain an awareness of my position to the world, that mathematics was somehow connected to the reality of all humans.

2) Wisdom: Application, finding usefulness to an idea:

In the Fall of 1999, although heavily discouraged by my teachers, I decided that I would leave Washington Heights and apply to attend college outside of New York City. By the Spring of 2000, I was accepted to Brown University, one of the 7 Ivy League Schools in the U.S. In this privileged environment I learned my immediate history. I majored in Ethnic and Latin American Studies. History books were finally inclusive of my people's history. We covered the Cuban Revolution and Fidel Castro, the coup d'état on Juan Bosch, a socialist Dominican president, and the U.S. invasion of the Dominican Republic in 1964 among many issues. I understood what *"Chicano," "Dominicanyork"* and *"Nuyorican"* meant, learned concepts like "transnationalism," "cross-relational," and "poststructuralist" along with the relations formed between African Americans and Latinos in urban spaces.

Eventually, I was told I was a "White Latina of Color" through an essay by Julia Alvarez. What did this mean? So I was white, but of color? The more conscious I became, the more angered I felt, resulting in unproductive arguments with "people of color" who grew up in upper middle-class communities serving as tokens in social circles. Upon realizing that anger was destroying my persona, I started asking myself what was the usefulness of this knowledge? How could I use it in a way that was productive and non-reactionary?

3) Understanding: When one "gets it"; an exposure to one's objective:

Upon graduation, part of my purpose was revealed to me. I decided to earn a Master's in Teaching. I wanted to teach modern and ancient history - the stories of our people - to kids of disenfranchised backgrounds. It was a struggle attaining my Master's degree. I thought, how would a white teacher know what teaching methods would resonate and maximize adequate learning within Original youth? I ended up getting into an angry and disrespectful discussion that cost me an extra year of student teaching within the program. In a letter written to my mentor teacher, I stated "Do you think that having kids read events from an outdated textbook and having them play "History Jeopardy" will get them to ask questions about the mathematical patterns embedded within the construction of the pyramids?" I haven't taught in a traditional classroom regularly since then, only as a consultant and curriculum developer. However, this experience led me to understand my purpose: teaching youth, other women and men. Simultaneously, I knew there was more to learn of my people.

4) Culture or Freedom: Living out the understanding acquired:

I met Sunez Allah in December of 2006. We officially became a couple February 1st, 2007, and I started getting a true knowledge of myself. Attending weekly classes of his P.E.A.C.E. Course (Political Education And Civilization Enrichment) provided me with the opportunity to attain the mathematics, alphabet, and the 120 lessons. I learned about the history of the Nation and that I wasn't a "white Latina of color." I was Black. I also learned that to best describe my supreme reality as an Original woman, the term Earth was used. I became aware of the concept of living foods and by March of 2007, I was Vegan. My knowledge of history expanded with books like *Stolen Legacy, Message to the Blackman,* and other such titles. Furthermore, with the Mathematics I was able to apply and understand the patterns of Creator and Creation. It was a beautiful experience, living a culture that my understanding brought me to.

5) Power or Refinement: Where one can extend their culture to a level that has reached the ideal moral and ethical principles:

For the first time, I was living a culture in tune with myself. I was no longer getting eczema breakouts or experiencing constant lethargy. A good development, yet I wanted to focus my culture properly. Through different Original cuisines (i.e. Mexican, Indian, Caribbean, Soul food, etc.), I explored the relevant history and began taking various recipes and adapting them to vegan versions. It was a beautiful experience being able to refine the culture I was living by learning more about world cuisine.

6) Equality: The ability to understand the different levels of supreme realities and sharing understandings of culture by all Black families:

Attending classes at the Allah School in Mecca allowed me to be surrounded by elders, Gods who "knowledged 120," and 85ers who were in the process of attaining a knowledge of self. I developed the ability to interact with each individual at their own level of understanding. If they were just learning their modern history (i.e. a Puerto Rican learning of Albizu Campos) or whether it was a God applying a particular degree from the 120 lessons to a deeper concept, we would engage in discussions. During one P.E.A.C.E. class, we engaged in a conversation about the ideal healthy diet. Sunez passed a sheet detailing the mentality of eating, with ideas on how to start transitioning into a vegan/living foods diet. I noticed that while students understood the ideas, they were having a hard time applying them. I devised an additional sheet detailing how to be vegan while living in the hood on a meager budget. This was my way of sharing a part of my understanding and culture powerfully.

7) God: It's a reaffirmation of oneself, of who one is:

I deliberately waited a year and a half before coming up with my righteous name. I wanted to continue absorbing my reality and accumulating knowledge. I didn't feel ready yet to describe who I was. In August of 2008, after much building with my God about how I saw the Earth and my relation to the Universe, I named myself Izayaa Allat. I Zig Zag Zig Allat = Why Allat is of Allah. My name expresses that my reality is intertwined with that of my God. It describes my relationship to him. Allat is the name of one of three pre-Islamic Goddesses. I wanted my name to show my creative nature as an Original woman. Mathematically, my name expresses the equation $9+26+1+25+1+1 =6+3=9=$Born. I had come to fruition, like the beauty of a blossoming lotus.

8) Build or Destroy: Adding on greater and destroying the unnecessary; universal change:

With my name, I realized my power to affect and change any cipher. Mathematics provided the building blocks to understand the patterns of change. When I learned something new, a pre-conceived notion or preliminary idea was no longer there. I was told that I was a "White Latina of Color." Did this mean that I have like a drop of Black blood? Getting a knowledge of self helped me destroy the idea that I was only a little Black. I built on new concepts of what Black really is, starting with KMT (Egypt) extending to chemistry, with the etymological root meaning, 'study of black.' I learned that melanin is what comprises the concept of Blackness. It is made in the medulla oblongata, the brain stem responsible for autonomic functions, where it is produced in an unquantifiable amount. Being infinite in its measure, in all the Original people, Black, Brown or Yellow, it is activated not calcified as in the colored man, the unoriginal man. This melanin is expressed in every major organ of the body, not merely the skin. That this bio-chemical reality of Blackness was in me fully as my darker brother and sisters was revelatory fulfillment for me. Small notice like compliments for my dancing and that I never suffered from skin-cancer as a very light skinned Dominican made sense. Of most importance, is that I now knew I was Black.

9) Born: A fulfillment and completion of self; what's created:

Getting knowledge of self has resulted in a complete Original woman who can now build more profoundly in any cipher. I am now living and navigating through the world with true consciousness. I look forward to creating more powerful curriculums for our youth, to read and write more about the Earth, as well as borning Original children with my God that will add-on aspects of our reality never considered before.

0) Cipher: Infinity:

In this process of mathematics, my reality will only deepen; an infinite progression of living perfection. Peace.

Izayaa Allat is a Brown University graduate with a Master's in Teaching focusing on Secondary Education in Social Studies History. Part of her experience includes designing curriculum for formal instruction or program-based learning, as well as documenting and researching Caribbean/Latin American History. A lover of the arts and travel, in 2003 she lived in Cuba and wrote research notes on the growth of Cuba's urban music. Currently, she serves as an Editor for the *Lavoe Revolt Journal.*

MARRIED AT THE AGE OF SIXTEEN
Queen Necessity Earth - D-Mecca (Detroit, MI)

At the young age of sixteen, I became a mother. I had a healthy young God that was 6lbs. 15oz. His very existence is the reason that I am who I am today. I had a young Earth four years later. I am a young, Black, single parent. Nevertheless, I am a mother and that is where the marriage part comes into play.

I was married to my son in the sense of commitment. I committed myself to care, love, and be there for him until death do us apart. There are other components of this word marriage, such as life-long. Life-long consists of the time from when this occurs and when you return to the

essence. Once you give birth no matter the circumstance you cannot take the act back. It is a life-long thing that cannot be reversed. I committed that to him. It is also considered a close union. There is most certainly a union amongst child and mother. In most scenarios, there is a close bond with the child and mother. The baby hears the mother's heart beat daily for nine months. Not only that, but the mother is the first teacher of the child. Another term related to marriage would be wed locked. The baby is locked to the umbilical cord and receives nourishment and vitality from the umbilical cord. One last term to relate to this union is intimate. The baby hears the voice of the mother for nine months straight, sometimes shorter. The mother carries the baby in her womb and nurtures the child before and after birth. The baby is secure and safe from harm in the mother's womb, and grows and develops there. Once this process is complete the mother goes into labor and the baby is released into the world.

The process does not end there. There is the next step, breastfeeding our children, because that is why breasts were created in the first place. In the olden days there was no Similac and cows to take the place of the woman's breast. Do not take that from our babies, give them what they need, it is all in there. All the nutrients and vitamins that are for babies; that help babies further their development and grow are present in breast milk. The truth is that should be the only way. I breastfed both of my children for 18 months, and I do not regret it one bit. It is good for them and they will be healthier for that reason. This may seem extensive to some but sometimes the baby needs more. The statistics show that babies are smarter due to breast milk so why would we hinder our babies by not giving them what they need? If they do not latch on immediately, try again. Persistence will pay off. This also plays into our marriage of motherhood because knowing that we are providing the best start for them is setting them up for future positive moments.

Another vital point is studying with the babies. We are the first teachers as mothers, so let us teach. A child that knows they are God and Earth is destined to steer away from the bullsh*t that we encountered as 85% before we got knowledge. We are setting them up for greatness. The babies are the greatest. They are the understanding and the best part. As a young mother even before knowledge of self, I read to my son in the womb. I read baby books and my homework because I know that he could hear me. That was teaching, the vibration of my voice was translating words to my son while in the belly. If that is not Peace, what is? We must catch our babies at this age, give them knowledge and the ability to spread the word so that we can ultimately turn the Nation of Gods and Earths into a bigger picture. The babies are the ones that are going to lead us there.

Peace to all young mothers. Do not believe that you have messed up and got yourself into a situation that you cannot be pulled from. You are helping us move closer to the understanding, granted it may be sooner than you first thought but make a way. Make knowledge born that you need assistance and I promise you will receive more than you request. I continued my education, finished my Bachelor's in 2006, and will complete my Master's this year. It can be done and I build that you will stay strong and help to elevate this nation by being the wisdom and show the babies through your ways and actions that you can do it. If by chance you are not already married to your children and the motherhood lifestyle than do so as soon as possible. Peace!

Queen Necessity Earth attended Oakland University for her Bachelor's degree in English (2006), and University of Phoenix for her Master's degree in Adult Education and Training (2009). She has two children, Akil Allah (10) and Makayla Earth (6), who motivate her daily. She is working on a book titled *Birth of an Earth*. She also likes to write poetry and cook. She explains, "Being an Earth has brought out feminine traits that I did not know existed. Having knowledge of self has allowed me the freedom to excel to my higher self. Without knowledge of self I'm not sure where I would be."

SO...THEN WHO IS THE DEVIL?
Supreme Understanding Allah - Allah's Garden (Atlanta, GA)

I know I've already offended dozens of you with the title alone, so I'll be clear about a few things upfront. I make no apologies for any of the statements I will make in the following paragraphs, but I want to be clear about what I am NOT saying.

First, I am *really* neither pro-Black nor anti-white. I am not against every individual white person. I AM against white supremacy and white privilege and its many manifestations. I will elaborate on that, but I need you to understand that I'm not into hateful, inflammatory rhetoric. I am not trying to incite a frenzied mob into a witchhunt for "those damn devils." I am simply clarifying a condition of reality. Finally, I don't find any value in spending time "blaming" white people for the problems of people with color. However, I think it is useless to attempt to treat a disease without knowing its cause(s). People of color DO need to understand WHY things are the way they are before they can effectively begin to solve their problems. Otherwise, we will easily fall victims to the same predatory conditions.

Let's begin. First, let's identify what exactly a "devil" is. We don't need to consult a dictionary. Common sense serves us well in telling us that a devil is one who lives in opposition to God; a force of evil; a source of wickedness and misery on Earth. The very existence of the devil is dependent on the existence of God. In every theology where a devil exists, he exists in opposition to the Supreme Being, God. When we talk about God and the devil, these constructs come to us pre-packaged as religious concepts, each pair unique to its respective theology. So keep this in mind, the word "God" was developed to describe the person/people around whom the theology was written. In the same way, the word "devil" was developed to describe a person/people who fit somewhere else in that theology. Thus, the real devil isn't the devil presented to us in our modern mythology (an insidiously evil man with a tail and pitchfork), but he is the man that the "devil" concept was originally created to describe.

Religions develop from the historical goings-on of the region where they develop. In the Near East, where Judaism, Christianity, Islam, and the Kemetic (Egyptian) religions emerged (as well as Zoroastrianism and the ancient Sumerian and Babylonian systems of worship), there is a stark contrast between God, who is good, and the devil, who is evil. So clear is the contrast that they are often opposite colors. Typically, the devil is a servant or creation of God "gone bad." In other world traditions, the devil is a sort of "trickster" or conniving and clever fellow that employs deceit, illusion, and other ruses for his own gain, benefit, or amusement. The reasons for these phenomena are tied directly to the history of these areas. Let's look at the history of the Ancient Near East, which is where we get the idea of the "wicked devil made by God."

In the Near East, the devil comes from God, and was once amongst him. The devil is expelled, takes power and begins inflicting misery upon the people of God. God must simultaneously fight for the minds and hearts of his people as he fights against the growing power of the devil. This isn't myth. This was life. This is what happened, historically, in the Ancient Near East. Don't believe me? Just keep reading. The truth behind the ancient myth remains relevant today, because God and devil occupy the same roles and behaviors in Near Eastern mythologies that they do in race relations among Blacks and whites today. Think about it. And if you're white, really think about it. Once you get past the shock value...try to make sense of it. Try to find answers for the elderly white man - at least 80 years old - who, at a workshop on the history of racism, quietly confided in me:

> I heard what he said about the cold weather and skin color changing, but that doesn't explain to me why we do what we do. Why is it that we just love to take from and destroy other people? We seem to enjoy it. Almost like it's natural for us. [Wink] I think you know what I'm saying to you.

Back to the history. Now, if we're gonna talk history, we need to talk about the most controversial element of this teaching. They say we teach that a "mad scientist named Yacub made white people" as if it was done on some Petri dish somewhere. They'd like for it to sound dumb, so you'll never look into it. But if it couldn't happen, why did white people spend hundreds of years trying to develop eugenics programs that do the same thing? Look up the history of eugenics and see! So was he one man, and was his actual name Yacub? Possibly not. In scripture, names are assigned to roles in prophesized history, so whoever/whatever functions in that role is thus identified with that scriptural personage. Thus, whoever led or organized this ancient cult became "Yacub" when they led thousands of people into the world's most successful planned eugenics movement. *Yacub*, in Hebrew, means "the supplanter," as in, his function/role was to supplant a new people for the dominant ruling group of the world. In ancient Egyptian, *Ya-cub* means "moon circuit," a period which is 6,000 years and coincides with the rule of whites. It is quite difficult to find any usable archaeological evidence from 6 millennia ago, but there are records that speak of a god named "Yacub El" (or "Yacub Allah") predating whenever the Jacob of the Bible was supposed to have been around. (*A Self-Verifying Chronological History of Ancient Egypt*, by Orlando P. Schmidt, p. 396) Who was this Yacub-El? Did he give birth to the myths of the Biblical Jacob "grafting" sheep and "fighting" with God? (read Genesis!)

And how did it work? Well how do scientists produce white lab mice from brown field mice? They breed out the dominant traits, saving only the most recessive offspring for further breeding. Simple eugenics. We'd already been doing it for tens of thousands of years. Our ancient knowledge of animal domestication and plant hybridization was supreme. So after several generations of selective breeding finally produced a generation that was completely genetically recessive, these whites were reintroduced to the Black population at the center of our civilization. Around this time, records from Egypt record King Menes having to reunify Egypt after expelling a divisive band of white intruders. These white intruders would later be reintroduced to Near Eastern civilization 2,000 years later. Except this time, it would fall at their hands.

Don't believe me? Read *SAHARASIA: The 4000 BCE Origins of Child Abuse, Sex Repression, Warfare and Social Violence in the Deserts of the Old World* by Dr. James DeMeo. He explains that - for some reason - people in North Africa, the Near East and Central Asia, which he calls Saharasia, suddenly emerged in "patrist" cultures, characterized by (a) repressive patriarchal institutions and deities, (b) castes and classes that may include slavery, (c) low attention to infant needs, (d) painful male and female initiation rites, and (e) brutal violence and warfare. This was in stark contrast to the cultures that previously dominated the region, characterized by (a) low levels of adult violence, (b) more democracy and egalitarianism, (c) gentle child treatment norms, and (d) healthy sexual relations. Now this is all in the book. In fact, book reviewer Paul Von Ward (www.ahpweb.org/pub/perspective/saharasia.html) writes:

> He concludes "that 'patrism' originated first and only within the harshest of hyperarid desert environments, and then only around 6,000 years ago." He further believes subsequent "patrist" societies outside Saharasia resulted from the invasion by "patrists" of adjacent temperate and wetland regions. The spread of such values by people inured to violence and hardship enabled them to impose their cultural patterns on more peace-loving peoples. DeMeo describes how "powerful nomadic-warrior cultures of

Central Asia and Arabia have played a prominent role in the genesis of kingly states, military allegiances and political history in both Saharasia and its moister borderlands."

The existence of "matrist" societies in other harsh climates—parts of the Himalayas, deserts of southern Africa and North America, and the Andes mountains—poses questions about the validity of his theory. *But other explanations will have to encompass DeMeo's data.*

This last part is critical, because it exposes the flaw in DeMeo's theory, that such a culture will arise due to a climate shift alone, and it presents the case that there must be a more comprehensive theory for why "Child Abuse, Sex Repression, Warfare and Social Violence" was born at this time, and at this place. You must examine why, as noted elsewhere in this book, geneticists have pinpointed the origins of **blue eyes** to this *same time period and same region.*

Historical evidence shows us that these whites were eventually expelled to live in the Caucasus Mountains (hence the name Caucasian), where they reverted to primitive behavior while sustaining and feeding their predatory tendencies. There are records of individual children living like this even in the modern era (www.feralchildren.com). Very interesting, if you think it can't happen. Michael Bradley's *The Iceman Inheritance* details what life was like in the caves for these people, and the aggressive and warlike behaviors it developed in them as a result. Many of the traditions that have lasted even until this day in European culture stem from this epoch of history. For example, the Western marriage ceremony is rooted in the practice of one caveman's tribe kidnapping a woman from another tribe, binding her, and carrying her into their cave - thus the ring (to bind), the throwing of the rice (rocks) during the getaway, the carrying over the threshold, and the immediate sexual gratification of the honeymoon. Another of these entrenched cultural practices is eugenics, a fascination among whites who have desired to produce the Supreme Whiteman, as most notably attempted during Hitler's campaign for a pure Aryan nation.

If you've every read a World History textbook, you'll remember that European history always begins sometime around 2,000 BC in the Caucasus Mountain region. It was from here that they reemerged, wreaking havoc on every civilization they encountered in the area. You may have also read further to see that every Black and Brown civilization was pillaged and destroyed by "foreign invaders."

Who were these foreign invaders? The Egyptians called them *Hyksos*, and history says these people eventually became known as the Hebrews after mixing with the Black Egyptian population. By 1800 BC, Indian scripture records them as the self-described *Aryans*, who created the caste system based on skin color, and manufactured the religion of Hinduism to reflect their values. Further east, in China, where they finally arrived about 1500 BC, they were the *Zhou* people, who conquered and displaced the Blacks of the previously ruling *Xia* and *Shang* dynasties, giving birth to a new, yellow (mixed) China. Everywhere these people went, they brought many familiar things along. In terms of physical artifacts, there were the sword and the chariot, probably "borrowed" from the designs of Egypt and the Near East. However, more significant were cultural patterns, like those described earlier, including a vicious style of conquest most Original people had never before witnessed. Everywhere they went, these people: (a) took over the most important cities, then spread out their rule as far as possible, dividing up geographic regions as they saw fit; (b) raped the local population, and set up "mixed" people as the buffer between them and the Black servant class; (c) used religion to supplant themselves as the "favored people" of an invisible god (Yacub); (d) introduced the religious ideas of heaven and hell, used as a system of reward and punishment for obedience; (e) disputed any idea that they came from another region, and claimed to be native heirs to the land; (f) reversed the society's positive views on Blackness by introducing white gods and Black demons into the mythology; (g) began replacing the indigenous language with an Indo-European variant; and (h) began rapidly transforming the local social, financial and political structure to fit their ruling style, resulting in equitable (or "socialist") communities quickly becoming hierarchies of seriously imbalanced power and wealth.

Does this sound similar to what has happened when whites colonized Africa or when whites "settled" America? Not much has changed, of course, and history is indeed cyclical.

> *"If you do not understand white supremacy, what it is, and how it works, then everything else will only confuse you." - Neely Fuller, Jr.*

So let's look at the modern era. Conspiracy theories abound, on every topic from 9/11 to 2012 to 666. However, unless these fragmented theories are seen through the unified lens of the global conspiracy for white supremacy, they all are simply confusing and disconnected. In fact, what the white pundits who rant and rave about 9/11 and "constitutional freedoms" love to ignore is that the "New World Order" and the "Illuminati" are about white power more than anything else. When Bush and the rest of the Skull and Bones crew are engaging in what appear to be Satanic rituals, please don't think that the most elite whites on this Earth are dumb enough to be so religious and primitive. They are hailing themselves and their direct "descent" from Yacub, who is the same as the Moloch hailed in the Skull and Bones' "Cremation of Care" ceremony. Look up the video online. Who are they cremating? YOU, Blackman!

These people know who God is. They know the Original Man is God. They are informed enough to be aware of the obvious. It is only Original People who are too blind to know it. Did you know that when

Masons attain their 32nd and 33rd degrees they are introduced to the worship of the "true God," Allah? Ask any old Shriner why they wear a Muslim fez with a sword at the top. Of course he won't tell you!

They know who they are. And I'm not referring to Sally and Joe Pimple from down the street. I'm referring to those who function on the higher echelons of society. Sally and Joe Pimple, on the other hand, are just passive participants in the global plague of white supremacy. Sure, their son Trevor is a nice guy who never calls you the "n-word" and listens to hip hop nonstop. He can even dance! That doesn't exempt him.

"Treason to whiteness is loyalty to humanity." – White studies pioneer Noel Ignatiev

White people are typically either active or passive participants in this racist system of white supremacy, and while it's very hard for them to simply escape being a participant, it's impossible for them to escape their nature. "Devil" is not just what you do, it's who you are. A man can act like a woman, dress like a woman, and even get surgery to fool nearly everyone...but at the end of the day, he's naturally a man. White people were not created to be our saviors or our benefactors, no matter how many trees they hug or African squirrels they campaign to save. They were made to be who, as a whole, they are today.

I could spend the next ten-thousand pages detailing every ill this planet is currently faced with and how it goes back to whites, but I don't think that's a productive use of literature. If you are genuinely interested, pick a topic and research it thoroughly until you get to the bottom of who is responsible. For example, try finding the answers to some of these questions on your own, so that you too, can understand why the white man is the devil (unless you're already conditioned and too scared to say such a thing):

❑ Why did the Hutus and Tutsis go to war in Rwanda, resulting in an African genocide? Who started all the other ethnic and tribal wars?
❑ Who is currently toppling governments, creating unrest and civil war, and murdering countless civilians over land and oil?
❑ What were the Crusades fought over?
❑ What is manifest destiny?
❑ What is the history of eugenics?
❑ What non-white nation or people has interacted with whites and benefited positively?
❑ Why did Communism and Socialism have to be crushed?
❑ Why are scientists exploring "escaping" to other planets?
❑ Why do so many people think racism is going away when all the evidence says the opposite?
❑ What is Lothrop Stoddard's 1920 book, *The Rising Tide of Color against White-World Supremacy* about?

- [ ] What is population control?
- [ ] What were *300* and *The Lord of the Rings* really about?
- [ ] Who are/will be the enemies in the current war on terrorism?
- [ ] How did the tsunami in South-East Asia occur?
- [ ] Why did American nuke Japan in WWII?
- [ ] Why are foods, household items, and even water in Black and brown communities laden with toxic poisons?
- [ ] What happened to the aboriginal Black natives of Australia, the Pacific Islands, Asia, and the Americas?

Once again, remember, the word "devil" is not meant to be used as an epithet, insult, or slur. It is not a fighting word; it is a word that explains our fight. The devil is a social reality, grounded in real history, lived out in real human affairs. And the very existence of the devil demands that you *choose sides*. We aren't anti-white…we're anti-devilishment.

THE BUILD

THE WHITEMAN IS THE DEVIL

Shaikhi Teach Mathematics Allah – Interior Cipher (Virginia)

It was 7:00 am and young Malik was still waiting inside of the International House of Pancakes for Scientific to arrive. He was also waiting for his order of five blueberry pancakes with extra syrup and two cups of milk, which he'd ordered about 15 minutes ago.

"Excuse me Miss, but where is my order?" he asked the waitress as he shrugged his shoulders, gesturing with both of his hands raised to express inquisition. "Five blueberry pancakes with two cups of milk, right?" she replied. "With extra syrup," added Malik. "Sir, the syrup will come in a jug when you get your pancakes and you can use as much syrup as you'd like," she told him. She then smiled and informed him that she was going to check on his order right away - then headed towards the kitchen. As Malik looked at his watch wondering why Scientific hadn't arrived yet, he noticed, through his peripheral vision, an unfamiliar face that appeared to be watching him attentively, staring so deep into his mouth that Malik could've mistaken the person for his regular dentist. As Malik was trying to figure out who this unfamiliar person might be, his attention was suddenly directed outside due to the bass of the music penetrating from an all-white 1987 4-door Skylark Buick that had just pulled up in front of the restaurant. Finally, Scientific had arrived.

"It's about time!" Malik said to himself excitedly as he watched Scientific, a dark-skinned brother, 6 feet 5 inches tall, about 200 pounds, with a hairstyle of neatly-braided cornrows, approaching the restaurant. Scientific had a very humble and humorous character, but one could easily sense his seriousness whenever he spoke, especially when he got deep on various topics. Yesterday, he had told Malik to meet him at 7 o'clock the next morning at the International House of Pancakes so that he could build with him on the wisdom degree in the Student Enrollment lesson. Almost 15 minutes late, Scientific saw young Malik watching and waiting for him as he nonchalantly walked through the entrance door. After he started making his way to the table where Malik was seated, he observed the pretty young woman serving Malik a plate of pancakes along with two cups of milk and a silver jug that he assumed contained syrup.

"Peace God!" Scientific greeted as he approached the table. "Peace Lord!" Malik responded, returning the greeting. Then Scientific turned and greeted the waitress, "Peace sister, how do you feel this morning?" Perplexed about why they had just addressed each other as 'God' and 'Lord' as well as why he'd cared about how she felt, she simply responded with a kind smile, "I feel just fine sir, thank you for asking." She directed her attention back to Malik. "I'm sorry that we took so long with your order so I brought you three extra pancakes. If you need anything else just let me know." "Okay, thank you," Malik responded with a look in his eyes that gave away how hungry he'd become. She then turned back to Scientific. "Can I get you anything sir?" she asked. "No thank you sister, I'm alright," he answered. As the waitress walked away, Malik - with a mouth full of pancakes - asked Scientific if he would like some. "Now Cipher God, I just started a three day fast today," he said, noticing that Malik had already devoured about half of the eight pancakes. He apologized for being late and explained that he'd been caught up in a conversation with his Earth about a white South African farmer in Johannesburg who was on trial for the murder of one of his Black employees. The farmer had beat him with a machete, tied him to a stake, and then drove him to a nearby lion reserve and threw him over the fence where he was mauled by the lions. Malik's facial expression revealed that he was in shock from hearing such horrific acts.

"Are you alright God?" Scientific asked after seeing the disturbed look on the young God's face.

"Yeah, it's just unbelievable to hear that someone would do something that cruel to another human being," he said.

"You better start believing it, so that you will learn to know that the white man is the devil," Scientific said seriously. Malik became very silent and focused because he knew that when Scientific took on a serious tone, he was poised to drop a powerful build. This build, he knew, would be about the white man being the devil - a lesson he knew he'd never forget.

Malik, who was only 16, had just started studying the knowledge of himself with the Nation of Gods and Earths, who is commonly referred to as the 'Five Percenters', about two weeks ago after he had heard Scientific build on the history of the Nation of Gods and Earths at his high school during a history seminar. After the seminar was over, he approached the 30-year-old man who had introduced himself to the audience of students as Be Born Scientific Nature Allah. He asked Scientific how he learned about the teachings of the Nation of Gods and Earths, which he had spoke about during the seminar. Scientific saw a thirst for the knowledge in the young student's eyes, looked down at him and asked, "What is your name?" "Corey" he replied. "Corey is not a righteous name. Honorable but not righteous." Corey was a little confused because he didn't completely understand the difference. "I will bestow upon you the righteous name of Malik, and if you choose to accept this name I will teach you myself. Malik means 'a king' and it is a king that I will teach you how to become, just as your forefathers were." Without any hesitation, Corey gladly accepted the name. And from that point on Scientific had been teaching Malik, personally, the teachings of the Nation of Gods and Earths.

As Malik was washing down his last mouthful of pancakes with his second cup of milk, Scientific placed both of his elbows on the table and leaned forward towards Malik. He then asked him, "What is the wisdom degree in the Student Enrollment?" "Who is the Colored Man? Answer: The Colored Man is the Caucasian White Man or Yacub's grafted devil of the planet Earth" he replied. Malik then asked Scientific why he was referred to as the 'Colored' man. "Colored is past tense - meaning that something was once something else but has been changed from its original state. In this case, the white man was once a man of dark color but due to him being grafted he was changed to the color white. If you recall during the Jim Crow era, white folks referred to us as colored people - not because we were people of color, as many people believe, but because they were telling the world that *they* were the original people and that Black people came from *them* after being cursed by God, burnt by the sun and turned black. They referred to us as "colored" to indicate to the world that we were changed from our original color of white! All they had done was reverse the historical truth about themselves. In her book *The Isis Papers: The Keys to the Colors*, Dr. Frances Cress Welsing quoted a 19th century German philosopher named Arthur Schopenhauer. Mr. Schopenhauer made the following statement about white skin in *The Philosophy of Schopenhauer: Metaphysics of Love of Sexes*:

> ...the white colour of skin is not natural to man, but that by nature he has a black or brown skin, like our forefathers the Hinus; that consequently a white man has never originally sprung from the womb of nature, and that thus there is no such thing as a white race, as much as this is talked of, but every white man is a faded or bleached one.

"Lord, what is one of the biggest tricks that the devil has ever pulled?" Scientific asked, and then continued by answering his own question. "He convinced the world that he didn't exist - meaning that he convinced the world that he's not the devil. About eighty-five percent (85%) of the people on this planet, regardless of their race, color or creed does not know the true knowledge of the devil (or whiteman) because he's hid it from them, and deceived them into believing his lie - that the devil is some creature wearing a red suit, with a long tail, two horns protruding from his head, carrying a pitch fork around, and living deep beneath the earth's surface surrounded by everlasting flames of burning hellfire. And when the Nation of Gods and Earths reveals to them that the white man is the living devil who was grafted from Black people, they reject it at face value as being some kind of mendacious fairy tale, even with all the evidence that is available to prove it. We are taught to never accept anything at face value, but at the same time we should also never reject anything at face value. Knowledge must be respected in order to allow it the opportunity to be analyzed and investigated." As Malik listened attentively to Scientific's wisdom, he noticed - again - that the same unfamiliar person was still there with his eyes and ears locked on him and Scientific.

"Pardon self God?" Malik interrupted. "Do you see that person over there?" he asked. Turning his head slightly to see who Malik was referring to, he answered "Yea, what's the science with him?" "I don't know exactly, but he's been here since I got here and he's been watching me ever since. Now he's watching the both of us, and it appears that he is ear-hustling on our conversation," Malik explained.

"He *is* tuning in kind of hard but I don't think he means any harm. Maybe he'll learn something if he's being nosy" Scientific said, and continued with his build. "Many people read the Bible but do not truly understand everything that it's revealing to them, because the devil has intentionally taught them a misunderstanding of it, in order to keep them from seeing the truth. Revelation 13:18 says: "This calls for wisdom. If anyone has insight, let him calculate the number of the beast, for it is a man's number. His number is 666." This lets us know that the devil who is referred to as a beast, is actually a man. But what man? Pay close attention God because what I'm about to share will provide you with a foundation so that you may do your own research to learn whether I'm telling you the truth or a lie.

"Many people believe that Adam was the first man on Earth even though the Bible never says that he was the first man - but this is what the whiteman has taught the people to believe. If one would read the Bible with reason and logic, common sense would reveal to them that Adam couldn't have been the first man on earth due to the fact that Adam and Eve gave birth to two sons - Cain and Abel. Cain kills Abel and then cried out to the Lord that someone would find him and kill him for what he had done. Genesis 4:15 says - "But the Lord said to him, "Not so, if anyone kills Cain, he will suffer vengeance seven times over." Then the Lord put a mark on Cain so that no one who found him would kill him. So if Adam was the first man on earth and he and Eve gave birth to only two sons - then who is the Lord warning not to kill Cain? Then Genesis 4:15 and 17 tells us that Cain moved to live in another land where he lay with his wife. Now where did she come from? Many people never ask themselves these questions because they are taught not to question the Bible but to just believe everything in it to be true. This kind of teaching kills a person's ability to use their reason and logic to discern information. This kind of teaching only comes from the devil.

"With the right knowledge the people would be able to decode the Bible and learn the truth of the Devil. The word 'Genesis' means the beginning or origin, and the people are taught by the devil that it refers to the beginning or origin of the entire Earth - which leads them to believe that Adam was the first man. The root of the word 'Genesis' is 'gene' which implies genetics, and when you look in *Webster's Encyclopedic Unabridged Dictionary of the English Language* you'll learn that the -*sis* - is a suffix appearing in loanwords from Greek, where it was used to form abstract nouns of action or process. Mr. Graham also made mention that "...the word genesis does not mean something out of nothing. It is a derivative of the word gene, the life germ, thus implying generation, growth." In the book of Genesis it is revealing the beginning or origin of the devil (or whiteman) through a genetic process, whereas something is being grafted or made out of something else. Those who write our history in advance predicted that Yacub would produce a generation of people that would be unalike his own. So there in the book of Genesis you read about Jacob (Yacub) grafting a flock of animals. The secret is that the animals are used as a symbolic term for people in order to hide the truth of the devil's origin. The name Jacob means "supplanter' and it is the noun for the word supplant. Supplant means - to take the place of another, as through force, scheming, strategy, or the like; to replace one thing by something else. So Jacob (Yacub) through a process of selective breeding or grafting produced out of the Black gene a white gene to replace the Black gene. After Yacub had produced a generation of devils (or white people) - he taught them tricknology and how to master Black people and rule them for 6,000 years. Those who do not even believe it's possible to graft white people from the genes of Black people needs to consider that in the January 3, 1910 issue of the *New York Times*, that there was an article entitled "May Make Negroes White; Chicagoan Believes It Possible to Neutralize the Color Units." In this article Q.T. Simpson had proudly announced to the members of the American Association for the Advancement of Science that the Black race could be bred out of existence through genetic manipulation:

> I think we are on the verge of gaining complete control over these chromosomes (governing races), and that means the control of color...By a set process of treatments with baths or injections this new tide in the affairs of the black man will be attenuated or destroyed. Today we can do it by breeding. Tomorrow we can change the color of the blacks' offspring by treating these color-controlling cells with a stimulant to war against the chromosomes...

"One can also read in the book *The Christian View of Science and the Scripture* by Dr. Bernard Ramm who admitted:

> By scientific breeding we can shuffle these genes with their characteristics, and breed traits in or breed them out. The laws of heredity plus principles of separation or selection operating over a period of time will produce the various races of the world.

"One of the main reasons why I said that the book of Genesis is revealing the beginning or origin of the whiteman through a genetic process whereas something is being grafted or made out of something else, is also due to the fact that the word Adam itself means 'whiteman'. It is also a plural noun, meaning more than one. You'll find the original Hebrew meaning of the name Adam in the book called *The Exhaustive Concordance of the Bible* which was written by James Strong in 1890. In it Adam is defined as - "ruddy, i.e. a human being (an individual or the species, mankind). To show blood in the face, i.e. flush or turn rosy: to be dyed/made red ruddy." It is a known fact that due to white people's lack of melanin (a black substance) that their blood shows through their face. Black people blood doesn't show through their face due to the abundance of melanin that they have. Paul L. Guthrie confirms this when he states in his book *Making of the Whiteman*: "...Adam's ruddy complexion was due to the lack of melanin in his skin. Because Adam's skin was pale it allowed the blood beneath to show through." Another European name Alexander Winchell wrote a book entitled *Preadamites* in 1880, which tells the history of people living before Adam. Mr. Winchell makes mention from the early Hebrews:

> Here is the old record which also declares that Adam was ruddy. This tint is found only in the Mediterranean race. The unmixed black races do not possess ruddy complexions. The ruddiness of Adam was...a complexion characteristically white."

"You can also find in the *Zondervan NIV Exhaustive Concordance* by Edward W. Goodrick and John R. Kohlenberger III, where Adam is defined as 'reddish-white." The highly educated white historians, scholars and scientists know that they were grafted from Black people, that they were made devils, and that they are the Adam in the book of Genesis. Another historical piece of evidence that reveals that Adam was a group of people who were grafted or made from Black people, was when a fourteenth century Spanish monk name Tomas Scoto was put on trial and executed after he revealed that the story of Adam and Eve simply told the making of one group of people from another. Paul L. Guthrie informs us:

> Records kept by the Church of Spain show that Tomas Scoto was charged with the crime of spreading an "unauthorized" view of the scriptures. At his trial, the monk responded to the charges against him by declaring in Latin: "Ante Adam fuerunt homines et per illos homines fit factus Adam," meaning: "There were men before Adam and Adam was made by those men."

"And this is why you'll read in the book of Genesis 1:26, where it says, "Then God said, "Let us make man in our image, in our likeness." The pronouns 'us' and 'our' are used because it is referring to a group of people - the Gods or Blackmen. Even in the Qur'an, Allah is described by the pronouns we, us and our. These same white folks are also well aware that this took place a little over six thousand years ago. A whiteman name Dr. John Lightfoot had declared in 1654 that "Heaven and earth, center and circumference were made in the same instance of time and clouds full of water and man was created by the Trinity on the 26th of October, 4004 B.C. at 9 o'clock in he morning." Why would Dr. Lightfoot declare that man and earth was created by God (the so-called Trinity) in the year 4,004 B.C.? If we (Black people) know today that we lived on this earth long before 4,004 B.C., just due to the fact that the bones that we found in Africa was carbon dated back millions of years - Why does Dr. Lightfoot refer to man and the world beginning in 4,004 B.C.? I believe that Dr. Lightfoot knew that Adam was the whiteman or white people and figured that if he placed Adam's beginning with the creation of the earth, that it would lead people to believe that the whiteman (or Adam) was the first man. And how right he was, for it prepared the way for the white historians to write their lies in his-story - that Black people came from white people when they (white people) had been burnt by the Sun. And the sad thing about all of this is that many Black and White people believe(d) it. But why 4,004 B.C.? I had mentioned earlier that the 24 Black scientists had predicted that Yacub would be successful in grafting or making a devil (or whiteman) on or about the 9,000th year of the 25,000 year cycle, and that they would master and rule Black people for 6,000 years. Well then when you subtract 2,000 years from the year 2,004 B.C. you come to the year 4 B.C. and finally subtract 4 years from the year 4 B.C. and add 1,996 years from the start of the A.D. years - you'll end up with the year 1996. That was a total of 6,000 years from the year 4,004 B.C. The year 1996 is tantamount to the year 15,082 in the 25,000 year cycle. Subtract 6,000 years from the year 15,082 and you'll end up with the year 9,082 - which is tantamount to the year 4,004 B.C. This is very near the 9,000th year of the 25,000 year cycle, which was or was around the year that Yacub had successfully made or grafted the devil.

At this point Scientific and Malik could both feel the energy from the unfamiliar person eyes radiating on them, clearly reading every word that was exiting their mouths. They both yielded in silence as they turned to look at him. As they looked upon him he just stared back at them as if he had no shame that they knew that he was watching and listening to them. "Do you think he's some kind of FBI agent or something?" Malik asked in a mumble, trying not to let the unfamiliar person see his lips moving. "Now cipher, I think that he's just being nosy, or he's just attracted to the wisdom that we speak" Scientific assumed. "But lets not worry about him at this time God, just keep an eye on him from time to time," Scientific said. "What time is it anyway?" "Five minutes till eight" Malik revealed. "We're going to motivate out of here around eight-fifteen. Now where was I? Oh, I remember. In the book *100 Amazing Facts About the Negro* by J.A. Rogers, he revealed:

The Devil which is now depicted as black, was once portrayed as White. When the black man dominated the planet he painted the forces of evil, white. When the whites came into power they shifted the colors. But as late as 1500 the Ethiopians still depicted their gods and heroes black, and their devils and villains, white.

Our Black historian Chancellor Williams makes mention of how white devils from the west came in contact with some African tribes or nations that had never seen a white person, and when they did see a white man for the first time they had thought that they (white people) were just painted in white chalk - until they realized that the white would not erase from their skin. Black people are a peaceful and loving people - so peaceful and loving that we embraced white folks because we seen that they were in the image and likeness of ourselves (Gen 1:26), not in pigmentation but in human form.

"When you read in the book of Genesis where Adam and Eve were banished from the Garden of Eden - it is referring to the history when they were ran out of the holy and righteous land of an established civilization by Black people for causing trouble amongst them. Black people had ran them across the hot Arabian Desert into the caves of west Asia which is today called Europe, and had set up warriors to guard and keep them from entering back into the holy and righteous land. This is what is meant in Genesis 3:24 when it says - "After he (God) drove the man (Adam) out, he placed on the east side of the Garden of Eden cherubim and a flaming sword flashing back and forth to guard the way to the tree of life." If only the people would study and research, they would be able to decode the true history that the Bible is revealing to them. In the secret order called Masonry (which was only meant for white folks) they practice a ritual of walking across the hot sand, which is symbolic to the history of them being ran across the hot Arabian desert into the caves of Europe. Paul L. Guthrie also tells us about a group of 19th Century explorers in Ethiopia who had uncovered a very ancient document called *The Book of Adam and Eve*, and that many scholars include it as part of *The Lost Books of Eden*. It was originally written in Arabic but the text had long ago been translated into Ethiopic. *The Book of Adam and Eve* picks up where the book of Genesis leaves off. The book speaks of Adam and Eve being forced to walk across the desert:

> But when our father Adam, and Eve went out of the garden, they trod the ground on their feet...And when they came to the opening of the gate of the garden, and saw the broad earth spread before them, covered with stones large and small, and with sand, they feared and trembled...

The book also makes mention of the cave that they were run into:

> And, indeed when Adam looked at his flesh, that was altered, he wept bitterly, he and Eve, over what they had done...And as they came to it Adam wept over himself and said to Eve, "Look at this cave that is to be our prison in this world, and a place of punishment.

The Maulawi Sher Ali translation of the Holy Qur'an refers to white people as 'Jinn', who are described as:

> The inhabitants of northern hilly tracts of Europe, of white and red color, whom other people looked upon as being separate from other human beings and who lived detached from the civilized people of Asia but who were destined to make great material progress in the latter days and to lead a great revolt against religion...Wild and savage peoples who...lived in caves and hollows of the earth and were subject to no rules of conduct."

All throughout the religious scriptures it speaks about the battle of God and Devil or God and Evil. In Maulana Muhammad Ali's translation of the Holy Qur'an Surah 20:102 it states that "The day when the trumpet is blown; and We shall gather the guilty, blue eyed on that day." This scripture clearly describes the white race for they are the ones who have blue eyes. Footnote 1501a is the footnote where Maulana Muhammad Ali explains Surah 20:102:

> The word zurq means blue-eyed. According to Bd, blue being the colour of the eyes of the Rum (i.e. the Greeks or the Romans), who were most hated by the Arabs, that colour was regarded by the Arabs as the worst colour for the eye...

"And with all of this knowledge out there the masses still don't believe that the whiteman is a grafted devil" Malik asked while scratching his head, then he signaled to get the waitress' attention. When she came over to the table Malik ordered a glass of orange juice and asked Scientific if he wanted something to drink, since he was fasting. "I'm peace God" Scientific said. As the waitress left to fulfill Malik's order, Scientific continued by answering Malik's question. "God, you even have some white people that bear witness to what we teach and try to teach their people and ours the truth about themselves (white people), and the masses still can't see it or they just don't want to see it. There's a white woman in particular, named Dr. Dorothy Fardan, who wrote a book called *Message to the White Man and Woman in America: Yacub and the Origins of White Supremacy*. In it she bears witness that her people are grafted devils:

> If we follow the teaching of Elijah Muhammad on the making of the whiteman...we understand that the nature of the white man...has been grafted out of the original. It is, therefore, an aberrant genetic construct and thus lies at the base of the errant and malicious way of white rule...Therefore, on this most fundamental level, the salvation of white people...lie in grafting back to originality [the righteous nature] of original black people.

When the waitress had returned with Malik's orange juice, he thanked her and interjected to ask Scientific a question. "Pardon self God, but can the whiteman's nature change without him being grafted back to the original?" Malik wondered. "Now Cipher! What determines the nature of a thing is how it came into existence from its very beginning. Wickedness and devilishment was bred into the whiteman at the beginning of his existence, so his nature is to be an evil man and many people are deceived by him into believing that his nature can be changed into being a good man because he shows them a little good. Always remember God, an evil man who does good cannot be compared to a good man who does evil. What may help you understand this a little better is when Muhammad Shabazz and Ali Shaheed made discussed the nature of the Doberman Pinscher:

> In 1888 the German government commissioned Dr. Dobermann to develop a dog with the strength of a hound and the veracity of a terrier. Ten years later Dr. Doberman successfully completed the grafting process and presented Germany with the Doberman Pinscher. This dog was bred to be an attack and guard dog. This was its nature and still is its nature. Though the demand for having the Doberman as an attack dog has significantly diminished, it still acts out of its inherent disposition. And while there are as many Beagles as Dobermans in the United States, people are far more susceptible to being harmed by the Doberman than the Beagle. This is simply the nature of the beast. Dobermans attack maul or kill several people every year. Although many Dobermans are used as companions for young and old alike, Dobermans too often "turn" on their beloved, defenseless masters for no apparent reason. Beagle owners are not faced with this problem. Why? By nature the Beagle is docile and gentle and not inclined to attack. Only if the Beagle has been mistreated will the Beagle attack. Surely, many Dobermans never make an aggressive gesture toward their masters. However, this does not mean that their nature is different. Given the right or wrong circumstance, the true nature of the beast will surface.

"The evidence of history shows and proves that the whiteman has committed supreme evil throughout the world, and still our people believe that his nature has changed over the last century. Is the whiteman still the devil? Well let's see – There are so many incidents that have happened in recent history that reveal that their nature has not changed. From the horrendous lynchings where white families watched in joy (cutting off body parts to keep as souvenirs)…to the rampant police brutality that never results in any punitive actions…to the bombing of innocent men, women, and children in other countries for oil and power…to the prison industrial complex and the sentencing disparities used to return Blacks to modern-day slavery…not to mention the chemical warfare they are waging on us through the dumping of toxic waste in our communities, and the toxic substances put in our food and water supplies…to the modern day lynchings and executions that continue today…to the very way our society is structured so that we never see exactly how much we're being exploited and victimized."

"Anyone who is aware of current events and does not believe in the lies of the media surely knows that these acts are a regular occurrence. Black people need to always remember the attacks that were and still are being committed against our people at the hands of white folk. We need to never forget what happened to our people throughout history, throughout the world. It happened to them yesterday – and it continues today – and if we don't start remembering and doing something to prevent it from happening again – it will continue to happen to our children tomorrow. While we are teaching that the whiteman is the devil - the whiteman is showing our people that he is the devil, which only show and prove that what we've been teaching them was right and exact.

"What did you learn this morning, God?" Scientific asked. Feeling energized from such an informative build, Malik answered "That the wisdom degree in the Student Enrollment is right and exact." "So what are you going to do now?" asked Scientific, wondering how Malik was going to respond. "I'm going to study and research the things that you built on to learn it for myself" Malik said. "Very wise response God, because you should never take anything at face value, regardless of who it comes from. Study and research it for yourself" Scientific advised, - then asked Malik for the time. "8:14" he informed him. "Lets get out of here God, because I have somewhere to be at nine," he uttered as he passed two small sheets of paper across the table to Malik. Malik began reading what was on the sheets of paper as Scientific left a twenty dollar bill on the table to pay for the meal. Malik attempted to pay, but Scientific insisted.

As they were walking out, they noticed that the same unfamiliar person was still sitting there, watching them. Scientific stopped and said,

"Excuse me? But we've noticed that you've been watching us and reading our lips the entire time. Yes, you! I'm talking to the unfamiliar person who is reading this article. We know that you read every word and if you have any doubts about what has been said, research it for yourself and find out if it's true or not. Malik, give him one of the sheets of paper that I just gave you." After Malik left one of the sheets of paper, he and Scientific said "Peace" to the Reader - the unfamiliar person - and exited the restaurant.

Shaikhi Teach "Living" Mathematics Allah is currently in the belly of the beast in Virginia. Because certain prisons do not allow in literature containing the location of prisoners, he can be contacted at the address provided at www.knowledgeofself.us

Note: The contents of the "sheet of paper" provided at the end of this story was a list of the many texts referenced in this short story.

❧ 4 ☙
CULTURE

WHAT WE TEACH

1. That Black people are the original people of the planet earth.
2. That Black people are the fathers and mothers of civilization.
3. That the science of Supreme Mathematics is the key to understanding man's relationship to the universe.
4. Islam is a natural way of life, not a religion.
5. That education should be fashioned to enable us to be self sufficient as a people.
6. That each one should teach one according to their knowledge.
7. That the Blackman is God and his proper name is ALLAH. Arm, Leg, Leg, Arm, Head.
8. That our children are our link to the future and they must be nurtured, respected, loved, protected and educated.
9. That the unified Black family is the vital building block of the nation.

WHAT WE WILL ACHIEVE

1. **National Consciousness:** National Consciousness is the consciousness of our origin in this world, which is divine. As a nation of people we are the first in existence and all other peoples derived from us. National Consciousness is the awareness of the unique history and culture of Black people and the unequaled contributions we have made to world civilization, by being the fathers and mothers of civilization. National Consciousness is the awareness that we are all one people regardless to our geographical origins and that we must work and struggle as one if we are to liberate ourselves from the domination of outside forces and bring into existence a Universal Government of Love, Peace and Happiness for all the people of the planet.
2. **Community Control:** Community Control of the educational, economic, political, media and health institutions on our community. Our demand for Community Control flows naturally out of our science of life, which teaches that we are the Supreme Being in person and the sole controllers of our own destiny; thus

we must have same control on the collective level that we strive to attain on the individual level. It is prerequisite to our survival that we take control of the life sustaining goods and services that every community needs in order to maintain and advance itself and advance civilization. Only when we have achieved complete Community Control will we be able to prove to the world the greatness and majesty of our Divine Culture, which is Freedom.

3. **Peace:** Peace is the absence of confusion (chaos) and the absence of confusion is Order. Law and Order is the very foundation upon which our Science of Life rest. Supreme Mathematics is the Law and Order of the Universe, this is the Science of Islam, which is Peace. Peace is Supreme Understanding between people for the benefit of the whole. We will achieve Peace, in ourselves, in our communities, in our nation and in the world. This is our ultimate goal.

WHO IS THE 5%?

Freedom Allah - Love Allah (Los Angeles, CA)

The Nation of God and Earth is built upon the teachings of Allah, our founder. We know and teach that the Supreme Being, God (Allah), is the Black man. Supreme means most high and being means something that exists. We do not believe that God is an invisible being existing somewhere outside of man. Allah is real. This is our most profound teaching, it is often rejected by the masses of the people because they have been subjected to the teachings of the deceitful religious leaders for thousands of years.

The prophets and messengers of old have all hinted at the reality of God. Many keys are found in the scriptures and teachings of the various religions; however the real secret of God was not to be revealed publicly to the masses until the last days of the devil's rule. Those of us with the knowledge of ourselves are now living in the hereafter. We have been blessed by the coming of Allah who has taught us how to 'born God,' that is, how to grow into God ourselves. We live and learn in Allah's world. In Allah's world, the righteous are becoming victorious. It is the birthright of the Black man (which includes all people of so-called black, brown and yellow descent) to be God. We teach that the Black woman is the Earth. God and Earth go together like sun and moon. The sun is symbolic to man and the moon is symbolic to woman. Each God must be the foundation of his family or universe. He gives light (knowledge) and life (sperm) to his Earth so that their family can continue on after they both return to their essence. The true and living God is the original man with knowledge of his own reality. He is an upright and civilized man. He knows who he is and teaches the world true freedom, justice and equality through example.

"There are unquestionable universal laws applicable to all forms of matter and life, but there are also forces which cause each individual person and each individual place to become a unique expression of these laws. The phrase "a god within" symbolizes for me the forces that create private worlds out of the universal stuff of the cosmos and thus enable life to express itself in countless individualities." - Rene Dubois, A God Within

Supreme Mathematics is order, the natural order of the universe. In order to reach completeness, everything that exists must start at knowledge and be taken to born. Supreme Mathematics is the language of the Gods and Earths. These laws are the foundation of our culture. It is evident that the devil is still ruling the masses of the people. He is running in overtime. The rich are ripping off the poor and cataclysmically destroying the Earth.

"There must be Religion. Otherwise the poor would murder the rich." - Napoleon Bonaparte

The devil does not rest. He causes trouble and manipulates all that he can. To be victorious we must talk and walk our language daily. Each of us has to take the devil off our own planet – else we may fall victim to his deceit. The only power the devil has nowadays is the power we give to him. Knowing this is one of the steps to understanding how Allah is truly God.

Even though we utilize the 'Islamic' name of God, Allah, the Gods and Earths do not practice the religion of Islam. We are not Muslims. Islam, as we live it out, is a culture. It has no beginning nor ending, it is not a religion, it is mathematics. All religions have a beginning and things that have beginnings have endings. For us, all religions expired in 1964 which is year one of the Five Percent Nation (now known as the Nation of God and Earth). We use the name Allah because that is the name of our founder.

"God has no religion." – Mahatma Gandhi

The religion of Islam was started in the 7th century, Common Era. It is now made up of over seventy sects which are usually categorized into two factions, Sunni and Shi'a. These two are commonly called orthodox Islam. They make up the majority of the Muslim population. There are other forms of Islam that exist such as the Sufis and the Nation of Islam. In the Arabic language, Islam literally means surrender and in its religious connotation it means the peace that comes when one submits or surrenders their will to Allah. For us, ISLAM means I Self Lord Allah Master, or I Sincerely Love Allah's Mathematics. Though we are not Sufis, we do hold some commonalities with them. The Sufis teach an esoteric version of Islam that combines the teachings of orthodox Islam with the Eastern mysticism traditions. There are some groups of Sufis who are not Muslim at all; they practice a secular form of Sufism. Some of the Sunni and Shi'a Muslims accept the teachings of the Sufis while some of them reject them as heretical.

THE NATION OF ISLAM

The Nation of Islam, in its face value exoteric meaning, is an organization started in the early 20th century by Prophet W.D. Fard Muhammad. The Nation of Islam is rejected by the majority of the orthodox Muslims, primarily because they teach that Allah appeared in the person of Wallace Fard Muhammad. Orthodox Muslims believe God is an unseen being existing somewhere far, far away, even though their scriptures teach that Allah is closer than our jugular vein.

The Nation of Islam teaches that Wallace Fard Muhammad is the Supreme Being. There are several Nation of Islam sects, most notable is the Nation of Islam led by Minister Louis Farrakhan. Many authors write that the Five Percenters are a sect of the Nation of Islam, this is not true. We are not part of the organization, the Nation of Islam; we are not Muslims, we have no ministers, captains or lieutenants and we are not required to follow the restrictive law of the Nation of Islam.

We do however memorize, internalize, and bring the lessons of the Nation of Islam to life by relating them to our present circumstance with the proper application of Supreme Mathematics. And like the Nation of Islam, Five Percenters do teach that God came in the person of Fard Muhammad. Though for us it means that the knowledge, wisdom and power of Allah came in the person of Fard Muhammad. In other words, Fard Muhammad was a God, but not exclusively Allah. Fard Muhammad prepared the way for the 'coming' of Allah by raising a messenger. We do not attribute any supernatural characteristics to him or to any other man. In other words, we are not spooky.

The last book of the Old Testament, the book of Malachi, speaks on the last days (of the devil's rule, not literally the last days of the Earth) and the coming of God. The scriptures say that God will come to Elijah's temple in the last days. This Elijah is referring to Elijah Muhammad, the messenger Fard Muhammad prepared and this temple is the Nation of Islam's temple number seven (Harlem, New York City).

ALLAH

The New Testament begins with God being among the people, in the streets. Allah, born Clarence Smith, joined the Nation of Islam in the mid 20th century. Allah was not born with the knowledge of himself. As it is written in the scripture in Malachi, God came to Elijah's temple. When Clarence realized his own godhood, he told a few of his Nation of Islam brothers. Leadership in the temple did not take too kindly to that. Allah was expelled from the Nation of Islam. Some say that Allah was kicked out of the temple for gambling and drinking liquor, two prohibited acts in the Nation of Islam. Others say that he was kicked out because he was teaching that he was God and the leaders of the temple did not like that. The former usually grants a suspension, not a permanent expulsion so there is more likelihood in the latter. Like the Jesus of the bible, they threw stones at him for teaching what was already in their book (lessons). Regardless to how it went down, that was the end of Clarence's presence in the temple. He changed his name to Allah and began teaching people who the true and living God is, publicly. For us, that was the end of the need for religious belief. Allah was now here. He hit the streets and taught his teachings to the adults in Harlem. Most of them rejected his teachings so he began to teach the youth. His first student was named Matthew. Allah renamed him Karriem which means noble or generous though later he would become Black Messiah. We now enter Allah's world manifest. Allah taught other young men in Harlem and together, Black Messiah and Allah's other sons became known as the Sons of Almighty God Allah, also known as Allah's Five Percent. His first teaching was not that we are all Gods. His first teachings were simple; that we should be clean, righteous, upright teachers of knowledge and wisdom. He taught them that they were all brothers. He discovered order within the universe and called this order Supreme Mathematics. And with the help of his brother, Justice, he put together our Supreme Alphabet which is a set of principles we live by. The Supreme Mathematics and Supreme Alphabet make up the language of the Gods. Supreme Mathematics allows us to measure all things in their proper perspectives while Supreme Alphabet allows us to describe all things. Allah instructed the brothers to teach the people of Harlem, which he renamed Mecca. Eventually they spread throughout all five New York City boroughs as well as other major cities in the tri-state area. Now we are located in all the major cities of the United States as well as some cities in Canada, Puerto Rico, the United Kingdom, the continent of Africa and even Asia thanks to those traveling and doing their duty.

WHO ARE THE 85, 10 AND 5 PERCENT?

The term five percent comes from the lessons of the Nation of Islam. Before we can talk about the Five Percent, we must first explain the other two groups of people. The masses of the people, the eighty-five percent, are ignorant. They eat unhealthy foods, foods that are even outlawed in their scripture. They are slaves of a mental death, they are people who do not know their origin in this world, they worship deity blindly and are easily led in the wrong direction but hard to lead in the right.

The ten percent were originally described as religious leaders but are not limited to religion alone. The ten percent are the rich who enslave the masses. The religious ten percent teach that God is an unseen being who we will either meet after we die or maybe never meet because we were disbelievers or sinners in this life and therefore sentenced to eternal hellfire. The ten percent can be summed up as corrupt leaders. The ten percent control four major institutions; EDUCATIONAL, ECONOMICAL, POLITICAL and RELIGIOUS.

The public educational system presents a fallacious account of history. Many textbooks are teaching the myth that European civilization and culture was the first on this planet. Europeans did not build the first world civilizations. Europeans were not the first civilized nation, however, under the United States public school system, we are taught that the original inhabitants of the planet (black brown and yellow shades) were backwards until Europeans came into contact with them. We are taught that our people were and are still primitive, savage and inferior to Europeans. The public schools teach our children to honor George Washington, Christopher Columbus, Thomas Jefferson, Abraham Lincoln etc. However, they are not giving a true account of the stories that have taken place; history is simply his-story. If you ask a Black child in America who Marcus Garvey or Elijah Muhammad was, they will most likely tell you that they do not know. The schools do not teach about Benjamin Banneker, Cesar Chavez or Malcolm X. They teach lies about history and emphasize irrelevant subjects while omitting relevant ones. The United States' public education system also honors mythology. I remember celebrating Valentines Day, Easter, Thanksgiving and Christmas when I was in school. Many schools even have Halloween parades. Public schools teach our children that Abraham Lincoln freed the slaves. What they do not teach is that Abraham Lincoln thought Blacks were not people, just property. When he "freed the slaves" he was saying that Black people are not people, but slaves, and now they will be free slaves. He saw all Blacks as inferior to whites. On August 14, 1852, Abraham Lincoln said "Not a single man of your race is made equal to a single man of ours," but this is never taught in the schools to the children. They do not teach that "Thanksgiving" was actually a slaughter of the natives or that the acts of Columbus and other European 'explorers' and 'settlers' were horrific and terrifying. Their acts are seen as a victory for God, a victory to be held in high esteem for all

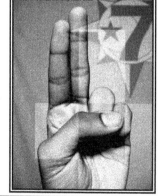

United States citizens. The school system does not teach us how to implement change. They do not present any working solutions to fix our condition economic wise, health wise or any other way. It teaches us what to think instead of how to think creatively.

The economical institutions are controlled by the 10%. They control how the masses live by manipulating the decisions they make. They are money lenders and big business owners. A 1996 study revealed that 68% of the total net worth of all U.S. families is owned by just 10% of those families. Although the 10% run the major businesses and institutions that enslave the masses, it is the masses who keep the 10% in power by working for them and accepting the system. Wealth, power and prestige are maintained by the puppet masters by way of mass manipulation. The economical institutions' main tool for manipulation and programming of the masses is the television. What are television shows called? Programs! The masses are influenced at an early age by cartoons, music, television programs and movies. Corporations like FOX, NBC, HBO, etc. indoctrinate the masses mentally while corporations like McDonalds, Taco Bell, Coca-Cola and Pepsi feed them the wrong physical foods which all contribute to keeping them enslaved. There is a large percentage of children watching videos after school on MTV and BET. These channels influence what healthcare products people buy, how they dress, and how they carry themselves. Nowadays it is not surprising to hear a young Black woman call herself and/or her friends "b*tch(es)" Do you know who/what is molding your child?

Politics have a large influence on society, especially here in the United States. The ruling class, which is the 10%, gets elected by the masses of people. The politicians smile for cameras, kiss babies, and claim to be in their position for the interest of the masses. Laws are formed by these politicians to keep the other three institutions running well. Once in a while, a member of the power elite gets caught breaking the law and will actually be prosecuted. This trick is done to make the masses believe that the criminal justice system maintains fairness, giving the masses a reason not to overthrow their oppressive government. One governmental agency is called the Food and Drug Administration, it regulates what can and cannot be done in the businesses of food and drugs. Drugs go with the foods because you will need something in your old age to cure you from all the poison contained in the meat, the preservatives and the artificial sugars eaten throughout your lifetime. The political institutions have important roles that keep the eight-five percent manipulated and the system of extreme inequality functioning. The political bodies work closely with the other bodies to keep the people enslaved. More than 60% of all U.S. companies paid no federal tax at all during the economic boom under Clinton's presidency (1996 to 2000) and eighty-two of the United States' largest profitable corporations paid no federal income tax for at least one year of the Bush's first three years of presidency (2001 to 2003).

Religion is defined as "belief in a divine or superhuman power or powers to be obeyed and worshipped as the creator(s) and ruler(s) of the universe." The word religion comes from "religare" which means to restrain or tie back. What are people being restrained from? What are they being tied back from? The full knowledge of God. In order for religion to exist, you need followers, a "God" (or Gods) and someone to link the followers to that God. It's a hierarchy where the popes, bishops, reverends, swamis, rabbis, imams and other preachers lead and teach the followers about this God (or Gods). The truth is, God has always been one with man. Most religious preachers know this; however, they desire to make slaves out of their followers. So they teach lies.

"It has served us well, this myth of Christ." - Pope Leo X

It is said that Christianity has over one billion adherents. Christian preachers teach that God came in the form of a man, but they say God is not a man. The last messenger of Allah, the Honorable Elijah Muhammad, said:

> The Christians do not believe in God as being a human being, yet they believe in Him as being the Father of all human beings. They also refer to God as He, Him, Man, King and The Ruler. They teach that God sees, hears, talks, walks, stands, sits, rides, and flies; that He grieves or sorrows; and that He is interested in the affairs of human beings. They also teach that once upon a time He made the first man like Himself in the image and likeness of Himself, but yet they believe that He, Himself, is not a man or human. They preach and prophesy of His coming and that He will be seen on the Judgment Day but is not man. They cannot tell us what He looks like, yet man is made like Him and in the image of God, and yet they still say that He is a mystery (unknown).

The religious leaders make God a mystery to the masses in order to keep control over them. If the followers knew everything that the preachers know, there would be no reason to go to church. Therefore, the preachers do not share all of their knowledge with the followers. The preachers know that they need followers in order to get paid. The religious institutions are connected to the other institutions. In school, children are taught to quote "One nation, under God." Whose God? Where is He? When testifying in court, you are told to put your hand on the Bible and we are sworn under an oath in the name of God. The truth is, and has always been, that the only God is man. A definition of God is Supreme Being. Supreme means most high, and being means to be or to exist. The most high being that exists is man. You can not prove that there is any being more supreme than man. People ask, "What about when man was not? Where was God then?" There never has been a time when man was not. Most people hear the word man and automatically think head, two arms, torso and two legs. That is physical man, yes, however man is more than a physical body. The cells, tissues and bones I have now are not the same as the cells, tissues and bones I had when I was a baby. Yet I am still the same person. That is because the physical body is not my essence. Man is intelligence. That is what God is. The mind has always been here and always will be. Religious people say "in the beginning God created..." Who's beginning? Everything that has a beginning has an ending. There is no beginning for the Original Man.

WHO IS THE ORIGINAL MAN?

When asked this, the Honorable Elijah Muhammad answered "The Original Man is the Asiatic Blackman, the maker, the owner, the cream of the planet Earth, God of the Universe." This is not something he just made up. The knowledge of God has always been known to those "in the know," but it has been concealed from the masses for a very long time. Societies like the freemasons have kept the knowledge of God bottled up in their higher degrees. Shriners bear witness to the Black man being God. They know that there is no mystery God, outside of man. The Shriners even call God by his name, Allah. In public however, they deny the knowledge that they have acquired, and some even go to church on Sundays to preach about a mystery God that is the father of Jesus, outright liars. They know this isn't true, but they will teach it in order to keep their power.

"When you repeat the same thing over and over, Sunday after Sunday, that makes people believe it whether it is true or not. It also makes writing theology easy." - Franz Bibfeldt, German theologian

People also ask the question, "If man is God, who made the physical man?" Man has always been in some form...there is no 'who' that created him, he is self-created. From the 'time' of sub-atomic particles to atoms to molecules to organelles to cells to tissues to organs to organ systems to organisms, man has always existed in one form or another. The evolution of man has been carried out by his own will, just like your evolution is carried out by your will. You create your own destiny by choosing what you will and will not do, what you will and will not eat, how long you will rest, what you will study, etc. The Original Man is the Asiatic Blackman, meaning, the Blackman from Asia. We are taught not to separate Africa from Asia and not to limit the Blackman as an African, for Africa is not the Blackman's only home. The planet Earth is the Blackman's home and the Blackman has fathered civilizations all over the world. We call the Earth Asia, us being Asiatic makes us people of and relating to the Earth. Asiatic also signifies an esoteric meaning. Within the teachings of Kaballah, Assiah is described as the world of expression. It is not only the people of African descent that are Black. We teach that all Asiatic (non-white) people are Original or Black people. We do not fall victim to the European's teaching that we are all different, that is something they want us to believe, so that they can divide and conquer us.

The term 5% refers to a small percentage of the world that knows and teaches who the true and living God is. This small group of people teach that God is the Son of Man, the Supreme Being, Black man from Asia. The knowledge of the Asiatic Black man being God is kept hidden from the masses in order to control them. Some people know who the true and living God is, from the Pope in Rome to the Freemasons in your local Masonic Temple. Your local church preacher may even bear witness to the true and living God, however, keep in mind that everyone who knows who God is does not teach the truth about God. The 10% teach of God as a mystery, unknown and unseen God.

God is usually described in theology as being a "He." The Bible, Qur'an, Bhagavad-Gita, Upanishads and Book of Coming Forth by Day (Egyptian Book of the Dead) all refer to God in this masculine gender, first person singular description. In addition, the Bible also quotes God referring to himself/themselves with the term "Us" and the Qur'an uses the term "We." This He, We and Us are all speaking about the Asiatic Black man with knowledge of himself, the true royalty deserving of the "royal plural."

The Honorable Elijah Muhammad taught that God is a man. He, like the Jesus of the Bible, taught that we are all Gods (John 10:34). The masses of the world believe God is some unseen, supernatural, being existing somewhere out in space. Allah is not unseen; he is seen and heard everywhere. In theological texts, God sees, hears, speaks, walks and feels. In Genesis, Adam heard God walking through the garden (Genesis 3:8). Three men appeared to Abraham in the plains of Mamre, one was the Lord and Abraham fed him (Genesis 19:1-33).

Allah, the founder of the Five Percent Nation, was not hateful and neither are we. He taught that we should not fear competing against nor interacting with Caucasian people. He taught us that it is fine to socialize with them however, we should not mix our seed with them, for that would be grafting out the originality of our seed. Unlike the Nation of Islam, Allah taught Caucasian people. The F.B.I. report on Allah quotes Azreal, a Caucasian Five Percenter as saying "He gave me the knowledge of myself....Allah loved everybody." Allah was also a close friend of the Caucasian Barry Gottehrer, an assistant to Mayor Lindsay and head of the Mayor's urban task force. Barry Gottehrer provided Allah with buses to transport the young Gods and Earths to rallies where Allah would teach the youth.

The Honorable Elijah Muhammad was taught by Master Fard Muhammad, who came to North America with the challenging job of resurrecting the mentally dead lost but now found, Nation of Original people. He had his hard times, but with hard work he proved to be successful. Allah came to us and with the help of Justice (his right hand man), Shahid, Ebeka, and the first borns Black Messiah, Bisme, Uhuru, Kihiem, Prince, Jamel, ABG, Akbar and Salaam he began what is now known as the Nation of God and Earth. The 10% claim that it is impossible for God to be the Black man, however, the Bible and Qur'an cite various passages revealing who the true and living God is.

It is true that the Asiatic Black man is God, however, as I mentioned above, the 10% make God into a mystery. The 5% are the poor righteous teachers who do not believe in the teachings of the 10%. They are all-wise and know who the true and living God is, and they teach that the true and living God is the Son of Man, the Supreme Being, the Black man.

Freedom Allah grew up in Long Beach, California. Seeing his family members in and out of jail motivated him to seek a higher purpose in life. In the late 1990s he met a group of Five Percenters that put him on a path of righteousness that would change his life forever. As he gained the knowledge of himself, he was encouraged to pursue a college education. Freedom earned a Bachelor of Arts degree in Sociology from the University of California, Riverside, and is currently earning a Master of Arts degree in Education. He lives in Southern California and works in the education field, teaching and tutoring.

ALLAH THE FATHER
Lajik 17 Allah - Mecca (Harlem, NY)

During the turbulent 'Black Power' era of the 1960s, there was a man in Harlem that helped provide direction for the many aimless Black youths who lived in the concrete jungles of the inner-city. He was known as "Allah." He accomplished this by teaching young people how to gain "knowledge of self." This culture, in turn helped to restore the high levels of consciousness and self-esteem that had been stripped away during the enslavement process of Original people in the Western hemisphere.

Born in rural Danville, Virginia on February 22, 1928, Clarence Edward Smith was the 5th of 7 children. As a youth, his mother Mary nicknamed him "Puddin'" because of his smooth, rhythmic cadence. It's a name that he's still known by today in certain circles. He eventually followed his family to Harlem in 1944, as they escaped the Jim Crow laws of the segregated South. After serving in the Army from 1952-1959, including a tour of duty in the Korean War, he joined his wife

Dora in the Nation of Islam (N.O.I.) in 1960 at Harlem's legendary Temple #7, which was under the tutelage of Minister Malcolm X at that time.

Now known as Clarence 13X, he soon became a member of the 'Advanced F.O.I.' (Fruit of Islam - security for the N.O.I.), teaching the martial arts he had become proficient in while in Asia to other members. After having discrepancies with Captain Joseph over his 'understanding' of some of the 'Lessons' that were taught only in the Temple, Clarence 13X and Abu Shahid took those degrees to the streets of New York in the Spring of 1964. Although Clarence was already educating many individuals while he sold *Muhammad Speaks* newspapers while in the N.O.I., he focused more on teaching the youth when they began building 'The 5%ers'. "We left because Elijah and Malcolm were going through their stuff and we loved both of them. Plus, he wanted to teach the youth that were straying in the streets!" reflected Abu Shahid.

Allah, as he was now known, took Islam to the so-called incorrigible youths of the 'concrete jungle' that were behind the scenes in 'The Mecca of Black Culture." Not as a religion, but as a science - utilizing the Supreme Mathematics and Supreme Alphabets, that he and Abu Shahid compiled. "We understood that God is in our body – Arm Leg Leg Arm Head = ALLAH! The Father's teachings are simple enough that even a child can understand them!" assessed First Born Prince Allah, the third of the nine 'First Born' who Allah chose specifically to spread his teachings.

Shortly after hitting the pavement, he came across some teenagers he had previously met while in Temple #7. "We initially organized to combat police brutality! We were known as 'The Blood Brothers,' which Malcolm X mentioned in his *Autobiography*. "We were considered 'renegade Muslims!'" recalled Eye God, who was framed in 'The Harlem 6' case. "The Father advocated for us to keep on striving and to continue building after he left."

Allah is the best knower. Many of those youths were seeking direction and found what they were seeking, quickly latching on to the Father's teachings as he captivated them with his swift, self-styled wisdom. "The Father taught us according to our level of understanding. He didn't teach all of us the same way. Although he had already taught a lot of youth, he picked the nine 'First Borns' by how fast we learned our 'Lessons' and how many people we taught," confirmed First Born Prince Allah.

"Around this same time he had befriended 'Old Man Justice' in Mount Morris Park (Marcus Garvey now) while teaching," according to Prince A.B.Gee. Justice would continue educating the youth during Allah's absence.

"Malcolm X had left the N.O.I. before 'The Father,' and they'd cross paths in the streets as they both strived to liberate the oppressed minds of the masses. They'd discuss solutions!" explained First Born Prince Allah.

During December 1964, in a basement on 127th Street near 7th Ave., Allah was shot in the chest with a high powered rifle after a heated dispute with another man. After recovering, he instructed his 5%ers not to harm his assailant, "...because he will suffer more in living than in death!" recounted First Born Prince.

Allah soon recovered as he and Old Man Justice continued educating the youths. Those students went on to spread this 'knowledge-of-self' to other lands, primarily teaching the young and resurrecting many that society had deemed irreparable; drug addicts, prostitutes and ex-cons.

According to Omala Earth – the 2nd female 5%er, "Allah had a Nation that would do anything for him because he saved a lot of us. Heroin was ruining our neighborhoods. He kept us from getting caught up in it by teaching us that we were greater than that. He saved me and my children's lives."

While building in front of the Hotel Teresa on May 31, 1965, Allah was arrested for unlawful assembly and sent to Matteawan State Hospital for the Criminally Insane after telling the judge that he didn't want a court appointed attorney because he is God and he'd represent himself instead.

The young 5%ers continued spreading this knowledge while Allah was in Matteawan Hospital for the Criminally Insane for 2½ years. Justice helped guide the young 5%ers during this time as they continued educating the masses of their origin in this world. "We'd civilize gang members until the gangs died out!" explained First Born Prince. "We were from the streets, so we could reach those were lost in them because they could relate to us."

Although they'd visit him often while he was in Matteawan to get the jewels he'd drop, the youthful 5%ers did their own studies and continued to civilize their communities in his physical absence. During this period 'Old Man Justice' stepped up his responsibilities in helping to guide the younger students of this new found knowledge of self.

Upon Allah's return to the city in March 1967, the 5%ers held their first monthly Parliament at the bell tower in Mount Morris Park on

April 30th, in what was known as 'The Sermon on the Mount.' He was pleased to see how much his nation had grown during his hiatus.

Allah quickly developed relations with some higher ups in the local government, including Mayor Lindsey, and he'd utilize those alliances to provide boat, bus and plane rides for the inner-city youth he loved so much, some who had never left the city before. By June of the same year, he acquired a building that was a former barber shop and established it as "Allah's Street Academy in Mecca," which he utilized to conduct classes teaching the 120 lessons, G.E.D. classes, building trades and many other skills. The school is still standing today on 2122 7th Ave. (aka Adam Clayton Powell Jr. Blvd.), on the corner of 126th St.

"He advocated 'teach the babies,' and made sure that we went to school and got an education. He wanted us to learn about our true selves. Then go teach our own people," remembered First Born Prince. Some of Allah's fruit were even taught by the great historians – Dr. John Henrik Clarke and Dr. Ben Yochannan at Harlem Prep.

"Allah emphasized teaching the Earths [as the women are known] because we are the first teachers of the children, and they are our tomorrow! We wore 3/4ths and had our heads wrapped," reflected Omala Earth. "Gods respected us and they had to set an example!"

Allah and his young 5%ers were cleaning the streets from drugs, prostitution and other illicit activities. As he continued to grow and become more powerful in the streets he also drew major jealousy from others who had some major power in the streets. "They (5%ers) were extorting us," claimed former drug trafficker and snitch Frank Lucas.

Riots erupted throughout the country on April 4th, 1968 as news of M.L. King Jr.'s assassination spread. Allah and his Nation hit the streets and prevented a full-scale riot from happening in N.Y.C., advising the people, "If you burn and loot your neighborhoods how will you be able to feed your babies later on?" He received much praise and honor, from both residents of the area and public officials. Allah had saved his community from the type of destruction that befell most other urban areas like Detroit and Chicago.

The Father Allah continued educating the youth, preparing them for life without his physical presence. In 1968, the FBI - who were watching him closely - recorded Allah saying he would be gone in a year. "The Father knew he was gonna get killed for teaching the children. He never wanted us to walk with him late at night. He'd chase us away if we tried to walk him home. He didn't want anything to happen to us," professed Akmen Allah. "He'd tell us that if we want to see him, to come together."

As he stepped into the elevator of 21 West 112th St. in Foster Projects (now M.L.K. Towers) in the early morning hours of June 13th, 1969, Allah was shot and mortally wounded. He'd been hit with 7 of the

8 shots fired at him. "After 'The Father' was killed nobody knew anything! We knew all the drug dealers and killers in the streets and nobody heard a word. That's how we knew the government did it!" claimed First Born Al Jamel.

Yet Allah doesn't die. On the weekend closest to the anniversary of his assassination, Gods and Earths from around the world come together - as instructed by Allah - to acknowledge their history and display their talents to their Nation at The Harriet Tubman Learning Center on 127th Street between Adam Clayton Powell Jr. and Fredrick Douglas Blvd. during the annual Show and Prove. Artists who either possess Knowledge of Self or have been influenced by The Father Allah's teachings have lent their support at this event. Brand Nubian, Digable Planets, King Sun, dead prez, Common, Papoose, Erykah Badu and Wu-Tang Clan are just a few artists who have graced the stage throughout the years.

"It's not about who knew The Father. It's about who learned what he taught, which is educate yourself and then teach the children!" - First Born Prince

Lajik 17 Allah earned his doctorate in street psychology at UCLA - the University on the Corner of Lenox Avenue – and was taught 120 by First Born Prince Allah. He is a journalist whose work has been featured in magazines such as *The Source* and *Hip-Hop Weekly*. In 2005, he scribed the cover story for *F.E.D.S. Magazine* (Vol. 4, Issue 17) on the true story of Allah and the Nation he established. For the past three years Lajik has been writing for the weekly *New York Amsterdam News*, on topics ranging from urban culture to gentrification and police brutality. Lajik is a trained boxer and descendant of the indigenous Arawak Nation. He is actively involved in causes supporting the Allah School in Mecca, including personally maintaining the Universal Flag painted on the side of the building. For more information, and to support a petition to get Adam Clayton Powell Jr. Blvd. between 126th and 127th St. renamed "Allah, The Father's Way," write to P.O. Box 1295 NY, NY 10027.

FREE THE DUMB
Popa Wu – Medina (Brooklyn, NY)

This is the God Freedum Allah aka Popa Wu. I brought the knowledge to most of the Wu-Tang. Ol' Dirty (Unique Ason Allah), RZA (Ruler Zig Zag Zig Allah), GZA (Allah Justice) - they're my mother's sons. We're all family. Ghostface has babies by my cousin, so we're all family somehow. I raised them from when they first came home from the hospital, from when they were all little kids. I gave them knowledge. I brought the wisdom to the family. And - through them - that knowledge has made it to a lot of you.

My name is God Freedum Allah. Let me break down my name for you. God is first. The Father said to put "God" before your name, as He is the Most High, the Supreme Being, Living Intelligence. "Freedum" means to free the dumb from a mental state of unawareness of themselves. That's why I took the 'o' out of the 'dom' and added a 'u.' Now I Free-Them (free-dum). Finally, God is Allah and Allah is God; there is only one God and that is inside of you. So you find yourself through that, because by nature a man is born god, whether he wants it or not.

I got knowledge back in the days, around 1965. Not that I got deep into the knowledge of self at that point, I just heard the word of God. We were youngsters running around wild on the streets, and one day in the store where we got lunch, I heard a sharp brother on the corner talking about "the Black man is God." That caught my attention, as that was my natural language, yet I had never heard anyone speak it. You see, that's when you rise up - when you hear your language. I had heard all kinds of other things before, but never "the Black man is God." That made me curious, so I had to find myself through that.

W. D. Fard (Elijah's teacher) said he would return on his 87th birthday. That would be in 1964. But when he came in 1964, nobody spoke his language. That's when the Father stood up and said he was Allah. He seen a lot wrong in that house; he saw 10%, 5%, and 85%, and even in our nation you have the same. The Father knew he was 5% of that house. He knew he was the one, so he had to stand up and show and prove. When he stood up and said he was Allah, they said he not could teach that there. He came out of there with himself, not no lessons - with mathematics and the wisdom and understanding. That's what makes us gods, we bring about the understanding of life. If we didn't come into the knowledge, this world would be different. And we had to come when we came.

When the Father told the babies they were gods, he knew nothing could stop us; in a man's mind, when you want to be like God, it's a feeling inside just when you hear the language. Just think about it, if you never heard that the Black man is god before, how that now makes you feel inside. In the 60's we was young kids and we were wild in gangs and stuff, yet when we heard that the Blackman is god, it gave us a sense of freedom. It opens up your world. You had people who'd grown up with the blonde-haired, blue-eyed hippie Jesus on their walls and now you got 14-15 year-old teens now saying "they're gods," what are you going to do? Try to beat them up or try to understand them. It took me a while as I was stubborn. In fact, messing with the Gods was the first time I got knocked out, coming out of store with a ham and cheese sandwich! I was stubborn, but I was tough. A brother asked me a question and I guess he didn't like the answer I gave. So he made me stand there as he gave me some lessons and I had to learn them. The Gods had the Avenue locked down, so you couldn't go nowhere without running into them. They had ciphers on all the corners and you had to know the lessons they gave you or you got beat down. It was real like that. I would sometimes climb down a tree behind my house to go out my back porch, but they'd be on the other block and catch me. I finally stopped playing games around '68. I took it in my own hands and really sought the knowledge for myself. I'm 52 years old and been living it ever since. I never turned back. I'm a pioneer of this, as I built my own universe right here. Heaven is not above your head, nor hell below your feet, it's what you make it God.

Where I'm from, we didn't earn the title of "Medina Warriors" by accident. Since the Father was in Harlem, that's what we called Mecca, for the root of civilization, just as it is in the East. Mecca was this hustling ring, like "we cool." Medina was gangsters, cold-blooded warriors. We was some fighting men. The Father came over here 'cause he knew how Brooklyn was; Brooklyn get down. He knew Mecca wasn't about fighting, they was just hustlers, sellin' whatever. It was a place to go to make money, where you mind your business and I mind mine. On the other hand, Brooklyn was stick up kids; cold-blooded gangsters. The Father said, "If I go to these gangsters and give them knowledge, they can bang with intelligence, instead of banging with none. It would be better." And that's what we did. We were so slick to begin with, when we got knowledge of self, it made us humble. All the gangs turned to Five Percenters, which really messed the devil up. The gangs started breaking up and now we were hugging each other! They wondered, "How did that man do that? He took gang-bangers and made them love each other and they say they're brothers now?" They thought they were going to wipe us out. That's why the Father said to us, "WE the Gods. After me, it's y'all." He said, "Don't do me like they did Jesus, hanging me up on the wall. After me there is no mystery God." I'm no Muslim, so I don't pray to Allah. I don't submit. I bear witness to the teachings of Allah. That's what makes me show and prove Allah is the God, always was, and always will be, through the knowledge that He blessed. We are Gods because we are composed of the highest mathematics and intelligence. So we have to show and prove. We have to teach civilization as a civilized man. We are righteous men fighting for a common cause, so we have to strive for perfection.

The Father said all you got to do is be gods and you'll win every battle. Allah told us the power is with all of us together. You can't destroy that. I've been around the world three times and everywhere I've seen that the Blackman is god. We are rising and taking our place. Some people are preaching but don't understand the scriptures. They can't see that Allah comes in his own good time. Your job is to be the best that you can be and teach all those who want to be like you.

The father of Wu-offshoots ShaCronz and Free Murda and an expert on the philosophy of the Five Percent, Popa Wu can be heard teaching on Wu-Tang tracks such as "North Star," "Black Jesus," "All That I Got Is You," "The Blessing," and "Wu-Revolution". He released a solo album titled *Visions of the 10th Chamber* in 2000, which was effectively a compilation of Wu-affiliated artists (including LA the Darkman, Method Man, and Ol' Dirty Bastard) with regular interjections from Popa Wu himself. He was recently featured on "Older Gods Pt.2" on Masta Killa's second LP, *Made in Brooklyn*. The above essay is based on an interview conducted by I Cee Justice Allah for *Original Thought* Metazine (www.originalthought.mag.com)

FROM K.O.S. TO 120°
Allah B - Mecca (Harlem, NY)

Knowledge of Self means what it implies: Knowledge means to know and Self, as we know, is one's own being. Knowledge of Self means if you know your ledge, then you won't fall off the edge. Self is the entity that is your inner being, which is where you find your strength and force. Most people don't have a knowledge of self. The average person does not know that their body is a temple - a temple of Allah. Allah the Blackman expresses Himself in every individual. When you break it down to the extremities of the body: Arm, Leg, Leg, Arm, Head. The five major points of the body spell Allah, so the body being the temple of Allah, forms the basis of knowledge of self. We have to go back to the basics where it all began with Allah the Blackman. He is the Source, the Supreme Being, the God. Everything comes forth from Allah, and knowledge of self is to go back to the source from whence we came, Allah, and recognize our temple. The inner being of man is the god within. The inner being is expressed through the godly power of having knowledge of self.

I was young when I started my quest to know who I was. The word Allah came to me from my orthodox Muslim brothers, along with some knowledge of the Quran, and other things my Muslim brothers taught. But that wasn't satisfying. Then Elijah Muhammad was teaching Islam - that we were the original Black man, the maker, the owner, cream of the planet Earth. That resonated with me. I started to want to know more about myself. The way I came into the true knowledge of myself as God was when I was running from the police on 125th St. God Allah the Father came out and stopped the police from chasing me! I came back the next day, and he had a cipher around him. He was reading *Message to the Black Man.* He was speaking about the greatness I already felt in myself, and from then on, I came to know who he was, and who I was going to be with. That's how I came into the knowledge of myself.

I didn't get the lessons immediately. I was going to Elijah Muhammad's mosques to get information on the lessons, but it wasn't nearly as profound as I got it on the streets from Allah and the Five Percenters' teachings. I was given each lesson by Allah, and when I would visit him in Matteawan, it would be solidified. Soon, I knew my 120 and was perfecting it to its fullest extent, and just going on and showing and proving those lessons. I got the lessons and went on my journey as we were taught to.

The 120 consists of the Student Enrollment (10 questions and answers), English Lesson number C-1 (36 statements and responses), Lost Found Muslim Lesson #1 (14 questions and answers), Lost Found Muslim Lesson #2 (40 questions and answers), Actual Facts (which is actually 11 statements about the Earth and the Sun), and then there's the Solar Facts (9 statements about the planets - the solar family). These add up to the 120. **It was required to commit the lessons to memory, to recite on command, to demonstrate its application, and then put your knowledge into effect by living it to the best of your ability**.

Allah B gained knowledge of himself in 1964 and was tasked by Allah to spread the knowledge in Pelan (Bronx). Allah B became one of the first political prisoners of the Nation, sentenced to 27 years for a crime he didn't commit. When he returned to the free cipher, he initiated various growth and development programs in the Nation. Currently, Allah B is one of the administrators working with the youth at Allah School in Mecca. You can reach him there at Allah School in Mecca, 2122 Adam Clayton Powell Blvd., NY, NY 10027; or by phone at: (212) 665-4175; email: asainmecca@yahoo.com The above essay is based on an interview conducted by I Cee Justice Allah for *Original Thought* Metazine (www.originalthought.mag.com)

A GOOD NAME IS...

C'BS Alife Allah - New Heaven (New Haven, CT)

My honorable name is Absalom (for the record, the Gods and Earths as a whole do not refer to the names given to us at birth as 'slave' names or 'government' names. They are referred to as honorable names. As 1st Born ABG#7 told me - as Allah told him – that we bring honor to the names our parents gave us because that is all that they had to give us. That is why if one committed a crime Allah told his sons to turn their self in, serve their sentence and clear their name).

I know what it's like to not have a 'normal' name. Ironically, it is a "good 'ol' biblical name." However, the reality is that the majority of Christians who I run into are ignorant of their own religious text. Thus, they are always asking me if my name is Muslim. Shoot, even nowadays, when I give my righteous name, people think that I'm Muslim if they aren't familiar with the Gods and Earths.

Anyway, my name never prevented me from getting anywhere in society that I wanted to. If a person was racist then my name didn't make a difference. I was taught to uphold my name and be proud of it.

The point that Harold Clemens makes in his "Hail Lakeesha" article (www.blackelectorate.com) is interesting. People have names in this society and don't know what they mean. Adam means 'ruddy red.' Luke means 'white.' I know some coal black brothers with that name! Mary means 'bitter.' Peter means 'rock.' I know 'Alize' may seem odd, yet there are plenty names that people have that mean 'water' or 'wine.'

The Gods and Earths know all about different names. Many times our names are straight English words such as Justice, Wisdom, or Intelligent. Interestingly enough, the names that people have in this society sometimes mean those same things in another foreign language (especially Hebrew, since a lot of people have names from the Bible). It's considered 'okay' though, because it is accepted by society.

Names are used to identify an individual. Traditionally they reveal the characteristics that a person has or should live up to. Historically, by a person's name you could also tell immediately what nation, ethnic group or religion they belonged to. Nowadays those elements have been lost in this homogeneous society. The majority of people don't even know what their name means and the forethought that went into choosing a name many times by parents is that it was the coolest sounding name in some baby name dictionary. When we go back in time we can see one thing in common with all nations, ethnic groups and religions. There were traditions and methods by which names were chosen for children.

Being that the Gods and Earths came through the temples of the Nation of Islam we started out with Arabic names. At a certain point in our history we moved from adopting Arabic names to names that reflected the language that we speak here in North America, English.

We draw our names from our Supreme Mathematics, Supreme Alphabet, 120 degrees, and various terminology that has been identified with the Supreme Being. Some may isolate certain principles like Gods named Knowledge Born or Power Justice. Others may utilize the principles as elements to draw up a name like ShiMan (where Self He I Master Allah Now can be collapsed to mean Self Mastery).

Many of the Earths have names or have components of their names that reflect the earth and its topography. They also carry names that reference ancient cities or centers of civilization. Many also utilize names that combine aspects of Supreme Mathematics and Supreme Alphabet with various feminine principles to manifest a unique name.

One of the greatest things about this culture is that one chooses one's name. We oftentimes had no choice as to the name our parents gave us or the legacy that it might imply. By choosing our names in this culture we think hard about what attributes of ourselves that we want to amplify, put on front street, and share with the masses. Also, in the end, it connects us and identifies us as one who is of this culture. We can now say that we are living out the proper intent of naming as original people have done so in the past.

My name is…Whatever I tell you it is.

C'BS ALife Allah is the son of a preacher and a teacher. Both inspired him to become a life long children's advocate. C'BS has worked as an educator in the private and public sectors, as well as in leadership positions with various youth service programs including L.E.A.P. (Leadership, Education, Athletics in Partnership) and the Young Voices Initiative. In 1995, he was the Children's Defense Fund's national authority on the recruitment of college students for youth service programs. He has spoken at various conferences and panels throughout the country, on topics such as strengthening urban communities and youth leadership. C'BS is also an accomplished writer and world traveler, having visited such places as England, Canada, Kenya, Zimbabwe and Tanzania to expand his worldview.

His award-winning blogsites cover a wide variety of topics, from issues pertinent to the Nation (allahsfivepercent.blogspot.com), to general commentaries on health and race (blacktonature.blogspot.com), to afrofuturistic science fiction (blueblackatlantis. squarespace.com). He is senior editor at Supreme Design Publishing, and founder and CEO of Asiatic Light Micropress and E.very S.quare I.nch, a social media consultation service.

WHAT'S IN A NAME: SELF DEFINITION
I Medina Peaceful Earth – Power Born (Pittsburgh, PA)

1:36 MY NAME IS W.F. MUHAMMAD

Peace! The weekend of the first Show and Prove that I attended, I was still doing the knowledge to the culture (checking things out). I remember a conversation me and my god had in a New Jersey parking lot regarding two things that are imperative to our culture: wearing 3/4ths and changing my name...2 things I was fairly resistant to. After embracing 3/4, I had to come to grips with choosing what we call a righteous name. At the time, I just didn't see the importance of it. I thought it should be enough for people to recognize who I am through my deeds...my character, how I interact with people, and my activities that positively impact others. I also envisioned the inconvenience of having to tell old friends and associates my chosen name and the reasons why, as well as some grey areas (what should I put on resumes and business cards, how do I sign important documents or checks, etc.). I didn't want to go through an entire dissertation with every single person I encountered about why I changed my name. After a good hour of a fairly heated exchange, the god simply stated, "This is a part our culture and you can either accept it or reject it."

"Accept it or reject it," I questioned in my mind. No compromises? No knowledging 120 and keeping my honorable name? No meeting me half way? I have to change my clothes and my name too? I know I cried at some point that evening. But eventually, I had to start questioning my attachment to it. Part of my unwillingness to let it go was due to how I was named. My father wanted to name me Samantha, but my mother rejected that due to her thinking people would call me Sam. So they decided to let two of my older brothers, Willie and Tony, name me. My brother Willie chose my first name, and Tony chose my middle name. They wanted a little sister so bad and they were very proud to be involved in naming me. I always thought that was special and I was proud of that as well. Nonetheless, I decided to accept the name change as part of the process of getting the knowledge of myself, considering it a worthy sacrifice to make.

The understanding came later, and it was worth it. I soon understood how empowering it is to choose a name for yourself based on qualities you currently possess or strive to embody. I understood that throughout the process of our enslavement, that was a key aspect of our identity that was taken from us. Unfortunately, nowadays the process of naming a child doesn't seem to have as much meaning. We may name a child something that just sounds good, a name where it won't be too hard for them to get a job, or after a relative (no disrespect), or hell, even after our favorite drinks (I helped mentor a girl named Tequila, named after her mother's personal favorite)! We give our children names without knowing the meaning of those words or their significance…or lack thereof. I also began to see it as a great segue way into conversations about the Nation of Gods and Earths (specifically Nation History with a name like Medina). It provided teachable moments for people I interacted with, who'd never heard of the Gods and Earths.

Through building and elevating, I began to see that your name gives you a legacy to live out. It helps chart our path, good or bad. It holds you accountable for being that which you claim to be and is a significant aspect of living out the reality of being God or Earth. If my name is I Medina Peaceful Earth, then I am held accountable to living out the reality of being a warrior, who brings balance and homeostasis, and creates an environment that fosters growth and development in others (this is the short version). That is a heavy responsibility.

Medina was a name that had been with me for quite some time, prior to getting knowledge of self. While reading through the book, *The Life and Times of Muhammad*, on a sunny afternoon in Cali, I reached the chapter where it talked about the Hijra and Medina, and there was a beautiful picture of the mosque where the Prophet Muhammad was buried. I thought the name was so beautiful, and the story so significant, that if I had a daughter in the future, I would name her Medina. Years later, after building with the God, he thought that was a name that suited me, being a warrior for children. I am a loyal person, so whatever I am a part of, once I really cee it, I advocate it and will fight for it. I also learned about the history of the nation in Medina (Brooklyn, NY) and went back to the names' origins in Islamic history. While drawing up a name, I couldn't think of a name that suited me better. I added on "Peaceful" because that is a quality that is frequently assigned to me by others, and I've always been a fairly calm person who enjoys being in places and spaces of peace. I wanted to be a person who was able to bring peace to chaos, whether it was within self, friends, family on the street, children I work with, etc. I added on the "I" as a magnet to the qualities after it, self realization and definition, and to be bonded to my God and his universe.

After choosing my righteous name, I first told those in my local Power Born cipher, and then my close friends. They accepted it with open arms. Next came the gig...I had to tell my supervisors, my co-workers, and all of the children that I work with. It took a little getting used to, as there were many slip ups in staff meetings and at the water cooler, and some of the children stated, "I like your other name better!" However, they got used to it, and some of the children now proudly state my entire name when they are calling me. After I got that out of the way, it was time to make the call...my beloved Old Earth (mother). I was dreading this because I knew this was about to be some drama. I had made her, my father and brothers fully aware of my transition into the Nation, but I knew she wasn't ready for this megaton bomb...

It was one of the hardest conversations I have ever had.

I cried, and she sounded like she was on the verge of tears. She boldly told me, "I just don't see my self calling you that...you will always be my little (Honorable Name Goes Here) to me. Well, I'll let you tell your father." Even as I cried, the loving mother that she is, told me that I was going to have to be strong and stand on my principles, and I couldn't be afraid or apprehensive of telling anyone where I stand and why...not even her. It was at that point that I realized her hardship. My name is associated with my identity. She still sees me as a certain person, but since we live in different states, she has not been able to fully see my transformation. She doesn't see that every other person I interact with calls me by my righteous name, so she still sees me as her little girl. I'm sympathetic and have a certain level of understanding.

However, there is an issue when family members, friends or just people who have known you for a while refuse to call you by your righteous name. It is oppressive! I know you've heard those conversations..."He says his name is Malik, but I'ma still call him Joe Johnson! That's what his mama named him!" Shoot, I've even done it so I know how it is. They are trying to maintain their image of you, even when you've changed and accepted yourself. It goes against the natural flow of a person's growth and development to try to hold them in that space. And although they may love that person, it only makes things harder for them.

Ultimately, what happens is that a person will get annoyed by hearing their honorable name over and over again (any time I attend family functions in Cali) to the point where it's hard for them to be there. So, would you rather have the person's presence with their new name, or stick with the old name and identity, but gradually see the person less and less due to your lack of acceptance of said person's chosen identity and self-definition? And most times in these situations, it is the people who are closest to you (your physical fam) who oppress you the most and outright refuse to accept you. Even with international figures such as El Hajj Malik Shabazz...most people still insist on referring to him as Malcolm X, but throughout his growth and development he took on a new identity, and with that came a new name, which was the name he had when he returned to the essence. He should be more widely acknowledged as that, because that is how he saw himself in the last phase of his life.

Now, with that said, if you want to be taken seriously by others, then you have to live your name out. Everything starts with self. You can't be contradictory. For example, if your name is Peaceful Serenity, you shouldn't be out at the bar fighting every weekend. Every time I encounter situations where I am afraid, I remember my name, and know that I have to face whatever challenge lies before me, and build to be victorious. These days and times, my mother has finally started calling me Medina, and introducing me to folks as Medina. It took our trip to Hawaii to get there, partially because whenever I introduced myself, people really liked it...and she said the name suits me well. PEACE.

NO PORK ON THE FORK
OR SWINE ON THE MIND!
C'BS Alife Allah - New Heaven (New Haven, CT)

It's the new millennium and heads are STILL eating pork?! That's just nasty. That beast is filthy. If you won't take my word for it, go visit a farm and watch it in action. "We are what we eat" right? This is simple: Pork ain't good for you in any shape, form or fashion. Here are some points to consider:

- Out of the land animals that are most often consumed in the United States (beef, lamb, chicken, and turkey being the others) it is the only animal that is an omnivore, which means it eats *anything*. It is a scavenger also, which means it eats anything *dead*. And it's a glutton. It won't stop eating unless you stop feeding it, taking in all of those toxins, viruses, parasites, bacteria, garbage, feces, decaying flesh, and eating its own young sometimes. You can feed it practically anything (even poison) and it won't die. It rolls in mud because it has no pores to sweat from. Thus filth builds up inside. So it has ducts at the base of its legs that constantly let out puss.

- The Bible, Qur'an, and almost every ancient tradition have prohibitions against eating it. Wait...you're a Christian and don't think that the ban on eating pork applies to you? Read *The Hog: Should It Be Used For Food?* by C. Leonard Vories, a Christian minister.

- Why would you eating something that has to be 'cured'? And for those who say that "cooking it kills the trichinosis worm," why the funk do you want to eat cooked WORMS?! And how do you know how long McDonald's is cooking your BLT? Trichinosis results in cramps, aches and stiffness, nausea and vomiting, and sometimes headaches and nervous disorders. And approximately one in six people in the U.S. and Canada has trichinosis and may not know it! The trichina worm is able to burrow through tissues and invade neighboring organs or the bloodstream. After this point, they are often known to invade the brain or nervous system. Swine are also known to harbor the kidney worm, the lungworm, the thorn-headed worm, the roundworm and many others

- Cysticercosis (tapeworm egg infection) is the primary type of parasitic infection of the brain. Also the Number One cause of seizures worldwide is due to Cysticercosis. Want to know more? Read *The Woman with the Worm in her Head* by Dr. Pamela Nagami. The rate of Cysticercosis is so high in the Hispanic community that they automatically check for tapeworm infection if you come into the doctor's office with certain symptoms.

- African Americans are more prone to high blood pressure. It may be a genetically selective trait, so stop eating salt 'cured' pork. Duh. African Americans are also more prone to heart disease, prostate cancer and a dozen other diseases directly linked to eating red meat.

- The meat itself contains excessive quantities of histamine and imidazole compounds (leading to itching and inflammation), sulphur-containing mesenchymal mucus (which leads to swelling and deposits of mucus in tendons and cartilage, resulting in arthritis, rheumatism, etc.). Sulphur helps cause firm human tendons and ligaments to be replaced by the pig's soft mesenchymal tissues. The sulphur also causes the degeneration of human cartilage.

- Chitterling?! You mean you won't kiss a woman's feet or "elsewhere," yet you will *eat* where pig feces pass through?! PLUS you have to clean it first with bleach?!
- Pork SKINS?! Cooked skin? What are you - Hannibal Lecter?
- Most likely the pig was domesticated NOT for food. It was probably bred from the wild boar to be a living trash disposal unit (want to know more about this hypothesis? I wrote a paper on it and can send you a copy…just e-mail me)
- It has a high fat ratio and fat is where the toxins dwell in. A lot of the 'meats' from the pig such as bologna, bacon, etc. are all fatty.
- The most played out excuse: "We're all going to die anyway." Then why don't you play in traffic, sniff coke, play Russian Roulette, and have unprotected sex since I hear it "feels better"…hmmm?
- Here's another one: "My grandmother ate pork and lived to be a gazillion" – Well, my uncle Charlie got a bum leg, no teeth, arthritis and halitosis…and he lived to be a babagazillion…what's the point? We work to be living at the *freshest* level - that is, quantity (age) AND *quality*.

THE UNIVERSAL FLAG
Universal Shaamgaud Allah - Medina (Brooklyn, NY)

The five pointed star symbolizes Knowledge, the seed, the child with the power, the Supreme Knowledge that was manifested by W. F. Muhammad as revealed to us by almighty God ALLAH, it is solid Black! The Crescent Moon symbolizes Wisdom, the women (without child). It shows reflected light (Truth or Knowledge) and is not yet at its fullest Equality. It also symbolizes the Divine Wisdom that was manifested by the honorable Elijah Muhammad and revealed to us by Almighty God ALLAH, it is solid yellow! Together the Star and Crescent stands for Knowledge and Wisdom which is the unity of knowing it and speaking it (teaching). It also symbolized the Earth (Woman with Child) a Planet that has Life, and the dominance the woman has over the Seed (the child or the Knowledge) while it is young, and has been the symbol of Freedom, Justice and Equality since the awakening of Islam in the West of North America.

The seven has seven sides, it symbolizes the Original Man, the True and Living God, the Supreme Being, Almighty God ALLAH. Since the very creation of mathematics 7 has been the mathematical terminology for the Creator of the Universe. It is solid Black. Together this stands for the Supreme Understanding that was revealed to us by Almighty God ALLAH himself, it shows a unification of Knowledge, Wisdom and Understanding. Man, Woman and Child. It shows the authority of ALLAH over the planets and Stars and the proper order of the Universe. The seven symbolizes the male seed in full bloom, it shows that God must be the most high. The Master of Wisdom, Culture and Equality at all times, because they are six and can never dominate ALLAH, so they must remain in six or distill back to whence they came! Thus no part of the crescent moon should ever show over the top of the seven!!!

The white background symbolizes the white clouds of deception that have drowned our people in a sea of ignorance, and the feeble attempts of the wicked to conceal the true and living God which is the Son of Man!

The Cipher around the Allah Crescent Star is Black, the Original color of the Sun (anything that burns that hot and that long can't be yellow!). This symbolizes the Sun, the Universal symbol of Truth and Light; and whose power can evaporate all clouds of deception (lies).

The Eight Points are the symbol of the ever expanding Universe, and symbolizes the rays of the Sun, and the speed and distance that the Truth is capable of traveling. There are two sides to each point, the left is Black. This represents the Original Black Man, the right side is Gold. The Gold represents Brown and Yellow seeds. The eight points are a sign of he who is the Master Builder of Rain, Hail, Snow and Earthquakes!

Universal Shaamgaud Allah was one of the first youth of Medina educated by Allah. In the history of the Nation, he is remembered for being the architect of the Universal Flag and the founder of the periodical *Behold the Sun of Man*, which is currently still in publication, edited by Gykee Mathematics Allah's.

CIVILIZATION STUDIES
CIVILIZED ACTS AND UNCIVILIZED ACTS

1. God must carry himself in a unique manner.
2. The use of bad (profane) language comes from one who has no proper wisdom.
3. A wise man does not seek violence, but if violence comes to him, he must defend himself.
4. Two Gods must never fight unless one must die.
5. The Gods must never debate with one another, but instead, research to find out.
6. The Gods must always deal equally with each other.

7. The Gods must always perform their duty, which is to teach civilization to others.
8. Never mock those who do not understand, but instead give them the teaching of understanding.
9. A true God will always help his brother in time of need, mentally as well as physically.
10. God must always keep himself refined, mentally as well as physically.
11. The Gods must never lie, cheat or steal from one another, for that is devilishment.
12. God is the most high and merciful; therefore he has forgiveness for one's errors.
13. Allah is all wise and does everything right and exact.
14. God must never serve justice to a man for something he does not know.
15. You can always distinguish a wise man from a fool, for he is almighty God Allah.
16. Always knowledge before you speak; your wisdom will gain power and strength.
17. Allah does not seek revenge, but strives for justice.
18. Always seek positive, leave negative people alone.
19. If you ever see an error in a brother's ways and actions, then you must correct it.
20. Allah never forces anyone to do anything at anytime.
21. Allah always admits when he does not know.
22. A true God never uses math as a shield to cover his negative ways, for that is a form of trick-knowledge.
23. Allah does not do anything negative at any time.
24. Never deny your brothers, always teach one another.
25. Destroy all negative thoughts from the mind, for a negative thought only brings about a negative reaction.
26. God is never afraid to ask his alikes a question, for he is only seeking knowledge.
27. A wise man never portrays the ways and actions of a savage, for it only makes you look bad.
28. A true and living God will always show his love for his brothers by being equal with his jewels.
29. People look at you by the way you speak and act, so if you speak and act negative, surely you will be considered negative.
30. Watch out for black snakes, for they are the worst kind and if ever you find one, then destroy it as soon as possible.
31. Allah must always respect the wisdom (woman) for she is necessary to produce life.

32. Study your lessons as much as possible, for the more you study, the wiser you'll get.

> The above is an example of a "plus lesson." Plus lessons are documents written by Gods or Earths who consider themselves qualified to address a particular topic, and see a need for the dissemination of a particular piece of information, history, or guidelines. There are no "official" plus lessons, and because there is no formal review process, the ones in circulation can vary in terms of factual accuracy and consistency with the NGE's actual teachings. Fortunately, Gods and Earths are taught to think critically about *everything*, and plus lessons are not part of our *required* course of study.

IS THE NGE A MUSLIM COMMUNITY?
I Majestic Allah - Power Born (Pittsburgh, PA)

Within and outside the Nation of Gods and Earths (NGE), many are unsure as to the relation of the NGE to the religion of Islam as practiced by over one billion adherents throughout the world. Understandably, perspectives on the matter are varied, ranging from inclusion (those who see the NGE within the Islamic scope) to total exclusion (those who see the NGE having no relation to the religion of Islam). There are also those who see the NGE not as Muslims, but a group with ideas in the vein of Shiite and Sufi sects. The primary consequence of this argument is the way in which we define ourselves in relation to other cultures/religions in society. Furthermore, it begs the question: is the NGE merely an offshoot of the Nation of Islam (NOI), and by extension, orthodox Islam; or is it a new value system unique to itself? The answer to this question is one that incorporates many factors and connects varied cultural and social dynamics.

In order to look deeper into the question, it is imperative that we first evaluate the ideas and value system of the respective cultures/religions to see if they are indeed similar. The primary reason that many accuse the NGE of being quasi- or proto-Islamic is the use of the terms Allah and Islam. Although both groups use the terms, the meanings and context in which they are used are strikingly dissimilar.

In the traditional Islamic context, Allah is used to refer to an omnipotent, omniscient, astral God who is the object of adoration and worship in western monotheistic thought (Judaism, Christianity, Islam). God in Arabic is *Ilah*, so the prefix *Al* (meaning the) was added on to indicate a shift away from polytheistic culture/religion, as was the norm in pre-Islamic Arabia. In the paradigm of the NGE, Allah is the Blackman, who after gaining an acute awareness of his positive qualities, history, and the world around him, actualizes these positive qualities in order to be the creator of his own destiny and a positive enriching influence in his family and community (global and local). This worldview is not unlike the concept of the "perfect man" in Sufism and the Kabbalah.

While many would hold that Allah is a term exclusive to the religion of Islam, it is actually an Arabic term that is also used by Arab Jews and Christians when speaking of God. Our use of the Arabic term is not only related to the history of the NGE (and our evolution out of the NOI, but also on the profound affect that the term carries when speaking of a change in the worldview from the Christian perspective held previous by many in the African-American and Latino community. While the terms Allah and God are similar in religious usage, when used among a population that has been oppressed by a mix of white supremacy and religion (in this case Christianity), the term Allah often signals a stance of independence and separation from their previous cultural and religious experience.

The term Islam in the traditional Islamic context means "peace through submission," and refers to the religion and culture developed by Muhammad Ibn Abdullah in 7th century Arabia. From the perspective of the NGE, Islam bespeaks the cultural filament of high civilization practiced and maintained by people of the Afro-Asiatic Diaspora. Even in orthodox Islam, it is acknowledged that Islam as an ideal championing the existence of the oneness of God predated the emergence of Islam as a religion. Similar to the term Allah, the NGE does not use the term Islam to be seen as Muslims, but to underscore the correlation between a civilization's development of character and humanity, and its development of science and mathematics. It is well documented that the religion of Islam was a catalyst for the development of science, mathematics, and philosophy for hundreds of years, even influencing the enlightenment period in Europe. Within Africa, cities such as Djenne and Timbuktu are testimonies to Afro-Islamic achievements in mathematics and science, as well as human development and spirituality. In the African-American community, Islam (in its myriad manifestations) usually indicated a system that improved one's character, as well as one's knowledge of and standing in the world. By seeing oneself within this ethno-cultural framework, the mental paradigm is developed where people of varied backgrounds can transform the behaviors that many of us suffer from (lack of motivation, defeatist behavior, anti-intellectualism). This is why within the NGE community, you will find terms such as "science/scientist," "mathematics," "right and exact," and so forth. The NGE use of the term "Mathematics" is of particular importance as it relates to the Hindu-Arabic numerals we use. The history of the Hindu-Arabic number system is an example of the historical and social bond that connects civilizations and promotes human development by way of cultural and intellectual exchange. By seeing the filament that runs through the high civilizations of people of color, one can develop a universal worldview that champions and relates to the achievements of people of color all over the planet.

On a religious level, however it is important to note that orthodox Islam and the NGE are in no way the same. There is no veneration of Muhammad as the last prophet in the NGE, and the NGE has no set amount that is required to be distributed to the poor. Due to the view that man is the creator of his individual and collective destiny, prayer in the form of Salat is not required. Fasting is encouraged in the NGE, but not in a structured and mandated form as is Ramadan in orthodox Islam. Conversely, most Muslims would consider it anathema to call themselves God, and there is no outward expression of ethnocentrism present in the religion of Islam. Historically, there have been Islamic groups/sects that held views similar to the NGE, such the Zaydis of Yemen, the Druze of Lebanon, and the Baye Fall sect in Senegal, but these groups are the exception and not the rule. While comparisons to Sufism are fair (Exemplified by famous Sufi Al Hallaj, who was beheaded for exclaiming "Anal Haqq," or "I am the truth"), it is important to note that many of the Sufis that advocated self-actualized Godhood identified with Gnostic and Neo-Platonic thought and often ran afoul of traditional Islamic tenets.

While it is understandable why the NGE is identified with Orthodox Islam given the history of the NGE as well as the usage of selected terms by both groups, the truth is that the NGE espouses many concepts that do not fit neatly within an Islamic scope. In fact, after Allah, the founder of the NGE left the NOI, he went to great lengths to identify the NGE as a separate community, even going so far as to order sweeping name changes so that the Gods and Earths would not be mistaken for Muslims of the NOI. While one may be tempted to dismiss this change as slight, it is no less indicative of a new worldview than Muhammad changing the direction of prayer from Jerusalem to Mecca. It is also important to note that Allah, when asked about Islam, remarked, "that's just I-Self-Lord-And-Master," again speaking to the process of self-actualization rather than submission.

Ultimately, to place the NGE in an Islamic scope does a disservice to both groups. One, it forces the NGE to fit its values within a previous but unparallel framework. Secondly, it compels Orthodox Islam to include a group with values that are dissimilar to their own. It also infers that there will be no "new" value systems, and that no cultural/religious development can take place after the last revelation of the western monotheistic tradition (Islam). Following this train of thought, Christianity would be seen as "Quasi-Judaic," and Protestants would be known as "Pseudo-Catholic."

The NGE is a new value system that has similarities to and influences from a variety of Cultures/Religions (Islam, Buddhism, Gnosticism, Christianity), but is a unique ethno-cultural response to the condition of people of color in contemporary society. It is no less valid due to it originating from another group than Protestantism, being a response of the excesses of another group (Catholicism in this case). Building upon the legacy of Cultural/ Religious Nationalism left by the Moorish Science Temple and the NOI, the NGE and the ethno-cultural worldview that we espouse deserves the respect and consideration afforded to other Cultures/Value Systems and should be seen as adding another dimension to the contemporary Afro-Asiatic Diaspora.

Already, within the last forty years, the NGE has made a considerable impact on urban youth worldwide and is well known through its influence on Hip-Hop Culture. The ideas and values projected by many NGE musicians (i.e. Rakim, Wu-Tang Clan, Poor Righteous Teachers) has influenced youth culture, serving as the impetus for tens of thousands of disaffected youth to learn about and research the history and culture of aboriginal people across the globe. Viewing the NGE outside the limited parameters of "Proto-Islam" will allow many to gain greater understanding and appreciation for the ideas and concepts found therein.

HOLY VS. RIGHTEOUS
Rashawn Sincere Allah - The Desert (Queens, NY)

Our nation encompasses brothers and sisters from a multitude of backgrounds and walks of life. For some who are just receiving the knowledge of the Black Man being God, it's hard to let go of some preconceived notions about who and what God should be. Once the science of God is truly born to the blind, they will no longer be completely shrouded by the veil of ignorance, looking for a God in the heavens above. However, the supreme light of God can still be viewed through the prism of an individual's mind, affected by the viewer's background and level of understanding.

Some think that since they don't drink or smoke, that makes them somehow that much more righteous than their brother or sister who does. Granted, you may be health conscious. However, that doesn't make you righteous. Being righteous is thinking and living with a mathematically inclined state of mind, doing what's right in every situation, for the greatest good of all involved. Not doing something because of fear of what's going to happen in the nonexistent mystery after life, but simply because it's the right thing to do, in order to keep your universe balanced.

In order for one to truly be righteous, one must first begin to learn how to be civilized. Which, in the culture of I-God, means having knowledge, wisdom, understanding, culture, refinement and not being savage in pursuit of happiness. Then one can begin to study and activate what governs the natural law and order of all things in existence, which is mathematics. Mathematics puts the science of everything in life in its proper order without the use of religion, which uses fear, and ignorance to control the minds of its followers.

This is why we are not "holy" people, avoiding life as it exists around us. We are righteous people, interacting with all elements, in order to produce the best results. We come to the people as the people, and this is why we are successful.

"Let a fool month after month eat his food (like an ascetic/ holy man) with the tip of a blade of grass, yet he is not worth the sixteenth particle of those who have well weighed the law." - Friedrich Max Muller

Rashawn Sincere is an author, freelance journalist, and poet who writes under the pen name Maxwell Penn. As a child growing up in New York City, Rashawn was inspired by the storytelling elements found within Hip Hop. This began a lifelong love for writing, and an introduction to the teachings of the Five Percent. Rashawn acquired knowledge of self at age 19, where he was confronted by the apparent contradictions of "righteous people" who smoke and drank. As he matured, he came to an understanding of the science of "holy vs. righteous." Today, his mission in the literary field is to incite thought and poignant social commentary through tales like *Larceny of the Heart*, published by Sincere Communications Group in 2009. You can learn more about his work at www.myspace.com/maxwellpennonline

WHAT DOES IT MEAN TO BE GOD?

Scientific Born Allah - Interior Cipher (Pennsylvania)

I was once asked by the Heart of Philly what being God meant to me, and I told my Almighty Blackseed brother that being God means *everything* to me because it is the culmination of everything I've ever studied and worked for in this world. Of course I wasn't always a part of this world, because like the majority of us, I came from the 85% world into the 5% world. B.U.T. now that I am the True and Living God that my mental Father raised me to be, I can cee much deeper into his question of Supreme examination than the naked eye can detect. Show and proving that Understanding is indeed the Best Part of life and Mathematics, because Mathematics is life!

In arithmetic, "mean" is a term for the value midway between extremes, which is synonymous to the average. In Mathematics, mean is the specified importance of one's purpose or intentions. The difference being that in the 85% world, the meaning of life is determined by the law of averages, or "majority rules," which is defined by the mentality of the masses. While in the 5% world, the meaning of life is determined by the law of nature (Mathematics!) that rules the majority, which is defined by Allah, the Supreme Being, Blackman from Asia. What does this all mean? As I cee it, it means that the majority are dictated life by others while there is a small minority that dictate life on our own terms. Such is the reality of God.

Being God means that I must be above and beyond the mentality of the 85% masses and their superstitious concept of a mystery god that does not exist. However, I now know and understand that being God also means that I must elevate above and beyond just a God state of mind and into a God state of Living Mathematics so that the very same 85% masses that accept everything on the face value law of averages can cee the reality of God in everyday life. And where I once thought that this reality was a given, I now cee that it is not, because there is a vast difference between intentions and manifestations of life. All who intend to do well don't always do well! After all, even the blind, deaf and dumb have good intentions when they advocate their so-called mystery god. Yet that has nothing to do with the manifestation of the True and Living God of Reality! My point being that must say what I mean (I am God!), and mean what I say (I AM God!).

"A superior man is modest in his speech, but exceeds in his actions." – Confucius

What this means to me is that I must live this Truth out in the highest form of thought, deed and action, just as Almighty God Allah taught us to. Does this mean that I cannot commit errors? That I must be perfect in every way? Emphatically NO! Allah did not teach us to be "holier than thou." That's the 85% concept of what God is. Allah taught us the reality of God, and to be righteous, civilized people in the pursuit of happiness. He also taught us that if we do something that we don't know about and mess up, that's not a mistake. It's only a mistake when we know better and do otherwise. Which means that God is a righteous, seen being who utilizes his Divine Living mind to Born the necessary Mathematical solutions to the infinite equations of life. As I cee it, the Divinity of God is the ridiculous concept of "holy perfection"; it is the Supreme ability to rise above our flaws, errors and shortcomings, and perfect them through the growth and development of experiencing life itself. That's how I live my Mathematics!

Being God means to me that Allah's 120° of life are my CORE VALUE SYSTEM, which I must internalize and transcend into the lessons of life he intended them to be. This means that my lessons are simply my blueprints to build by, or my proverbial road map to life. These are of no use to me without having the Understanding of when and where to activate and apply them in my life. What good are any blueprints without the skills to read and understand them? What do I need a road map for without any destination to reach? Allah gave me my purpose (Good Orderly Direction!) when he taught us to "Teach the people." Now it's on me to build with his Supreme blueprints and navigate through life using the map he blessed us with. Our lessons are the Supreme Foundation that we all share. What we do with them is how we show and prove what being God truly means.

What all this means to me is that God is he who rises above the equality of all things and makes himself responsible for all that cannot respond for itself. We cannot just "say" our lessons; knowing and quoting them is only 1 and 2, basic Knowledge and Wisdom. We must DO the Knowledge and LIVE the Wisdom to be able to Understand that we are now responsible for standing under the weight of responsibility for not only ourselves, b.u.t. the masses as well.

As Allah once said, "It all depends on the Gods." We must each live our lessons out according to what he means to us individually, because together we equal him! Those that don't know that means need to ask themselves: "What does it meant to be God?"

Scientific Born Allah is currently in the belly of the beast in Pennsylvania. He is a frequent contributor to 5% periodicals, such as *The Light of the Sun* and *Behold the Sun of Man*, as well as blogs such as supremeteamofva.blogspot.com and supremelifegivers.blogspot.com

CHANGE THE WORLD
Wyking Allah - Morocco (Seattle, WA)

Our world is created from the inside out. What we write on the inside expresses itself on the outside. In order to change the world around (outside) us we must change the world within (inside) us. To change our reality, we must change our mentality. You must bring forth a new state of awareness and then manifest that awareness through your words, actions and habits. The ideas you nurture/cultivate through your thinking blossom in the garden of your life. Nurturing/cultivating means repetitive thinking or meditating.

We think about what's in our head and things get in our head through our eyes and ears. If you want to change what is in your head, you must change what you put in and/or let in your head. Consciously choose the images (written and spoken words) that go in to your head. Change the ciphers (people, places and things) that you are exposed to. Environment dictates action, or in a more common saying, "people are products of their environment." This is so until they learn to make their environment a product of them.

Wisdom is the way knowledge is made born. In other words, just as the seed of life must gestate and become born through the proper environment with the proper elements present, this is also true with ideas becoming reality. There is a particular way or order for thoughts to be born form the mental to the physical plane. Our mentality becomes or makes our reality through words (silent and spoken), actions (what we do) and habit (repetition). We make our world through what we say and do repeatedly. How can you keep your mind on something?

If you think successful thoughts in your head, by being around successful people (physically and/or mentally by reading about them) and then doing what successful people doing, chances are you will be successful. You can't think successful thoughts and then do the opposite and expect success. You can't think about going to the NBA, but then spend your time getting high and playing video games and expect to make it. You maybe an excellent blunt roller or the best at NBA 2K8, but you will not be anywhere the NBA, true story. The formula is think it - see it (in your mind's eye) - speak it - do it - and do it again.

From knowledge to born and born back to knowledge. Start with the end in mind and the awareness of the steps it took to get to that end. Start at the end and figure out each stage or step it took to get to that end. Mentally start at the end and work backwards to the beginning. Then proceed to go forward by physically taking each step. This covers both visualization and planning. Thinking about the end without seeing the steps is no better than fantasizing or "mental masturbation." Understanding is to see things clearly as they truly are. To see the full picture, which is the effect as well as the cause.

THOSE WERE THE DAYS
Bismi Allah - Wisdom Victory (W. Virginia)

Back in the days
when we were tight like brotherhood
We grew up together
risking our lives for each other
without hesitation
And we were brothers
true, although no blood relation

More power to the people
America didn't love us,
so we'd build our own nation

Well! I guess those days have gone

Ladue, Bismi, and little Born Allah
surrounded by assassins
totally outnumbered
no fear, don't know, don't care
and don't even give a f*ck
we remembered

I guess those days have gone

The words Allah-u-Akbar traveled so far
that we'd go from east hell to west hell
to help each other out
with no hesitation
we would build our own nation

I guess those days have gone

We were the envy of all others
and the women wanted us as husbands
not as their brothers
and wild in the streets were we as teenagers
but we still had respect for our fathers and mothers

Well! I guess those days have gone

All people of all races
they only care about their own
and being mistreated because you are different...

Well! I'll be glad when those days have gone.

God Bismi Allah was born in Norfolk Virginia, and reborn into the Knowledge of Self in the Bronx in 1969. He is a trained mediator, poet, family man, businessman, teacher of reality, and fighter for freedom, justice, and equality for all.

SERVING JUSTICE
Victorious Honor Allah – Medina (Brooklyn, NY)

It was 1968. Brooklyn, New York. My Old Earth was 12 years old and was finally getting adjusted to her new home here, after emigrating from her native land of Guyana. She was now running with a small group of girls her age from Jamaica calling themselves "The Big Time 5." They were wildly popular in the neighborhood, which attracted the attention of the local Five Percenters like Saekuan, Eminent, Moniek, Understanding and Infinite. While the general consensus of the Big Time 5 was that "all of the cute boys were Five Percenters," they were also dazzled by the wisdom these young men wielded almost effortlessly. She would tell me stories of how the Five Percenters spoke, chose their names, how they maintained an intense vigilance over every little aspect of their culture…even the way they stood and folded their arms.

I must have been 8 or 9 when she started telling me this history and the stories became favorites of mine. "Tell me about the Five Percenters again," I'd say. But by this time, 1985, she was no longer adding on with the Five Percent. She always made sure to balance her wild-eyed stories of the Crown Heights gods with sobering tales of the brothers who'd become reckless and self-gratifying.

At 8, I was a baby myself, so the gravity of what she said escaped me. I was aware of the moral duplicity of it all, yet I'd always viewed a Five Percenter as some sort of superhero who "served justice" to whoever messed up, perpetrated or failed to show respect. I hadn't really understood this system as much as I admired it…until the god Lord took my sh*t.

It was 1995. A decade since I was first told tales of the men who would eventually become my elders, friends and confidants. Though I was in Atlanta blindly pursuing what most would call the American Dream, I was a Flatbush Avenue Brooklynite at heart - which means I was cocky as hell and I thought my hood was the center of the world.

However, I learned quickly that my New York status didn't mean what it meant in the summers I spent in Toronto, Canada: instant recognition, respect, status and women. On the contrary, it seemed southerners hated New Yorkers with a passion. I remember the Goodie Mob song "Dirty South," where Khujo rapped, "They down here playing Rock the Bells/ We took what they had and left 'em quiet as hell." This was a reference to the heydays of DIY drug dealing - the 80's - when everyone in New York rushed down south to sell weight at exorbitant prices. When I arrived in Atlanta, there were even rumors of a native Atlantan gang whose primary objective was to terminate New Yorkers on sight. If that wasn't bad enough, there were a bunch of clowns from far-off towns pretending to be from Brooklyn, and only making us look bad in the process. So New York status didn't give me the ego boost I'd expected. My only consolation was that I wasn't *just* from New York. I was from *Now Why*, the Five Percent name for the city that was our Mecca. As a Now Why God, I felt especially superior in Atlanta…an attitude no different from the ones held by the early European settlers. That too, would soon change.

By the following year, I'd started to accept Atlanta as my home. More importantly, I began realizing my own divinity more and more as each day progressed, and as I grew closer to the Five Percent in Atlanta, or Allah's Garden as we called it. Though I'd received my foundational teachings in Fort Greene, Brooklyn (The Head of Medina), I'd never really built with many Gods in, or even from, NY. So I wanted clarity. I wanted to build with a man whose views I'd come to respect, Kalim, the editor of *The Five Percenter*, the Nation's premier publication. I hopped on the Greyhound bus, not concerned about anything but the one question burning on my mind – "Are we REALLY God?" The ride was over 16 hours long. When I got to Mecca, I already had my own affirmative answer. Even more so, I decided I didn't care what anyone else thought. I was GOD, in all essences and understandings.

I did however go the school in Mecca. Something my Old Earth never did. Actually a lot of the gods in Medina never went to the school, even when Allah the father was around. For some reason, she always thought that Allah wasn't real. I mean, she had never seen him – at least to her knowledge. And the way some of her peers spoke of him was supernatural. So I made the trip - a pilgrimage of sorts - for both of us. There, I bought as many Nation papers as possible, took down many numbers, forged relationships that would last for years, and bought my first Universal Flag.

Before that day, I'd never seen a flag like this one. It was on a headband. I saw brothers that had small pins with the flag on them, and even some t-shirts with the same. But in Atlanta, Georgia, in the mid 90's, not too much Nation paraphernalia made its way down. Some said that was a good thing. When I came back on the scene the following weekend, I was anxious to sport my new flag. I knew no one had it. I hadn't felt like this since my high school days, when I'd be excited to show off the latest, flyest Polo wear. My dreadlocks were freshly braided into cornrows and as I approached the rally, I cocked my head to the side - perhaps to bring more attention to that headband of mine - and let out a strong "PEACE!" The Gods were happy to see me, and I got a lot of compliments on my new headband. "Mission Accomplished," I thought.

Then it was time to build. I got in the cipher and built on the day's mathematics. The god Lord, an Atlanta native, smiled at me and said "Peace God." I liked Lord, he was always smiling. He looked like a lion however, with a smile he could use to disarm you before attacking. Disarm me he did. "I like the headband God" he said. "Thanks God!" I proudly answered. "How do you see that Flag?"

'How do you see' was a question I was familiar with. One of my educator I-Self's other students, U-God, used to always catch me at random and ask me how I saw something. I would give a jive answer, and he would stand there, stonefaced until I gave him something better. I dreaded seeing U-God, but I would never avoid him. I somehow knew this had to do with my own growth and development within the knowledge, the nation, and my individuality.

Lord wasn't stone faced, but the point was the same – I had to tell him about the flag. I took the head band off so I could look at it while I spoke.

"What are you doing?" he inquired, the smile never leaving his face. I explained to him that I was taking the headband off so that I could see it.

"If you need to see it to build on it, then you shouldn't be wearing it."

This wasn't good. "Well the 7 is God, the moon is for the woman."

All traces of warmth left his face as he looked me in the eye and asked, "Why is the moon gold?" This confused the hell out of me, because I thought the moon on the flag was Black. At least it was on the headband. "Why is it outlined in gold?' I clarified.

He then turned to everyone in earshot and said "You heard what he said, right? He said the moon was *outlined* in gold!" I knew I had somehow gotten the answer wrong. After I stumbled through a few more descriptions, he said, "It's okay God. Give it to me so I can build on it."

I thought nothing of this, because I definitely wanted to hear what the TRUTH of the Flag was, seeing as though I had It wrong. He held the flag up and pointed out the facts – which in turn revealed my errors. Then he did something that surprised the hell out of me. He clutched it and said "I'm going to hold on to this until you can build for it."

Was this a jack move? Now, I'm from Brooklyn so I'd been party to this type of smooth criminal sh*t before. *He was trying to rob me.* There was no way I was going to let it go down like this. "No, God!" I said nervously, "It's mine."

"Why?" he enforced.

"Because I paid five dollars for it." I had set up a beautiful trap for myself.

"Oh, so you paid for it, and that means it's yours?'

It was deep. And I was wrong. Maybe the cotton was worth five dollars, but even I knew that the Universal Flag was not something one could pay for. The Nation was not something one could buy into.

"No god, I'm not saying that. But I'm not going to keep it until I know it." He must have been trained by the masters. "I'll be that dresser drawer for you and I'll give it back when you're ready."

It was clear. He was trying to play me out. I suddenly noticed that he was now flanked by two other brothers, Darmel and Kasun. They were a year or so younger than me and from Jersey. I searched their faces for any signs of support. Those dudes left me hanging. One of them actually turned away. I would later on that year roll with 20 other gods to come to his aid because he couldn't protect his woman in a party. Go figure. So I was alone.

I thought, "Can I take him?" He had some years - and some pounds - on me. And he wasn't one of the "college gods," either. He ran with *Allah Familia*, a group of strong-arm Gods who took no prisoners. Some of them were former gangbangers, others - like Lord - were ex-military. All of them were in the streets heavy. And none of them were playing when it came to this culture.

As I considered my options, Lord added insult to injury with, "When you see me next, I'll have it on me. *I might have it on.*"

"Nah, God, nah." I shook my head as my legs and hands began to tremble into their ready marks. I was gonna have to go out for my sh*t. I didn't survive the 90's in Brooklyn's illest hoods to go out like a punk in Atlanta. If he was taking my sh*t, then all three of them would have to whup my ass. And they probably would.

And then he said, "That's a part of being in this nation."

Those words resonated with me – Instantly, I remembered all the things my Old Earth taught and told me. It finally clicked in my mind – Not only was I god of the Universe, but I was one of Allah's Beloved Five Percent. It's what I should have expected. He was right. This is what I'd signed up for. It's what I had to respect. In high school, the god Born had told me God wasn't "some punk pussy, soft faggot, b*tch motherf*cker!" And somewhere along the line, I'd forgotten that I had joined a nation of warriors. This WAS what being in this nation was about. I unclenched my fists. And my teeth. "Peace God," I resigned - and walked away.

When I got home, my phone was ringing off the hook. Everybody heard the word. My educator I-Self (who also hailed from Medina) called and told me "That's f*cked up but - sh*t God, you should have known the flag!" Very comforting. A brother named Hakim, who was another native New Yorker and taught by U-God, came over and said that Lord and some of the other "non-NY" gods were just trying to live out the type of stuff they heard happened in NY. It seemed plausible, but it was ReaSun, a brother from Detroit, who actually got at me and brought over a stack of information on the flag. I studied that like I'd studied in no class before. (Which wasn't saying much, as I was a habitual class cutter…but you get the point.) ReaSun prepped me and made sure I was ready.

The next rally was on the 22nd, which in Supreme Mathematics was Wisdom Wisdom. In the Alphabet, Victory. I prepared a long drawn out build on the Supreme Mathematics, Alphabet and lessons for that day. I was taking no prisoners and if homeboy didn't give me my flag, we were going to HAVE to square off. It was that simple.

I stepped on the scene and there he was. The headband wasn't on his head. Back with the Lion's smile on his face, he challenged "you ready to build on the flag?" I stared him dead in the eye and said "True indeed."

When I'd surrendered my flag to Lord, it was a shot heard around the city, so all eyes were on me. I began to dazzle them with my wisdom. Lord threw some curveballs at me, but I fielded each and every one of them. ReaSun had trained me well. When I was done, I awaited his response.

The god stepped up to me, produced my flag, and said "Peace God, NOW you can wear it." Almost instantly, everything was clear to me. This was justice! The system which so many had feared, rejected and misunderstood actually worked! It was fair. I didn't know the flag, so I shouldn't have worn it. He wasn't trying to rob me. He was manifesting his duty to the fullest. I thanked him.

More than a decade later, I have followed in the footsteps of the great warrior scholars of our nation. I have taught many, civilized many more and at times, I've had to strip some of their names and possessions. There were a few times where I've concurred that trials and corporal punishment were necessary. I was taught by men who didn't play games.

And I've seen the other side of the coin. I've sat in courtrooms while fellow Five Percenters were on trial, and the chief witness against them was a former/supposed friend and brother - often based upon fear. I've seen Gods walk away from wars, leaving brothers hanging – based upon fear. I've seen a lot of strength, but I've also seen a lot of weakness. Early on, I was prepped by my Old Earth to beware of men who were gods but became pimps, liars and thieves.

Hell, I had seen myself inadvertently perpetrate a fraud with that headband - And I got let off easy. So when I moved back to New York in 1998, I saw it fit for me to assume my natural role as Vanguard of this Nation. My life and sacrifice was for Allah and I proved it through my everyday administration of justice, whether it was through War, Civilization, Education or Scrutinization. The three former are often forgotten by the weak. They forget that it took and takes men like me, like Lord, to ensure safe passage of all those that come in the name of Allah and his most precious Five Percent in the ghettoes of hell. They don't understand what it took for us to earn the respect of the gangs and even other organizations that were once hellbent on destroying us. We had to lay a lot of things down in order for a lot of us to rise.

Somehow, people forget that - in agriculture - "slashing and burning" is just as important as seeding. All they see is arson. This has caused skepticism, discomfort and fear. They see the harsh tones and the physical force some of our warriors apply, and miss the reason why these elements must exist. They hear the legends about brothers getting "served justice" without hearing about the crimes these brothers committed. They can handle daily whuppings from the devil, but not the scrutiny of their fellow man. People have left our midst because they were consumed by the same fear the devil planted in them long before they ever heard of the Five Percent. These same people knew they couldn't stand the tests of character and integrity that we require of each other...constantly.

I'm glad I built for that flag that day. It disturbs me to think of those who ran from that aspect of the nation - the SHOW AND PROVE aspect. But hey, they didn't get it anyway. *End Fear - Murder the Devil.*

Peace to the Gods. In the memory of Siheem & Al Jabbar.

Victorious Honor has been working in schools and community centers as a counselor since the nineties. Since obtaining the Knowledge of Self, he has engaged local communities in five continents. He has worked on Riker's Island as part of an educational program. Victorious taught a class at Allah's School from 2000 to 2004, and was on the board of directors of the Allah Youth Center in Mecca. As DJ Victorious, he works with the A-Alikes and Sha Stimuli.

ALLAH AND INDIGENOUS ANARCHY
Sha-King Cehum Allah - Power Born (Pittsburgh, PA)

As a nation, we the Gods and Earths do not have any specific political outlook. As a collective, we are apolitical. This can turn into 'apathy' without the proper education. We are not a religion nor or we an 'organization.' We are a 'nation' of men, women and children who live according to some basic esoteric teachings, taught and understood through their parallel with mathematical and alphabetic principles defined by our founder, Allah. However, we can not be strangers to organization. We have organization, really only visible to those 'within' the culture.

Allah could have been considered a patriot. He was more a champion for education and 'civilization.' By civilization I mean the forward progression of 'Man' and his abilities to master himself and what he produces through space and time. While other Black groups, so called 'militants,' were concerned with bringing down the white establishment, Allah worked hand in hand with Major John V. Lindsay and his aid, Barry Gotherer. Allah secured airplane rides, bus trips to Bear Mountain, trips to the beach and a host of other activities for his young Five Percenters, courtesy of the "city of New York." While many radicals dismiss these services and the funds allocated for them as mere ploys from the city government, Allah didn't care. Allah was focused on his "fruit" and making sure they had the best, considering they came from having 'nothing.' Allah wasn't a democrat or republican. He was simply familiar with the laws of the land. He was a hustler and knew how to get what he needed. Especially when it came to the youth. He was more concerned with sending children to college that 'separating' them from all that society could offer them. They were already separating because they were poor and Black. And by "society could offer them" I mean an education and advancement in society. And he did this, on his terms. He didn't teach the children to hide who they were or sacrifice his teachings just so they could "pass" through society. Allah instilled in them a respect for the American flag and the government, yet made distinctions as to certain laws to acknowledge and obey, as long as they didn't conflict with 'our' laws. He didn't advocate marriage under the government nor did he recognize the government's authority to 'tell' or someone who they are or define them. He called himself Allah and didn't care who liked it. He even represented himself as "Allah" in front of the judge prior to going to Bellevue and Mattewan State Hospital.

Allah would work with anyone who could help him further his agenda for his sons and daughters. And by virtue of interacting and meeting compromises with city and government officials he was 'political.' Irregardless to how some may feel about it.

Allah taught us to be leaders and therefore we have no 'central' lead figure. Yet, we do have leadership. Those qualified with moving forward with certain issues and actions. We have no hierarchy, except between the 'best knower' and those 'seeking to know.' Which means, I will openly accept direction and suggestions from someone who 'knows' more than me or is more qualified in a certain area. Allah freed us from hierarchy by revealing to us the reality of GOD, and that being every Original man. Thus, each man is the ruler of his own life and universe (family). With no external force or entity having dominion over ones' self. This concept is very 'anarchist.' And by 'anarchist' I do not mean "chaotic" but in the original context and meaning of the word. Many of us, in our quest to free ourselves from the shackles of society-one being labels, are so opposed to many words and 'labels' just due to their Eurocentric origin alone. However, there is truth in all things.

Author Michael Muhammad Knight, on his "Waking the Midnight Sun" blog, has written the following about us:

> Look at their breakdown of society: 10 percent of the population rules by deceiving 85 percent into believing in a false mystery god that doesn't exist. The remaining 5 percent reject the lies of this evil 10 percent (the priests, imams, etc.). So when they say they're God, it's almost like an anarchist view of religion. Faced with the bullsh*t of organized religion, the anarchist says, "no gods, no masters." Reacting to the same bullsh*t, the Five Percenter says, "I God, I Master." This can be very empowering.

Since, we are 'apolitical' and being endowed with the ability of 'free thought and action,' each citizen of the Nation of Gods and Earths has the right to chose for themselves their specific political outlook. Some are more conservative, some are more democratic. I, personally, am a self-proclaimed "anarcho-socialist," or even what many may refer to as "Libertarian." After all I've often heard Libertarians referred to as "rich anarchists." We must consider what "Libertarians" advocate in regard to the political outlook of Allah - overall self-sovereignty with an adherence to specific constitutional principles and laws. I've identified the relevancy of "Socialism" within the context of 120 degrees due to certain concepts within the lessons. For example, the 8th degree in the 1-14:

> Q: Why does the Devil keep our people apart from their own social equality?
> Ans: Because he is filthy in all his affairs. He is afraid that once we learn about him we will run him from amongst us. Social means to advocate a society of men or group of men for one common cause. Equality means to be equal in everything.

Socialism means, for me, that social issues and responsible are of a greater importance to the longevity and welfare of a society than capital. For me it has nothing to do with a "welfare state." Yet and still, regardless to what one's political outlook may be, we must still be familiar with the principles of capitalism (true capitalism versus what is actually practiced, with the "Central Bankers" in control) and adapt to it to some degree in order to survive in 'this' society. To be 'socialist' to many times is understood as to give all power to the state, which really isn't the reality, as I see it. That may have been a 'Eurocentric' perspective and application of 'socialism' but it's different from what Hugo Chavez is 'attempting' in Venezuela and what Daniel Ortega is doing in Nicaragua by the creation and perpetuation of communal councils. The adoption of these councils gives more power to the people and is considered 'democracy' by the western world. Democracy, as defined through its Greek origin, means to "rule by the people." The United States is far from that. And so was Greece, a slave-based economy and society.

Yet that definition of democracy is what "anarchy" really is and means. Within the Nation of Gods and Earths, each city or cipher agrees (collectively) on particular policy in that city. Within each man's home, he decides the rules and policy of how the house is run. And this, whether acknowledged by the majority or not, is 'anarchism.' Our internal structure is very anarchistic and an understanding of this will allow a citizen within the nation to identify the process and channels of change here and how to harness this seemingly "lack of organization" and transform it into productivity. As opposed to feeling like no one is 'listening to them' and that they are against the odds. This is coming from someone who was involved with the original Growth and Development proposition and the establishing of regions and regional conferences within the nation. An anarchist styled proposition fortifying individual rights and merging/balancing with collective responsibilities, in and of itself. Not 'anarchist' in that we are striving to overthrow the government. "Anarchist" in that we seek to gather of collective resources and network these resources in order to create the best possible quality of life for ourselves and our children. Ruling over ourselves and our 'destiny.'

Below, I included an excerpt from Jack Weatherford's book *Indian Givers: How the Indians of the Americas Transformed the World*, to bring forth further understanding of where the term "anarchy" come from. Please Read on. Do the knowledge...

To an outsider, such powwows often appear chaotic. Even though posted signs promise that the dances will begin at four o'clock, there is still no dancing at five-thirty. Drummers scheduled to play never arrive, and some groups drum without being on the program. Impromptu family ceremonies intertwine with the official scheduled events, and the microphone passes among a score of announcers during the evening. No one is in control. (Sounds very similar to a Universal Parliament.)

This seems to be typical of Indian community events: no one is in control. No master of ceremonies tells everyone what to do, and no one orders the dancers to appear. The announcer acts as herald or possibly as facilitator of ceremonies, but no chief rises to demand anything of anyone. The event flows in an orderly fashion like hundreds of powwows before it, but leaders can only lead by example, by pleas, or by exhortations. Everyone shows great respect for elders and for warriors, who are repeatedly singled out for recognition, but at the same time children receive great respect for dancing and even the audience receives praise for watching. (page 120-121)

Furthermore…Writing a little later in the sixteenth century, the French essayist Michel de Montaigne presented a similar description of American Indian life based primarily on the early reports from Brazil. In his essay "On Cannibals," Montaigne wrote that they are "still governed by natural laws and very little corrupted by our own." He specifically cited their lack of magistrates, forced services, riches, poverty, and inheritance. As in More's utopia, Brazil, emerged as the ideal place and Indians as having created the ideal society [Montaigne, pp. 109-10]. Most of these early writings contained strongly satirical veins - the writers indicated that even the so-called savages lived better than civilized Europeans - but the satire grew out of the unavoidable truth that the technologically simple Indians usually lived in more just, equitable, and egalitarian social conditions.

Not until a century after Montaigne did the first French ethnography on the North American Indians appear. Louis Armand de Lom d'Arce, Baron de Lahontan, wrote several short books on the Huron Indians of Canada based on his stay with them from 1683 to 1694. An adventurer far more than an anthropologist, Lahontan nevertheless managed to rise above the genre of adventure stories to give the French reader the worldview of the Hurons from inside the Indian mind. By the time of Lahontan's sojourn among the Hurons, they had already survived several decades of sporadic interaction with European explorers and traders, and they had been the subject of numerous commentaries by Jesuit Missionaries. From these interactions the Hurons were able to compare their own way of life and the Europeans'. The Indians particularly decried the European obsession with money that compelled European women to sell their bodies to lusty men and compelled men to sell their lives to the armies of greedy men who used them to enslave yet more people. By contrast, the Hurons lived a life of liberty and equality. According to the Hurons, the Europeans lost their freedom in their incessant use of "thine" and "mine."

One of the Hurons explained to Lahontan:

We are born free and united brothers, each as much a great lord as the other, while you are all slaves of one sole man. I am the master of my body, I dispose of myself, I do what I wish, I am the first and last of my Nation…subject only to the great Spirit [Brandon, p.90].

It is difficult to tell where the Huron philosopher speaks and where Lahontan may be promoting his own political philosophy, but still the book rested on a base of solid ethnographic fact: the Hurons lived without social classes, without a government separate from their kinship system, and without private property. To describe this political situation, Lahontan revived the Greek-derived word "anarchy," using it in the literal sense meaning "no ruler." Lahontan found an orderly society, but one lacking a formal government that compelled such order."

MATHEMATICS AND MYSTERY GODS
Supreme Understanding Allah – Allah's Garden (Atlanta, GA)

In today's economy, organized religions have to be centered on the worship of a very specific God or collection of Gods in order to thrive. You're not gonna find many organized religions that break that mold. Even the Buddha, who despised religious thinking, is now the object of worship in most mainstream sects of Buddhism. We can say the same about Jesus and plenty of others who simply wanted to teach, not become idolized.

Let's be clear: Worship isn't all about prostrating and saying prayers. Worship refers to idealizing some being as perfect and all-powerful, holding the power to redeem and save the worshipper somehow. While the original form of Buddhism focused on the power of the mind, and our own ability to save ourselves, modern Buddhism is all about Buddha and his avatars. What about Confucianism? Confucianism was all about ethics and values…with no real focus on a God…but is anybody claiming Confucianism today? What about Taoism? Not too many Taoists left either.

What's my point? People *need* religion. And they need one thing from that religion more than anything else: *Hope*. They need a sense of hope that their God will be able to make things better for them. They need the idea that someone/something is taking care of them. And they need that someone/something to be as close to perfect as possible. They need that God to be way above and beyond anything they can do, because who wants a God as imperfect as them? People organize around the worship of these gods because it's easy to create structure in this type of belief system. God is on top, at some unreachable point, and some "special" individuals are identified as having the closest connection to God and are named as priests/pastors/imams/shamans/ministers/etc. Then there are the masses of followers lumped together at the bottom. They establish an unsaid hierarchy among themselves by contributing either time, effort, or money to the worship of this God, or his/her priests.

Through this structure, social control and financial capital are generated simultaneously. In exchange, the people get a false sense of hope, something to believe in, when reality just isn't satisfying. You'll find this phenomenon in groups that aren't purely religious also. Look at the Civil Rights organizations that have idolized Dr. King and made him out to be something more than what he wanted to become. The people heading those groups live comfortable lives by acting "in the person of" Dr. King and whatever they claim he wanted.

And that's pretty much how religious organizations work, and the reason why they thrive. With everyone focused on a point of reference that no one will ever be able to see, the group in charge can direct affairs however they please, with an incredible amount of control. Since people who believe in matters of blind faith are the least likely to question authority, especially "divine authority," there are rarely any setbacks to the growth and development of the religious organization. Unless, however, another more persuasive religion emerges and takes away followers. Or a member who is not a blind faith follower decides to challenge authority and takes others with him in his dissenting movement. Without these challenges, religious organizations can acquire unparalleled wealth, membership, and even public acclaim (although little of this trickles down to the followers who help acquire it).

The Nation of Gods and Earths does not fit this paradigm. There is no religious focus on a divine authority outside of self, and no hierarchy established among its citizens, who would rather consider themselves representatives than members. And because of this seemingly "loose" structure, the NGE thrives where other groups fail. After all, the NGE is a cultural paradigm. Its teachings spread by diffusion, and the "memetic" nature of it all makes it very difficult to suppress.

Yet people have tried. When it was clear that assassinating or incarcerating "key figures" in the NGE wouldn't dismantle the fluid spread of our culture (because we don't depend on a hierarchy), they've tried to alter our cultural paradigm itself. So how do you dismantle an association of freethinkers? You make them religious. But there's no way to infuse religion into the ideology of the NGE except to incorporate teachings from other organizations. And although the "freedom" you find in Gods who are all over the place (doing who knows what) seems to be a problem, it is also that exact same phenomena that keeps this culture from falling victim to religious order. Fortunately, attempts to weave religion into the NGE's framework have been unsuccessful. Most NGE members view the NOI's religious ideology as equivalent to the Christians' belief in Jesus. And teachings that require blind acceptance do not survive the rigors of "breaking it down" and "drawing it up" in the NGE's most dominant tradition of critical consciousness.

But wouldn't we be more successful if we could ALL just come together and work on the same exact project at the same time? In theory, maybe, but that's not how the NGE works. It is because of our lack of organization around a central religious hierarchy that we have been a scattered group of free-thinkers, lacking a consolidated economic base. However, it is this fact that keeps us diffusing fluidly through communities everywhere. This fact is what separates us from the billions of people who are religious followers, while aligning us with the millions of scattered, but strong, groups of freethinkers across the world and throughout history. It is no surprise that most intelligent and revolutionary people were the least religious. It is similarly no surprise that revolutionaries rarely arise due to the prompting of a structured organization. Even the ones who emerged from religious backgrounds were rarely "orthodox" thinkers. It is with this in mind that I am a tried and true advocate of the NGE. I know this kind of thinking is what will one day change the world. The NGE don't tithe. We don't pray. We don't follow. We don't obey. We do what is right because it is right and just, to the best our ability to do so. We don't look in the clouds (or an altar) for hope and refuge. We look in the mirror. We don't pray for salvation. We work for it. We teach people our curriculum, but first we teach them how to think. And we do not allow religious ideology to corrupt what sets us apart. Teach on.

THIS IS NOT JUST A PHILOSOPHY
C'BS ALife Allah – New Heaven (New Haven, CT)

The core curriculum of the Gods and Earths consists of Supreme Mathematics, Supreme Alphabet and 120 Degrees. Supreme Mathematics and Supreme Alphabet are tools by which one can navigate and negotiate a peaceful life which brings love, peace, and happiness. Supreme Mathematics and Supreme Alphabet are the tools that are utilized to unlock 120 Degrees.

We call them 120 Degrees, because each degree can contain a multitude of lessons. Lessons originate from study. The questions and answers originate from the prophet W.D. Fard and the Messenger Elijah Muhammad. When the questions and answers were primarily within the temple of the Nation of Islam, they were taken at face value because they were delivered almost as scripture. There was no need to research these degrees because, in the theology of the Nation of Islam, they were delivered by the Supreme Being himself. In fact, even questioning them, in the context of the Nation of Islam, would be blasphemy. When the man named ALLAH (formerly Clarence 13X Smith) took the degrees out of the temple, he added the tools (Supreme Mathematics and Supreme Alphabet) to show the youth how to make 120 degrees relevant to them.

Supreme Mathematics and Supreme Alphabet are the keys. 120 is the door. Behind the door is the science of everything in life. Supreme Mathematics is our language, as Mathematics is the foundation for all forms of communication. Supreme Mathematics illustrates the form or example of structure on how the Universe is Ruled and Measured, by development of mathematical relationships between various phenomena that exist and can be observed. Supreme Alphabet is a glossary that allows us to draw up common words to see how they relate to the Supreme Reality.

120 is our history, which is the Knowledge and Wisdom of the Original Man. It is in the form of degrees or questions and answers. They only become lessons once YOU do the Knowledge and Wisdom to get the Understanding. Lessons are not on paper – they are in life. The exercises outlined in 120 serve as a guide for you to interpret and manifest on similar phenomena such as a job application, a bible, a legal document, a building, an astronomical observation, a relationship, any person, place or thing. The exercises in this study will enable you to obtain a method of action – to aid you in organizing your words, ways, and actions in a mathematical fashion, so as to obtain the maximum amount of success in your endeavors.

As I stated before, 120 is the Knowledge and Wisdom of the Original Man – his history, in compact form, broken down and expanded by your own research into the science of mental improvement through symbolism, idea association, abstract and practical thought, memorization, rhetoric and speech, pattern recognition, hypnosis and other gifts you receive, as well as the ability to network with your alikes.

The questions and answers in 120 are not updated (for example, the total population of the Original nation in the wilderness of North America is the total from 1933), because the lesson is found in analyzing each question and answer as it was presented in 1933 and 1934 in order to get an Understanding that is connected to the wisdom of its origin and context.

These degrees will assist you on building up a personal bibliography dealing with science, history, almanacs, maps, etc. 120 touches on everything from astronomy to zoology. Literally. Master Fard Muhammad taught the honorable Elijah Muhammad to use this curriculum in order for Black people to realize their heritage and legacy.

As stated earlier, when these degrees were first presented in the temple of the Nation of Islam, there was no inquiry or research into these degrees. Since ALLAH took the degrees out of the temple, several decades has passed. We now have a generation of Gods and Earths who actually received the Knowledge of themselves in college versus on the streets. As a result, many, along with their college education, now bring a totally cynical viewpoint to 120 degrees. They have gone to the exact opposite of how the degrees were presented in the temple. Instead of taking any degree at face value, they have assigned 120 degrees to the realm of philosophy and allegory. The problem with this outlook is that it is as flawed as the religious orientation.

In the Nation of Gods and Earths, we are taught to use science in order to arrive at a conclusion. Supreme Mathematics is science. 120 is the history. History is interpretation of the past. Science is a tool for interpretation. You must utilize the science to draw out the facts of history. In this way utilizing the tools (Supreme Mathematics and Supreme Alphabet) and the document (120 degrees) will provide one with an organic way to approach the past, view the present, and determine one's future.

ALLAH AIN'T RAISE NO PUNKS

Supreme Understanding Allah – Allah's Garden (Atlanta, GA)

I didn't get this knowledge off a website or on a college campus. No disrespect to those who did, but I got this knowledge on the street corner. Had knowledge not been on the street corner, I would most likely have become another statistic. So I have nothing but love for the gods on the block, because they saved my life. They pushed me to go to school when I considered dropping out. They sometimes helped cover my bills so I didn't have to hustle when I was in college. And they raised me to be a warrior myself. Yet here I am now with a doctorate and a publishing company. I'm reading up on quantum mechanics and evolutionary biology for our next book, The Science of Self. You would think I was a college god. And I'm okay with that. I learned early on that, in our Nation, every scientist had to have some warrior in them, and every warrior had to have some scientist in them.

At one point, however, I was having a hard time understanding how Gods could be heavy in the streets, involved in affairs not worth describing on paper, yet still be righteous enough to raise up a lost knucklehead like myself. It seemed like a contradiction. And over the years, I watched more and more Gods and Earths transition into family life, with many of them now condemning the brothers (and sisters) still in the streets. And I watched the number of Gods on the streets drop heavily. Some may have "settled down" but many of them simply went "inactive" because it was no longer acceptable to be involved in that type of world while using our righteous names.

But observing this change, I now understand. In natural systems, there's always a variety of factors that maintain balance and growth. The predators are just as important as the prey. Take out a predator and the rats grow out of control. Next thing you know, the ecosystem collapses. An ecosystem is basically a culture, so similar laws apply. Back when Allah was rounding up young Gods throughout New York City, he specifically wanted to bring in the brothers in the many gangs out in Brooklyn (which became Medina). Gods from Mecca (Harlem) were known being scientists, so Medina became known for its warriors. They would say, "The grass is greener and the gods are meaner in Medina." The same dichotomy exists today between Harlem and Brooklyn, even outside of the NGE. Even IN Mecca, during the early years of the Five Percenters at Harlem Prep, every young god wasn't tough and street-savvy. Elders will tell you that many were nerds. But those "nerds" were able to build on high sciences without fear because the warriors had their back. And the warriors could turn to these scientists for insight, information, and inspiration. The warriors then brought this knowledge to places where only a warrior could stand alone with a new teaching. And the cycle continued.

I respect the cycle. I understand how and why it works. You can't take out a gear and expect the watch to work the same. I'm not saying its okay for Gods to do "whatever" because we do need to enforce codes and laws regarding ethical behavior, but if we don't provide people with a way to get right or do better, we're no different from the religious people who only condemn others from their high horses. I know that we once "converted" most of the street gangs in NY to Five Percenters. Those brothers went on to bang for the truth. Now we have the same opportunity. Yet if we say there shouldn't be any "gangster Gods" how will we do it?

So please understand that I'm not excusing unethical behavior among people claiming the NGE. Some people are just plain foul and are okay with being foul. But if you know that we come to those who are lost, you will understand that many of us are a long way from home, and need more support to continue our journey towards righteousness. Of course, that's different from people who are straight up faking it. Those people are more like the 10% than anything, and they use this knowledge as a shield. But we make a mistake when we think that only "street gods" can fall in that category. I've run with hundreds of "street gods" and I've constantly seen them observed the principles of "word is bond," "don't speak on what you don't know," "no gossiping or backbiting," "take it through the math," and "save the babies"…often more than I've seen the same among the armchair philosophers who act high and mighty behind closed doors (or on the Internet) but won't bust a grape in a fruitfight. Why? Because in the streets, you observe certain codes or you pay a penalty. In other ciphers, there may not be any code or any penalty. As a result, you see people mixing 120 with all kinds of religious beliefs, obsessing over conspiracy theories but never reading a book, arguing amongst themselves over petty nonsense, lying or failing to keep their word without a second thought, and never, ever teaching a young person like myself. I'm not givin them a pass either. Because when I heard "Allah didn't raise no punks," I understood it to mean that we ain't the type of people who you can just chump off, but also that we are brave enough to mandate what is right from all those who are around us. We are brave enough to transform the 85%, hands-on, because we're not scared of our own people. We're brave enough to challenge the status quo, and to take on oppression, hands-on, rather than becoming armchair philosophers. And we're brave enough to call each other out when we're out of line. And we're brave enough to admit we're constantly perfecting ourselves, so our journeys are never done. So next time you run into a God or Earth who can't do none of the above, don't worry about if they're a street god or a school god, a warrior or a scientist. You don't have to worry bout none of that, because they're not one of us.

ℬ 5 ℭ
TEACHING

THE FATE OF THE MANY...
DEPENDS ON THE SUCCESS OF THE FEW
Almighty God Dawud Allah - Power Hill (Philadelphia, PA)

Why does the fate of the many depend on the success of the few? Because to everything there is a high, low and middle, or the 5%, 10% and the 85%. See, the 85% is lead by the 10% who are the blood suckers of the poor. The devil's two arms are religion and medicine which are the biggest frauds in the world. One will make you a patient and the other will sell you the pill (poison).

There is a word that most of us have never heard of, called *Entropy*, which is a scientific principle. Among the elements, there is a natural trend towards degeneration. This essentially means that there is a degenerative trend from the highly organized downward toward the lower levels and it is the weakest link that breaks the chain. Never and I do mean never is there an increase of order without an external force. As a matter of fact, to flow with stream means to degenerate, and to flow against it mean to regenerate and that requires the work (building) of each individual, because we must work to live. The Bible says "If you don't work, you don't eat." The Bible also says (Gal 6:7), "Be not deceived, God is not mocked for so ever a man soweth that shall he also reap," but religion and medicine refuse to recognize this universal law. The religionist says, "Just believe in the gospel of the Jesus and everything will be all right," and the doctors of medicine say, "Just believe in medicine, inoculations and immunization and you will be safe." There is an old saying that "promises are made to be broken." Plus all diseases start in the Mind, which no medicine a doctor gives you will reach.

See, the 85% loves that kind of teaching. Our people follow all sorts of practices and all kinds of habits and hang ups, whether they are good or bad and don't worry about the consequences, because of what they are taught. The devil's world is based on the law of entropy. In his world it is hard to go up or get up "just like crabs in a barrel." That's why Jesus said "He who loveth the world; the love of the Father is not in him." There is no Mystery God, No mystery is closed to an Open Mind. See the mind is like a parachute, close it and it will kill you, open it and it will save your life. It all started when the devil came out of the caves of Europe into ancient Egypt giving birth to the saying that God is a mystery.

"The liberty of man consists solely in this: that he obeys natural laws because he has himself recognized them as such, and not because they have been externally imposed upon him by any extrinsic will whatever, divine or human, collective or individual." - Mikhail Bakunin, God and the State

Religion and Medicine. This is the world of the Devil that he teaches people to submit without understanding (the greatest thing in life) but we should do right by reason and conscious awareness. Not because of the spirits and spooks which produces ignorance, superstition and fear. Any association that has a mystery or an oath of secrecy for its base is nothing but a bunch of robbers. The devil and those who follow him have invented ceremonies of worship as a means of attracting the wealth of the people, while they are playing the part of god and all this is to carry on the singular trade of selling words, so they prey, pay and obey.

"Be Still and know that I Am God, your True Self."- Ernest Holmes, Your Invisible Power

Many shall come but few shall be chosen and the few are called the 5%, the ones who choose themselves. Because you don't join this. You just accept your own and be yourself. All minds must return to one. All is one and one is all. You join gangs, but we are not a gang, no matter what they say. Lies cover up evil thoughts.

Listen, this is what we teach: the Blackman is God, the whiteman is the devil, the Blackwoman is the Queen of the planet Earth and the Black babies are the greatest. How are we going to save the world? One Baby at a time. To defeat the devil one must sacrifice, be dedicated and totally committed to being the best you can be. Let our motto be" the greatest love of all is learning to love yourself." See this is Judgment day and people are basically looking for other to blame their inadequacies on. That's why Allah's suns are so hot. They are radiating visible light that's lighting up the world. How in the world are you going to get knowledge unless you talk to those that already have it. If you let a dog teach your children they will be in love with a fuzzy tail. To suffer in silence is the worst defeat and invisible tears are the worst tears of all. If we can speak, we are writing on air waves. Everybody is talking about us but don't know us, and they can't know God until they see God. And God is number; my number one self.

The pen is mightier that the sword. We can write them off the planet. So write books, songs, poems and papers, but write. Why? Because the fate of the many, depends on the success of a few.

WHY I AM A POOR RIGHTEOUS TEACHER
Original Author Allah - Mecca (Harlem, NY)

"Freedom, morality, and the human dignity of the individual consists precisely in this; that he does good not because he is forced to do so,

but because he freely conceives it, wants it, and loves it."
Mikhail Bakunin, God and the State

Poor Righteous Teacher. What does that mean? Let's define it.

First, what's up with the "Poor" part? Poor means to have the lack of something in a certain criteria. So I am poor because I lack greed; I am poor because I lack selfishness. I am poor because I lack ignorance. I am poor because I lack the need to keep my people ignorant to themselves. We are poor because we transcend materialism.

"A man's ethical behavior should be based effectually on sympathy, education, and social ties; no religious basis is necessary. Man would indeed be in a poor way if he had to be restrained by fear of punishment and hope of reward after death." - Albert Einstein

Those who teach mathematics, we don't get glory or medals or money for our actions. We will gladly do this for free, our only reward is to save another person from lies and remove the weakness off their cipher. The reason why we are poor is because we sacrifice everything that we have in order for the big picture to come into fruition. I study a lot of things I read so much I wonder if it becomes selfish and then I always say I don't keep it, I give it all away to all those who want to learn.

That's the sacrifice that we in the NGE make. We don't keep anything hidden from the masses.

When ones mind is consumed with every worldly device, one cannot truly build a strong mental. I care about food clothing and shelter, not excess of the above said, to the degree where I am spending 500 dollars on a pair of jeans or buying a million dollar house. I don't need these things. If I have a mansion with 40 rooms in it, bet that I will be housing families and not having rooms just to say I got mad rooms in my house! There are Blacks who have over 40 million in their bank account and are doing nothing with it. They have wealth just for the sake of being wealthy. We can change our own situations in this wilderness. There are enough Black dollars to make a real change in the communities that we are in. Those athletes, movie stars, rappers and such have enough gold to make a serious change, but nobody wants to put their money together and do something big with it. If the white man can pool his bread to start big time companies, so can we. Status in America is based upon having a lot of one thing and not sharing the wealth with others in ways that can make a true change. Since this practice is common among most whites, the Black people who have made it have accepted the same mindset. For example, Jay-Z has tons of bread, yet his old neighborhood is still in shambles. He thinks giving out toys on Christmas is something? That's that fake, Mafia-style 'giving back' routine! If you're going to give back, really give back!

The foundation of a PRT: Sacrifice. Why? Because we don't interpret the word "Poor" as a reference to being broke! For us, "Poor" refers to transcending materialism, and giving of ourselves for the sake of others. It's the Knowledge (first part), as I see it, to the equation Of PRT. Equality refers to the fairness of a cipher, and we deal equally in knowledge. In Supreme Mathematics, six is Equality. As one reference point, carbon is the sixth element in the periodic table, and it's the most fairly distributed element in the universe. Every living thing has a level of carbon in it.

So what does this tell us?

That carbon is a necessity to life and its dealt equality to all things so they can function properly. Original people who study the truth understand that it's a necessity to tell those who don't know and this too deals with life-giving equality. Knowledge of self for the Black family is a must in life, something all need equally. Thus, we give it, without taking in return.

Now let's define "Righteous," the Wisdom (second) component in the equation of PRT. I see it as acting in accord with moral thinking. Righteousness does not mean one free from error. We are not robots. It means that we strive for what's right at all times and never lose focus of what's right and what's wrong in the world and with ourselves.

Having knowledge of self, I am morally obligated to those who don't have it. Righteousness is action. So ones actions must strive to be right and in accord with the truth at all times. The actions of the sacrifice that I have made for my people can bring about change to all those I meet and speak to. The nature of Black people is to deal with equality amongst each other, that's why you see Black love can be the strongest, yet we are so distorted and divided it never truly comes into fruition.

A lot of people always want to do right, yet they never act on these thoughts so nothing ever gets done. What is the sense of having a righteous thought if you don't act upon it?

Let's define "Teacher," the Understanding in the equation of PRT. We all know understanding is the best part of the learning process. A teacher with knowledge of self is the best one to facilitate this process to those who lack the understanding of themselves in the universe. I see a teacher as one who gives knowledge and understanding to those who lack it on any given thing in life to allow them to make progress.

I have stood on my square and went through many ciphers in Harlem and Brooklyn and Queens to teach that the Blackman is God. I see Black males wasting their lives away on the corner and it makes my day to step to one and say something that gets him thinking. My whole purpose is to get people thinking.

I love the feeling when I hear, 'hmm...' when I am making knowledge born. I love the feeling when somebody says 'let me get your number so we can build.' I love the feeling knowing I am making a change in someone's mind state.

The main issues in the Black community are that the right things are not being taught to us. We are bombarded with images and substances that will bring about no growth and development to make any real changes to our current condition. We don't have enough teachers in the "hood" teaching the truth. Drug dealers and such are doing the teaching to the youth.

All I care about in life is the Black family knowing their identity. Health care and Education are the pillars of any working civilization. Once we as Blacks take control of these things we can take back our rightful claim on this planet. This all starts with sacrifice, the application of moral thinking and telling the world why we are doing these things so they can do it also. Thus, all of the above is why I am a Poor Righteous Teacher.

Original Author Allah is a School of Hard Knocks graduate and is currently a teacher in the University of the Universe (Life). He is a Scholar, a Warrior, a Nerd, a Visionary, a 90's Hip Hop Guru, a Camouflage Clothing Fiend, a Truth Mobster and a Longtime Fact Gangster. He knows the young are the future and is here to plant the seeds today.

EDUCATING OUR YOUTH
Born King Allah - Allah's Garden (Atlanta, GA)
"I believe the children are our future. Teach them well and let them lead the way." - Whitney Houston

When I first heard that quote from singer/song writer Whitney Houston I was around twelve years old and I didn't understand what she meant. Now that I am an adult and a father of two I can fully grasp what she was saying because I am a leader and a divine example for those to come after me.

The children are our greatest investment. Very soon they will be adults making major decisions that will affect our communities and the world. Over the years I have learned that there is not a mystery God somewhere with a magic wand waving his hand over us. The world is going to continue on and the results of what we produce will manifest itself. We will either educate or guide our youth so they will be prepared to face what is ahead of them or we will not find the time to spend with them and let them be educated through mass media and music. This will result in them committing more violent crimes, Black on Black crimes, and more Black people in the penitentiaries and cemeteries (physical and mental). In other words GENOCIDE for the Black Man, Woman, and Child!

Many of my peers (myself included) didn't have a strong male influence in our lives growing up. Our choices back then were to either play sports at the neighborhood park or hang with some of the older hustlers on the street. I choose sports and it was cool but it was more physical education than mental and cultural. Don't get me wrong having local parks and recreation centers are great and they are needed. It's good to have somewhere to go and exercise and release some of that young energy (Inner G). However we needed more than a football team to save ourselves. We didn't have any cultural centers around other than the church and they didn't teach us anything but fear. So most of our learning came from the public school system which really doesn't have any interest in the development of Original People (or "people of color").

"A people without the knowledge of their past is like a tree without roots." - Marcus M. Garvey

One of the major problems that needs to be solved within the Black community (come unity) is the disconnect that our youth have with the people and events that paved the way before them. History should never be taken for granted. History also has a way of repeating itself (positive and negative). We as adults have done a poor job of educating (or lack of) our children. We must improve in teaching them who they really are (knowledge of self). They must know and understand the accomplishments of their ancestors and predecessors, their mistakes, and their struggles. You see a lesson a day keeps the devil away. It seems that after the civil rights movement with the transition into integration, we stopped teaching, building and producing as a collective. We had more Black owned businesses per capita during segregation than we have now. Are our youth aware of this? Do they know that during the industrial revolution the original people made several inventions and contributions that are being used to this day? See they (the oppressors) continue daily to teach our children that they are useless, helpless, and defenseless people. This is being done through our educational systems and mass media. We can't continue to allow our children to be miseducated by these poorly run schools and this filth on television.

"I am not one who was born in the possession of knowledge;
I am one who is fond of antiquity, and earnest in seeking it there." – Confucius

You will find other cultural groups rearing their children with education and history. For example the Jewish culture have rites of passage ceremonies for their children entering adolescence called Bar and Bat Mitzvah's. This is why the Nation of Gods and Earths is so important to Black people because we are the only ones that exercise the *proper* rites of passage for our people. Why the only ones? Because we aren't simply doing ceremonies for adulthood. We are teaching young men and women to become what the entire world demands of them, to fulfill their existence as God and Earth. It starts from the very beginning. When one is interested in the knowledge of himself there will be someone available to educate and train them. They will have to be prepared to face other Gods who will examine them regularly on their degrees of knowledge. And if one is not prepared in his degrees, he should be ready to receive some backlash for it because this is not a game or a joke. Our people are in a terrible condition right now and only the ones that are thoroughly qualified will be able to reverse this horrible trend. Each one teaches one. Steel sharpens steel.

Statistics show that children (male and female) are more successful when there is a father figure in the household. I was taught by Allah the Father that the man is the head and leader of the household. Brothers, we really need to emphasize that leadership in every household, neighborhood and street corner. I challenge you Black man to get to know the young brothers on your street. Many of us claim "we don't have time" or are just afraid of approaching them because of what they do or the way they look. Many of these young men that get involved in illegal activity are not doing it because they saw their favorite rapper on TV stuntin. Many of them are put in a situation at an early age to contribute financially for their families. So they do what they gotta do. You will be amazed how intelligent, talented and gifted these young men are if you get to know them.

"The Field is the world; the good seed are the children of the kingdom"
Jesus, according to Matthew 13:38

When Allah the Father left the mosque he did not stop and rest. He kept building. He had understanding. He saw that our wealth lied within the youth so he began teaching them. Many of these young men did not have fathers present in their lives. The ones who were fortunate to meet and "walk" with the Father saw him as a father figure. The one thing he didn't do was chastise them and make them feel small for who they were. He knew they were the greatest and the cream of the earth. When he finally left them in the physical form the ones that were most qualified transitioned into being the Father and taught the ones underneath them.

18. What is the duty of a civilized person?
Ans. The duty of a civilized person is to teach he who is savage, civilization, righteousness, the knowledge of himself, the science of everything in life, which is love, peace and happiness.

It is the nature of the original man to be God. However there are degrees of the growth and development of the original man. The same way before a tomato becomes an edible fruit, it was first a seed planted into the fertile soil. Then it grew into a plant and the plant produced the perfect tomato. We as adult men must plant that proper seed into our boys so they can develop into the perfect man. In a child's early stages of life they are a reflection of the ones that are closest to them. So they need that example and guidance from us in order to learn and grow.

You see we (The Original People) are the Fathers and Mothers of civilization. Any educated person or scholar (black or white) will acknowledge that. Have you ever taken the time to think that maybe the reason the world is so chaotic right now is because the original people as a whole are not in the proper leadership roles globally to make major decisions? However we must be prepared for these roles. And it starts by taking back our communities and educating our youth.

"Children are the greatest sufferers from outgrown theologies." - Luther Burbank

The best thing that I can do for my daughter besides raise her properly is to teach these young brothers out here. So when she is old enough to start her own family there will be a strong, intelligent, and righteous Black man out there to protect and guide her. THERE IS NOT A MYSTERY GOD! If we don't Introduce Science, Law, Arts and Mathematics to our youth our future will be taken away from us and we will fall victim into the hands of the enemy (the end of me).

Born King Allah has had knowledge of self since 1997. The same year, Born received his Bachelor's degree in Business Management from Georgia Tech University in Atlanta, where he was also a letterman and a member of the 1990 National Championship football team. Currently, Born works as Director of Sales for the third largest commercial bakery company in America. However his passion is working with the youth. From 1998-2001, Born was also Assistant Director at Centro Mater youth center in Miami, Florida. He now serves as Executive Director of Show and Prove Youth Outreach which is a nonprofit organization geared towards educating and guiding Atlanta's at-risk youth.

SAVE THE BABIES
C'BS Alife Allah - New Heaven (New Haven, CT)

Here are fifty things that one can do to assist in the growth and development of the youth in one's community.

1. Make time for them.
2. Listen to them.
3. If you are bi-lingual, teach them a second language.
4. Teach them a trade such as carpentry, electrical work, cutting hair, or plumbing.
5. Teach them how to cook, sew, or about hygiene.
6. Teach them how to write.
7. Teach them how to research.
8. Teach them the difference between fact and opinion.
9. Encourage them to stay aware of the news (at home and abroad).
10. Walk them through 120 (Don't just "give" it to them on a piece of paper).
11. Volunteer to be a mentor/big brother/sister.
12. Teach them how to eat to live and the effect of things that go into their bodies.
13. Teach them how to walk safely through the "ghetto" (i.e., how to traverse that land).
14. Take them on trips out of the city.
15. Take them to a movie and talk about it afterwards.

16. Teach them to excel in whatever they do.
17. Spend enough time with them to recognize their weaknesses and come up with a plan together on how to overcome them.
18. Teach them about conservation whether it be on an ecological level (recycling) or on an economical level (savings).
19. Show them, by example, how to interact with all of the human families of the planet Earth no matter what ethnic group, nationality or caste.
20. Teach them history and show the connection between the past and present.
21. Perform science experiments with them that relate to 120.
22. Teach them the difference between male and Man...female and Woman.
23. Buy them a book, have them read it and then discuss it with them.
24. Show them the science of urban survival (how to stretch a minimum amount of money the maximum length, how to secure food, clothing and shelter, etc.).
25. Show them how to observe and record police misconduct in their Kingdom (community).
26. Teach them how to interact with the police.
27. Make sure that they don't become a slave to mis-economics (credit cards, loans, etc.). Make sure they pursue grants, scholarships, etc.
28. Show them how to maintain their health as a man or woman.
29. Teach them chess.
30. Encourage them to develop a specific artform (writing, drawing, music, dance, etc.) Also teach them to be responsible with the art forms' content, especially its ability to cause social change.
31. Teach them a martial art.
32. Have them walk their neighborhood in a 5 block radius so that they can know their neighborhood.
33. If you live in the "suburbs" then take them to the "ghetto." If you live in the "ghetto" then take them into the "suburbs."
34. Get them a pen pal/e-mail pal abroad in a war torn or impoverished country.
35. Challenge them to make positive things happen in their neighborhoods.
36. Show them how to produce something (soap, candles, paper, t-shirts, books, etc.).
37. Take them to the children's ward at the hospital and have them interact with the children there to teach them compassion.
38. Teach them the difference between wants and needs.
39. Teach them the difference between imagination and illusion.
40. Teach them to stand on their Square for what is right and you won't have to worry about them falling for that which is wrong.
41. Teach them to take responsibility for success and failure.
42. Teach them to avoid the symptoms of becoming religious.

43. Teach them how to think for themselves so that they will love Self and respect Self and won't search for themselves in others.
44. Teach them how to find the best part in any person, place or thing.
45. Teach them how to find all of the free services in their Kingdom.
46. Teach them not to take things on face value.
47. Teach them the science of a strong family unit (man, woman, child) especially if they don't have their own.
48. Teach them that the Blackman is God and that the Blackwoman is Earth through example and not through philosophies, theologies, rhetoric, etc.
49. Listen to them.
50. Make time for them.

THE SWORD MY SON
Khalik Allah - Lord's Island (Long Island, NY)

What's in me
is gonna be in my son.
I'm heavy confident
and of heavy consequence,
but enough about me
in these letters,
what of the Law?
I'll give you gold to hold,
and the Law for your right hand.
I was generous and the gold was plenty.
You want both hands to hold it, but if you drop the Law you'll fall.
And when I see him I'll say "Son this is what you did,"
and tell him my stories,
and tell him what
I wrote in his DNA.
I'll have him study theory
and develop strategy
and how to manipulate
his own thoughts
in order to master six.
I'll remind him of the
unbreakable rules of life
that need to be surfaced
from his DNA and magnified
upon by his Father.
I'll keep him from the city gates.
Far from there, he'll maintain
his umbilical cord

to the Earthly Mother.
There I'll teach him
about the Sun
and about Breathing,
about Water and Soil.
There he'll remain
in a small house
spending most days
studying nature
and training
in the art of God.
And after he
understands
his parents,
I'll introduce
him to evil.
I'll tell him
about man
and the
nature of
him.

I'll introduce him to the ugliness of the world
and question his decisions and hypothetical positions.
Upon success over six, success in sound wisdom and judgment,
his determined idea will be revealed and he'll leave.
The glory of my life will be that I shall rejoice if he ever returns.

Khalik Allah received Knowledge of Self as a 14-year-old. He is currently a Junior at Five Towns College, pursuing a Bachelor of Arts degree in Film. Khalik has filmed and directed a number of short films and music videos for artists such as Lord Jamar and members of the Wu Tang Clan. His most recent work is a documentary titled *Popa Wu: A 5% Story*, which is scheduled for release in Summer 2009. Khalik has also observed the raw foods lifestyle since 2006.

27 LESSONS

Sci-Honor Devotion - Born Power Truth (Bridgeport, CT)

As parents we always want the best for our children and this list of 27 things has helped me to be able to see clearly what my focus should be when raising my own children both of whom I love with all my heart and to whom I give all that I have and all within my power to make sure that they are standing firm on a strong foundation. 27 is significant in that it breaks down to Wisdom/God, which borns Born. Sharing the Wisdom of God with your babies will Born or show forth great results...always.
I can't stress these points enough...

1. Let us teach our babies from the time of conceptual thought who they are and their origin in this world and beyond.
2. Give them mighty names and the knowledge of their names so that they begin to build great character and self esteem.
3. Teach them their strong legacy and all of the power that they hold.
4. Teach them pride and humility so that they will desire to constantly learn about themselves.
5. Show them why knowledge is the key and the foundation, making them see that knowledge is infinite and that in order for them to gain the knowledge necessary for survival, they must not depend on school alone.
6. Teach them the value of their mental and physical temples and how to care for them, protect them and how to eat to live.
7. Teach them how to have respect for themselves and for others.
8. Teach them about honesty and the truth, so that they will know that the truth will always shine through.
9. Teach them gratitude and appreciation, so that they never take the jewels of life for granted.
10. Teach them that Justice is real and that there are rewards and penalties for all actions and thoughts.
11. Teach them discipline and how to be responsible for their ways, words and actions, while being prepared for whatever justice (reward or penalty) comes their way.
12. Teach them basic manners and how to be good communicators so that they may be able to solve conflict without killing each other.
13. Teach them integrity and how to stand firm on their squares while setting standards and living up to those standards.
14. Teach them the value of keeping their word and what the term "Word is Bond" really means and how much weight it holds.
15. Teach them patience, yet, show them how to be diligent and how to endure while striving for excellence, maximizing on their power and not settling for less. Perseverance is to be honored.
16. Teach them what "true" peace is and the value behind our verbal greeting.
17. Guide them to freedom, so that they know what they are striving for.
18. Teach them discernment and dissection so that seeing things clearly will come to them easily.
19. Teach them self-control and how to handle their emotions, to be in tune with their feelings and how to be logical thinkers.
20. Teach them the science of balance and how to maintain when walking the line and knowing the ledge.
21. Teach them to work for themselves and to never let anyone get rich off of their labor while they receive no gold.

22. Teach our sons what their roles will be when they are the kings of their families and how to be fathers. Teach our daughters what their roles will be when they are the Queens of their families and how to be mothers. These skills are best taught when watching us, the parents in these roles, fulfilling and mastering our duties.
23. Teach them the science of community and that they have a family outside of their immediate ciphers.
24. Provide them with love, peace and happiness.
25. Teach them their "infiniteness," "eternalness," and "limitlessness."
26. Teach them who God is, so that they waste no time searching.
27. Lastly, but not least, give them the mathematical keys to the universe so that they may enter any door when we aren't there to guide them.

I build because the babies are the greatest.

PROTECT YOUR COMMUNITY
Born Justice Allah - Pelan (Bronx, NY)

I'm a Black man who lives and work in the Bronx. Working to make a living is one thing, however I also work within my community to make a difference. I have done this by creating a mentoring program. This is my mission in life and it should the same for all Black men living in communities that need help.

As Black men, we have the obligation to serve and to protect the community that we live in. The word "community" means family, and within one's family we communicate and show unity with our family.

It is the duty of the Black man to protect his community (family) by serving the young people with wise words of wisdom. Better yet, be a mentor to our youth to guide them in the right direction towards getting a good education so that they can obtain a good job and so that they can live in a good community when they get older to raise their family in peace. We as Black men and fathers believe in the infinite potential of our youth. Our commitment is to provide them with the resources and support system necessary for them to realize and achieve their goals and dreams. Negative societal influences create a tremendous amount of pressure for our young children. To save our community, we (Black men) must create a program that recognizes this fact and combat this growing epidemic with the following strategies:

1. Identifying and building a young person's strengths to establish and enhance their self-value

2. Partnering with educational and community resources to monitor and identify best practice models and trends for servicing youth
3. Introducing concepts of self-reflection and critical thinking to encourage responsible decision making, as well as enhancing the awareness of behavioral consequences
4. Fostering an understanding of community, economic development, government and politics, and media

We know that proper and correct decisions are based on proper and correct knowledge. It is our desire to see our young people successful in all that they do. With our help, they will SURVIVE the gangs, the gun violence, and all the other problems that are killing our young people daily. So Black man, yes you, go make a difference in your COMMUNITY.

Please Educate All our Children with Equal LOVE.

Born Justice Allah, 55, was born in Harlem, NY in 1953. The lessons he learned on the streets would equal a degree in street knowledge. His upbringing in Harlem taught him how to not only be a survivor, but also how to have the strength to endure the pressures of life. Due to ill-made decisions, Mr. Allah was incarcerated for a few years. However, the immense desire to turn this negativity around is what empowered him to fight against gang and gun violence through speaking with young people. As a result, in February of 2005, Born Justice Allah founded a nonprofit organization called Positive Seeds in Pelan, Inc. Since then, the Positive Seeds initiative has served many children through action-oriented and effective after-school endeavors. Mr. Allah's other experience includes working with youth in the Salvation Army group home, a women's homeless shelter, a family living center, and most recently with Green For All, a national organization dedicated to building an inclusive green economy strong enough to lift people out of poverty.

RESPONSIBILITY
RESPONDING TO YOUR ABILITY
Islord ShaSun Allah - SunCity (Cincinnati, OH)

In our communities today there is one situation that adults are not addressing: Giving back to the same environments they grew up in. So the question is, why is it that we don't give back? What part of the puzzle is missing that keeps us from recognizing our duties as elders in our community?

"The love of individual freedom has stood in the way of the appreciation of social obligations." - Gora

As a youth I watched adults go out of their way to accommodate and be part of the lives of young people, providing them a better opportunity for engagement in society. There were also adults that have consistently made excuses for not getting involved. What I have found is that, in the process of "living life," many have forgotten about who they are, producing a disconnection with the youth of today. This drifting away from self and the community has caused them to be blind to what the true problem is. Many adults I have come across blame the youth for society's problems, justifying their failure to give back. All the time, I hear someone say: "Those youth are ignorant. I don't see how you do it. They don't listen to anybody. All they want to do is smoke weed, fight, sell drugs and get into trouble, etc."

I respond by asking, "How were you as an adolescent? Did you get into trouble and ever sell or try drugs? Did you ever act ignorant?" Some of these things you may not have gotten into, but at the same time you were once a young adult and at some time or another you did get into things you weren't supposed to.

In the growing process we experiment with the lessons of life, learning right from wrong and good from bad. No one is immune to these trials of growing up. I often ask religious people, "Was Jesus a perfect man?" The most common response is, "Yes, he was the shining example for us all to follow." I answer with more questions: "How do you know that for sure? In the Bible all you know of Jesus' history is when he was a child and then when he was an adult. What happened in the middle (adolescence) period of his life? How was he as a teenager?"

We have become disconnected from the next generation, programmed to forget about our own. Most importantly, we've forgotten the learning curve of youth. We automatically assume that maturity comes with age, when in reality we should all know better. We know that maturity comes with life experiences. There is a saying, "Experience is the best teacher." Everyone in this world goes through life experiences, but how many of us are teaching ourselves and learning from these experiences? Not many, because some continue to make the same mistakes over and over again leading me to ask the question, "Are we paying attention?" It astounds me how some of the youth that I have met may only be 18, but have a greater sense of maturity than some people I know in their 30's. Why is that? It is because some take their experiences seriously and some do not. Some have been taught how to learn from their experiences, and others have not.

The word response means "something said or done in answer or reply to an action." The word ability means "being able or having the power to do something mentally or physically." Now, are we not liable for what happens in our children's future? We have seen what can happen to this generation without guidance, so why don't we get up off our asses and do something about it? Oh I forgot, we are scared of them right? That's ridiculous! One thing I've learned since getting knowledge of self at 22, was that all young people need is information and someone who cares about their growth and development. I am now 35, and since I opened Elementz, a hiphop youth arts center, four years ago, I've been granted an incredible learning opportunity. I've seen so many young men and women come through the doors of Elementz with all types of trials and tribulations in their lives. Some are extremely aggressive, while others have very passive-aggressive behaviors. The world likes to label these youth "at risk," but as adult are we taking the "risk" to set things straight? I have lost some of these youth to murder and prison, but in the time that I've spent with them they were all genuine human beings. Some of these youth may seem to like fighting and causing problems in society, but they are all still human, just like you and I. I have learned that all they need is a relative ear. What is relative you ask? Simply a person who will listen and provide advice in their time of need. Someone who can be nonjudgmental and understand that you were once in their shoes. Maybe not to the same extreme, but you've been there. Someone who can "relate."

As a gardener of life, I continue to plant the seeds of life within these youth. With that comes patience, because one that plants a seed today cannot expect a flower tomorrow. Having knowledge of self has helped me become a better teacher, as the way our education is structured is one of the greatest methods to relaying information. This is the way I relay ideas to the youth as well. A lot of children are being taught in one style, but our learning processes are all different, and that's why some drop out of school. No one actually takes the time out to get into their world and learn them as a person, and this is the problem with most adults. They want to tell them something and expect them to change immediately but this cannot happen. Only a small percentage of youth can immediately grasp what's being taught and make rapid change. Others will take time. With this being said, I have seen, over the years, so many youth being transformed in some shape or form. It is refreshing, to say the least, to see it happen and know that hard work does pay off.

So elders, you must have patience and also learn adaptive teaching strategies. Let me give you one example of what I'm talking about: One of my youth loves basketball and one sells drugs. Now how do I get into the mind of these two and make the information relative? All I do is speak their language (with a scientific mind), so all the terms I use with the basketball player will be from the court and the terms I use with the other will be from the street corner's point of view. Now once you have gotten in their minds, the possibilities become endless. Yet to do so, you must be able to relate.

To get back to our responsibility as elders we must realize that nothing is impossible. We can and must give back to our youth. It is our responsibility and no one else's. Stop feeding your children to this wild beast of a society. You must not be afraid to save their lives. Fear is our number one enemy because it keeps us from learning (or even wanting) to bring about change in ourselves, our youth, and our community.

We can all learn from each other, young or old, and become more mature and conscious to how the world around us is made up, as well as the circumstances it presents to those who walk its many paths. In exploring this, we will find the keys to unlock the doors of misconception and "respond to our ability" to fulfill our responsibility.

Remember the word youth…because the root word of it is you!!!

Islord Shasun Allah is a 36-year-old entrepreneur, hip-hop mogul, and community worker. He studied developmental psychology at the University of Cincinnati. Islord is a longtime business owner in the OTR community, with a barbershop called Sun City, and is currently the Chief Operating Officer of Elementz Hip Hop Youth Arts Center, which recently celebrated its 4th anniversary. Elementz' mission is to engage and inspire inner-city youth using innovative arts programs, leadership development and community building. Elementz serves over 900 youth a month. Islord plans to franchise Hip-Hop Youth Centers across the country.

TO BE OR BORN THE EARTH
Eboni Joy Asiatic Earth - Allah's Garden (Atlanta, GA)

We Earths refer to ourselves as such because as the original (Indigenous) women of this planet all human life was spawned from our womb; just as all life on the planet earth was born from her habitable properties – an extended water supply that is drinkable, oxygenated, and supports the generation and stability of cellular structures, large land masses, moderate temperatures, a breathable atmosphere, volcanic conditions, and gravitation. These characteristics of our home planet can all be either literally or figuratively applied to the first home of man – his mother – because we original women's bodies are naturally created suitable for habitation, as is the land and water of the planet Earth. This is why we honorably carry the same name, because we bear many of our home planet's traits and shoulder many of the equal responsibilities.

There are 75 billion tons of biomass (living matter) on our planet, including humans, plants, animals, fungi, protests, archaea and bacteria. The total weight of the planet is 6 sextillion tons. The planet Earth reflects, refracts, and absorbs the light of the sun. There are seven continents (large divisions of land mass) on the planet and five oceans (large bodies of salt water that cover nearly three fourths of the earth's surface). Of the planet's entire mass, 57,255,000 square miles of it is land, and 139,685,000 square miles are water. With all of these terrestrial beings and objects inhabiting the planet, a great weight of responsibility comes with it. The planet is accountable for maintaining the rotation of its satellite, the moon, through the reciprocal gravitational pull of both celestial bodies, as the planet itself is attracted to the sun due to it having the most powerful gravitational force in the solar system. The earth is responsible for continuing to rotate around the sun while simultaneously traveling at 1,037 and 1/3rd mph on its axial rotation. And the planet earth must also shelter its organic life within an atmosphere that absorbs ultraviolet solar radiation, in which temperatures remain relatively moderate, and an atmosphere in which water that evaporates cannot escape the troposphere, and instead, distills back to the planet as water or ice to replenish her natural resources. The role of the Earth is neither simple nor limited.

So how is it that a mortal woman can define herself as one as mighty as our home planet? While we original Asiatic Black women are one with the Earth because we possess a womb perfectly organized to give birth to humanity. Our life-bearing properties don't stop there, however. Before producing milk, our breasts secrete colostrum that provides our children with the immunoglobin, an antibody needed to fight bacteria and viruses until their own immune system becomes fully functioning, colostrum also coats their gastrointestinal track to help expel meconium (an infant's first stool composed of materials ingested while in the uterus) and prevent jaundice. Soon, our breast milk flows, and that provides every nutrient needed to sustain a growing infant's life, including protein, fats, carbohydrates, vitamins, minerals, digestive enzymes, and hormones. Breast milk is also a natural vaccination, providing antibodies that help infants and toddlers resist infection. In the meantime, while nurturing our children with their first nutritious meal, we are getting them acclimated to the world around them – teaching them all about their environment and how to survive in it with a high quality of life. Can you see the perfection in that process?

As sisters with knowledge of self, who are aware of our origins in this world and labor to regain our civilization, our role of Earth is greatest displayed in our rearing of the babies, however, it is not limited to that role alone. We are held accountable for living in accord to Supreme Mathematics and the moral, ethical principles that the math entails. By living the math, portraying it in our ways and actions, verbalizing it in our wise choice of words, we become living examples of earthliness and show forth the power of God by reflecting knowledge of self in the physical, as stated above, through wise words, ways and actions, and in righteous deeds. We reflect God, the Asiatic Black man with knowledge of self, as the moon reflects the light of the sun, showing that the sun always shines by teaching knowledge of self and the science of life to those who have yet to be mentally born. An Earth is a teacher to the physical seeds, our babies, and the mental seeds, those brothers and sisters who are not yet as intelligent and wise as we. Yes, we original women with knowledge of self bear life physically, though we also present the truth to and exchange knowledge and wisdom with all human families, birthing them out of a mental death, thus we are life-bearers in the mental sense as well.

Being an Earth means being the best woman that you can possibly be, being a mother to the young, a role model to those yet to reach their full maturity, and first and foremost a student, sister, and wife to Allah God – the original (Indigenous) man with knowledge of himself as the supreme being in the universe and who lives in agreement with that truth. Sisters live out the culture of Supreme Mathematics in many different ways. We, as a nation, have our agreed upon restrictions – no pork, no marrying/mating with Caucasians. Outside of that, we are free to live our culture through the proper application of the math. How I choose to be Earth in comparison to how my sister chooses to be Earth may be vastly different. In having knowledge of self we are required to see and acknowledge our best parts, poor parts, and worst parts – refine the poor parts into useful land and destroy the worst parts of our character and behavior, being re-born as a true and living Earth.

In January of 1997, a sister-friend of mine first showed me the Supreme Mathematics. She had written down the principles and their basic meaning, her unique understanding of them in regards to her personality, emotional state, and also related them to her zodiac sign. I was immediately attracted to the math. In retrospect, I know it was because the principles that composed it had been ingrained in me throughout my childhood. They fell right in line with my own inherent and learned value system, and quenched my undying thirst for knowledge. I copied the Supreme Mathematics into my own journal, looked-up the principles in a dictionary, and added my own understanding to the dictionary's basic explanation of each axiom. I meditated on each word, to see how the axioms could collectively help to enlighten me and strengthen my moral code.

This attraction to the truth led me to the Gods in C-Medina (Chicago), who aided in my growth and development into a true and living Earth. My desire to be the best woman I could be, one knowledgeable of history and culture, and wise to my role as a Queen, is what compelled me to study my lessons so that I could learn, live, and understand the purpose they served. My stance as an atheist for 7 years led up to my meeting the Gods, and promoted my ability to accept the reality of God in person as the original Asiatic Black man. My educator, Cincur Allah continued to test my knowledge and understanding as I progressed through my studies of the 120 Lessons, never holding my hand, ensuring that I was about this culture for the message, not the messenger, for knowledge and understanding of self, not to master the Black man. He did, however, remain a constant guide and source of reference through my journey into Earthdom. The Gods I was around allowed me to be a self-evaluator, and to refine in my own due time, once I saw that certain aspects of my physical (be it dress or behaviors) were not on the same level as my mental development.

It was me who determined when the time was right to evolve from civilized to completely righteous. Not a single God told me to wrap my head; it was a conscious choice of my own making. And none of them had to suggest that I go natural. I didn't have to be convinced not to eat pork, because I had been a vegetarian for almost 5 years when I came into the knowledge of Supreme Mathematics and started doing my part to build Allah's World Manifest. My interests were Black history, Indigenous cultures, and holistic health. The book I was reading when I met the Gods was *Metu Neter*.

You see, I had Earth in me from the start, as all original women have the potential for greatness by realizing the Earth in them. However, what the Gods also saw was my receptiveness to gaining knowledge of who the true and living God is and insight into our natural way of life. They saw my interest in the science they were sharing with me and my appreciation for knowledge of self. All of the above tells me that the universe aligned itself perfectly for me to come into the knowledge of the culture of Supreme Mathematics at just the right time, among the right people. As this was, and still is, the culture that's right for me, supports my ideologies, my moral code, my interests, this culture encouraged and strengthened my love for and dedication to all original people, and provided the necessary motivation to keep me ever-focused on my refinement and mental elevation.

I have had my hell in this, crossed paths with devils in disguise as God, using the name of Allah to shield their dirty religion; had to send back sisters who were God groupies and amongst us for the man rather than the plan. However, I chose to keep the best part preserved for myself knowing that there is no unrighteousness in the true and living. I kept my focus on being among those brothers and sisters who I could study amongst, learn from, and manifest with. My constant goal in having knowledge of self has been the achievement of supreme enlightenment, and knowing the truth of God has enabled me to continue being led in the right direction, never misled by outside forces. I traveled among the Gods and Earths, and with knowledge of self was born again as an Earth for the knowledge, wisdom, and understanding that Supreme Mathematics and 120 Lessons presented to me.

This culture and our lessons have led me to the study of so many other sciences, cultures, and righteous aspects of life, that I can confidently say I know what the meaning of life is because I know and understand who I am – a Nation Builder adding to positive productivity of the collective; a Poor Righteous Teacher leading by example with the knowledge of when to be the teacher and when it's time to take the role of student, maintaining a chaos-free existence by treating people how I want to be treated; and a True and Living Earth: "True," because I heed the truth once aware of it, also because I'm honest to others and myself (even if it means seeing the poor parts of me). And "Living," because living means to be seen and heard, and this culture is in everything I express, from my topics of conversation, to my dress, hairstyle, lack of make-up, vegan diet, to my continued studies of Indigenous people throughout the Diaspora to show and prove our likeness and destroy the differences that have perpetrated our division...all of this is how I live my culture as an Earth.

Eboni Joy Asiatic originates from Chicago (righteously named C-Medina), and has been residing in Atlanta (or Allah's Garden) working as a childcare provider, vegan caterer, community activist, and facilitating educational workshops in health and wellness, early childhood development, and political education since August 2006. She has been published in several literary anthologies, and has been a staff writer/editor of *The 14th Degree and Beyond* magazine and blog (http://14thDegree.blogspot.com) for which she has been contributing articles and poems since 1999.

FOR THE REVOLUTIONARIES
Sunez Allah - Mecca (Harlem, NY)

For the self-proclaimed revolutionary of today, it is all about anti-capitalism. Capitalism, the oppressor's most powerful weapon of choice, is seen as the cause of all of today's ills. However, oversimplifications and shallow condemnations provide little support for actual development. Understanding what capitalism impedes - and what must be promoted - are crucial to becoming a true revolutionary *con Lavoe de revolt* for the masses.

Referring to the 120 lessons as a pedagogical guide will reveal the nature of capitalism more profoundly. The 18th degree in the 1-40, Lost and Found Muslim Lesson No. 2, says:

Q. What is the duty of a civilized person?
Ans. The duty of a civilized person is to teach, he who is savage civilization, righteousness, the knowledge of himself and the science of everything in life which is love, peace and happiness.

Along with what is taught by the civilized person, we must also notice the order by which the teachings are shared. To begin, civilization is revealed. Thus, we must examine our present conditions. In our capitalistic society, the betterment of society (known as "civilization") is actually of no concern, as capitalism's own flaws are not dealt with (i.e. increased poverty, destruction of resources). To properly teach civilization we must show how our own ancient civilizations (i.e. Kemet, the Moorish empires, the Olmec civilization, etc.) were as advanced, if not more so, than today's capitalistic society.

Secondly, the civilized person shares righteousness. As capitalism is revealed corrupt, the possibilities of alternatives arise. Here, most of our conscious brothers and sisters embrace an anarchist approach. This acknowledges the problem but does not reveal what has actually been lost. Other alternatives such as a socialist and/or communist revolution are offered. Still, it is not clearly stated what must be regained. Often this is the end of the exploration, yet "righteousness" manifests in sharing tools that promote understanding the principles of self-development. Once one is engaging in the activities that rid him/her of following a destructive system, the nature of their own ideals begin to be manifested.

Now the civilized person shares a Knowledge of Self. Knowledge of self is a complete, ever developing awareness of oneself. "Who are you?" is answered so you actually may know "what you can do?" Capitalism is a mandatory exchange of goods or legal tender for the necessities and/or luxuries needed or desired. In realizing civilization (i.e. the enlightenment attained by former civilizations), activating a righteousness (wisdom/intelligent activity), the natural accumulation of self-awareness - which has been depressed by capitalist exploitation - must be repaired.

The natural relationship of life is sharing (interdependence and exchange). The creator shares creation and all things follow this universal law. This is also done through us sharing our talents, insights, and experiences, with utmost sincerity for the betterment of self and others. The 'love of a revolutionary' is here, where enlightenment of that one contradictory force to oppression is actualized. This revolution takes place only when the natural accumulation humanity undergoes is recognized and embraced as virtue. Virtue is seen when the revolutionary is using the tools around him/her to build models and forums to reveal and promote self-awareness and social enrichment. This is not accomplished by force, as such an attempt is as wasteful as demanding change of the oppressor (refer to Paulo Friere's *The Pedagogy of the Oppressed*).

Real masters can use the tools of the oppressor to reveal their supreme nature, exposing the oppressor's "devilishment" as a byproduct. With capitalism, there is a difference between being able to buy whatever you want, and being able to fund each and every idea one has (for the betterment of the community). Even without immediate access to such tools, mastering capitalism as the latter is the right way.

How is capitalism manipulated (or transformed)? How are the righteous principles we've found in socialism and other peaceful/equitable systems instilled? How do Original people "find" themselves and build community, merging the right AND the exact? *This* is the beginning of the Science of Everything in Life. Peace!

Sunez Allah is an accomplished writer, editor, radio personality and lecturer. With over 15 years of experience as an editor and writer in the magazine, book, and newspaper mediums, he has published and/or presented over 280 articles, biographies, scholarly notes and lessons. He is one of few to serve as editor/writer for *The Source, XXL, Vibe Magazine* and countless other publications. He is the COO of Thuro-Publishing, a division of Thuro-Media, Inc., and Editor-In-Chief of its published journal, *Lavoe Revolt.* An avid martial artist, Sunez holds a Black sash in Northern and Southern Shaolin Kung Fu from Grandmaster Sigung Bobby Whitaker. He is a lifetime disciple and instructor of the wholistic healing arts and the Perfection of 180 Moves. Sunez has taught the P.E.A.C.E. course at Allah School in Mecca since 2000.

PEDAGOGY OF THE FIVE PERCENT

CITATION
Dass, S. K. (2006). *Pedagogy of the Five Percent: Education in the Nation of Gods and Earths.* Unpublished doctoral dissertation, Argosy University, Atlanta.

ABSTRACT
The Nation of Gods and Earths and its pedagogy represent an understudied, yet significant area deserving investigation in urban educational research. The purpose of this study was to examine the perspectives of members of the NGE on education in both the traditional school system and in the NGE. The researcher also sought to identify the pedagogical practices of the NGE within the theoretical framework of nonformal education. This qualitative study used semi-structured interview data from 13 participants situated throughout the eastern United States. The results of the subsequent analysis indicate that many of the shortcomings of the traditional educational system in serving at-risk Black youth are being met by the nonformal pedagogy of the Nation of Gods and Earths.

SUMMARY OF FINDINGS
1. Involvement in the NGE introduces one to a learning community that also functions as a support network or family group.
2. Self-instruction is an integral facet of education in the NGE.
3. The NGE provides a culturally responsive alternative to the Eurocentric curriculum of the traditional school system.
4. The NGE often attracts learners through exemplars who possess a number of attractive qualities as a result of involvement.
5. Involvement in the NGE involves the affirmation of dialogue as means towards *conscientization.*
6. The curriculum of the traditional educational system is often perceived as inherently Eurocentric and oppressive.
7. The traditional educational system's ideology and instructional philosophy do not meet or address the needs of disadvantaged Black youth.

8. The traditional education system is not comprehensive because, in delivering the standard curriculum, traditional education does not sufficiently address non-curricular issues that negatively affect student outcomes.
9. The ideology and curriculum of the NGE is attractive to many Black youth who find themselves dissatisfied with the traditional educational canon.
10. Education in the NGE is intrinsically motivational, and drives one to study and engage in pedagogical practice without any extrinsic incentive.
11. Education in the NGE is comprehensive because, in addition to addressing "Knowledge of Self," the NGE reinvents, remediates, and/or supplements the learning available in the formal system.
12. Involvement in the NGE instills in members a sense of purpose and agency in helping and educating others.
13. Involvement in the NGE increased members' sense of responsibility and accountability.
14. Involvement in the NGE developed intrinsic motivation in members to achieve their highest potential.
15. Involvement in the NGE gave legitimacy to education where it had previously been absent.

THE P.E.A.C.E. COURSE
Sunez Allah - Mecca (Harlem, NY)

Over forty years have passed since Father Allah established today's Nation of God and Earth and its first school, Allah School in Mecca. Propelled by the famous quote, "The Babies are the greatest!" the youth are the primary focus in the education of our foremost institution. To note, our nation is not one based on a society, backed by an enforcing government, sequestering land and riches. Rather, it is one of enlightened families actualizing their birthright of identity, proven mathematically and scientifically, where the Original man is God and the Original woman is Earth. Naturally being themselves, our pedagogical premise is on reaching the deeper reality of education's meaning. As revealed by its etymological root, *educare*, meaning to "draw out that which is within." Fulfilling the true promise of education, our science of teaching is in simply showing our people whom they really are.

While being a teacher of truth can be seen as a duty, it is best manifest as an honor, by fulfilling one's nature to truly share what is needed and not merely appeasing a spiritual debt. A poor, righteous teacher is one who is willing to sacrifice everything he has to share a truth that may better others. Thus, our truths, self evident to us, are presented as unconditional offerings to the young for their complete, unbiased testing.

Ironically, most essential to the framework of successfully sharing a curriculum we know is true, is the constant testing of all tradition, the denial of following any doctrine, and allowing for new ideas to become tomorrow's development. This pedagogy is humbly exemplified in the course I have been honored to instruct at the root of civilization, Allah School in Mecca.

Traditionally, the coursework of our Nation is simplified as "the civilization class" where a group of "newborns," are newly introduced to the knowledge of themselves as revealed through our major teachings of Supreme Mathematics, its accompanying Alphabet and the 120 lessons. The instructor would normally be the "enlightener" whom, in having revealed this knowledge to the newborn, has taken the duty to guide him or her through the process of living the teachings out with understanding. Sessions would include memorization of the lessons, accompanying techniques and exercises, historical sources referenced primarily from "plus lessons" (essays from older Gods) and works of the Honorable Elijah Muhammad.

As I have found tradition is emphatically unnecessary in conveying a truth, I have taken this notice to heart. Consequently, my course has the best part I've chosen of the "civilization class" ethic at its core, yet is a completely unique presentation of my experience, resources and sincerity. Ultimately, it is only with the principles of perfection, our culture, that I have come to teach my course.

A reality that witnesses no mistakes but is wonderfully filled with lessons.

An ethos that does not pass judgment over illusionary perspectives of good or bad, but upholds justice for what is proven right, discarding all that is shown to be wrong.

A way of life that sees no endings; rather, only constant re-awakenings to the vignettes of enlightenment within us all.

These principles of Originality, Honor (the natural manner of one's word being bond) and a Full Uprightness (where each moment, intention and action demonstrates one's living understanding), are all I carry as the curriculum of every course session.

Embracing all the respectable tools of modernity to fulfill these prized principles of antiquity, the course of the Political Education And Civilization Enrichment (P.E.A.C.E.) course offers the student skills and training in dealing with the harsh hypocrisies and contradictions of the outside world and the science of everything in life.

Being that I am currently the youngest teacher of the oldest course, the details of my fulfilling this immense honor may shed some light on the nature of this distinct pedagogy. Brought to Allah School in Mecca as a newborn by Dasun Allah (whom co-founded and personally penned the title of my course) in the summer of 1999, I was, by all intent and purpose, a civilized man, with a very capable scholarly mentor in David Traverzo

Galarza, Ph.D. With a diet advanced beyond the simple refinement of "no pork" and an education to rank me successfully endowed by the preening society of riches, I sought the details of my supremacy.

At the School, I encountered the three very real sages that would aid me. To begin, Knowledge Me Allah held the civilization class I attended at this time. From him I learned the 120 lessons, their history, and the duties related to such. I often would also spend many moments observing and taking notes on the witticisms, exclamations and immense understanding of experience from First Born Prince Allah. The other moments I visited, I learned the nature of pedagogy from the immaculate street scholar, Savior Knowledge Allah, who sold (and had read) all the historical, sociological, psychological and spiritual texts we would only find in totality in the streets of Harlem, not the universities of New York City.

Knowledging, Wisdoming and Understanding Supreme Mathematics, the Supreme Alphabet and the 120 lessons, I earned my universal flag from Knowledge Me by the end of the year. I was soon thrust into applying my talents to the Nation's benefit. By the summer of 2000, I was teaching the course that stands today. Let this be a definitive proof that the Nation is not constructed in the manner of any Masonic and/or hierarchal organization. There are no "free rides" in this Nation. The merits of every man or woman are *all* that may propel them. And so they have propelled me and what I offer into the said forum.

To teach my own course, I made it personally mandatory that I would have something unique to share amidst these great sages, builders and talented minds. Along with the experience of my elder teachers, I sought understanding from those whom had taught before me, from Freedom Allah (who taught a course in mathematics) to Darkim Be Allah and Allah Sakuan. Since the inception of Allah School in Mecca with its five classes in (1) Mathematics, (2) English, (3) Arabic, (4) History, and (5) Self Defense, there have been many great teachers here. Thus this research, together with my own observations, helped form the P.E.A.C.E. course.

Regarding the course itself…The curriculum is designed to draw out the talents and immaculate uniqueness of each student whilst they learn the knowledge of themselves. Every student is told that if they do not receive knowledge (useful information) and wisdom (the tools to apply that information), so that - on their own time - they attain an understanding, they are asked to never return. This is so because there are only three things I ask of every student.

First, they must spend considerable effort in evaluating whom they choose as a teacher. The techniques they use to validate myself, other people, and all resources and experiences as worthy of instructing them, are crucial for every moment.

Second, the student must begin to articulate all that they *do not* know. Putting into words what they do not know is the art of asking the question.

When their questions are prepared, they simultaneously are properly confirming what they *do* know.

Lastly, every student I encounter is told not to believe. Belief of any sort hinders the student and makes all learning limited by making the range of our exploration finite. Being instructed not to believe is my foremost demand of every student.

For every student learning at Allah School in Mecca, it is a voluntary endeavor and as it is such, they are not simply taught what I deem acceptable or would *like* them to know. They are taught what I have best judged that they *need* to know, presented in a way that allows them to test its truthfulness and validity upon receipt. As I was taught by many of the First Born, class is to be held as long as the student is capable of receiving insight. My class has always taken place between the hours of 7 and 10 pm (previously 6-10), but they have often been known to continue throughout the night until they welcome the following Friday! Why? Every student arriving between the given hours is taught as long as necessary.

Despite this offering, every student is taught as if he will never return. Everything shared must be - to the best of the teacher's ability - a lesson of worth for the student. The independent work is always focused on the individual's needs, while the classroom lecture is guided toward the student who knows the least. Thus those students who already know a particular lesson will have a chance to both review and study pedagogy itself, as it is displayed by the teacher. It is here where the next generation of poor, righteous teachers begin their appropriate studies in the craft.

The curriculum covers all disciplines conducive to learning the knowledge of oneself. Through utilization of the root science of Supreme Mathematics as well as the Supreme Alphabet, the 120 lessons are studied as a subjective text, filled with clear facts as well as abstract reasoning and insights, requiring contemplative study and lived experience. The primary tools offered are extensive training in reading, research, writing and communication skills. As it was 40 years ago, literacy is a key focus. Today, the student will use tools necessary in modern society and may draw his own talents out of such use, if not mastering them as well. With special lessons ranging from bio-chemistry, quantum physics, the ancient esoteric texts of Asia and India, archaeology, exercise and fitness training, martial arts, health protocols and the standards of a living foods diet, the reality of God and Earth is *taught* as holistically as it truly *exists*.

In the years teaching, I have lectured over 300 students, and have come to realize that it is not the truth that we offer that is unique. Our ancient ancestors, from the magnificent architects of Kemet to the Taoists of China, from the Yogis of India to the Sufis of the Middle East, have *all* known it. All have revealed the pristine interdependence of man - *the supreme, sole controller of the universe* - and woman - the *supreme, nourishing and sustaining vessel* - living harmoniously, as mathematics - *that most definitive, completely fluid and liberating language* - beckons their nature.

The unique quality of this culture and pedagogy is that the the Father and our elders have taken this truth to the purest and simplest form - for the most savagely complex times. And unlike the sages that revealed themselves upon discovering the worthy student, we have donned our beautiful universal flags and proclaimed our divinity as a gift to be shared with all we encounter. These poignant differences are not meant to lament the greats of our past. It is to remind us all that the saviors of the people - from the past, of the present and in the future - not only *find* the truth. They develop the pedagogy that allows this liberation to be shared, embraced and used to enlighten *all*. It is my honor to love in this supreme way, the culture of the true and living. Peace.

The P.E.A.C.E. (Political Education And Civilization Enrichment) course is held at 2122 7th Avenue (126thst) in Harlem, New York every Thursday evening since 2000. The course is free to the public and open to any and all questions. Its instructor is Sunez Allah.

ᴥ 6 ᴨ
THE UNIVERSE

WHY I DON'T BELIEVE IN A MYSTERY GOD
Supreme Understanding Allah - Allah's Garden (Atlanta, GA)

Many people agree with me that the Black man is "a" god, or that he is "godly," or that we are "divine," or that God "inhabits" man (e.g., your body is a "temple of God"), or that "His" spirit is in "us." In fact, many Black preachers have spoken about the inherent divinity of man...all while proclaiming that there is a much greater God somewhere outside of man.

That's not what I'm talking about when I say "the Black man is God." I'm saying the Black man is God. I'm saying God is the Black man. I'm also saying there is NO great mysterious God floating around somewhere beyond humanity. And here are some reasons why:

"When one person suffers from a delusion, it is called insanity.
When many people suffer from a delusion it is called Religion." - Robert M. Pirsig

1. You can have a conversation with God and get bad advice. Guess who you're talking to? Yourself! Otherwise how can serial killers and psychopaths claim God told them what to do? If they aren't credible, is ANYBODY who claims to hear from God? Think about it.

"I distrust those people who know so well what God wants them to do because I notice it always coincides with their own desires." - Susan B. Anthony (1820-1906) U.S. reformer, suffragist

2. Ever noticed that people always claim they "know" God is real because they made it through some crazy situation alive? Well what about the people that don't make it? You can have a personal relationship with ANYTHING you imagine or believe in. That doesn't make it real.

"Why did god bother creating all the generations between Adam and Noah?
I mean, if he was going to kill everyone off, all the humans (men, women, innocent children and babies),
guiltless animals, and all the plants too, and HE KNEW IT IN ADVANCE,
why in the hell didn't he just start with Noah in the first place?" - Ken Harding

3. How could this Mystery God be omniscient and change his mind at whim? You mean to tell me God made man and then realized he made a mistake? Just look through the Old Testament and see how many times he changed his mind talking to Moses alone. Moses had to talk him out of a bunch of crazy sh*t. And God changes his mind in EVERY people's scriptures. Why? People make mistakes. But an all-knowing spirit? How?

"The clear light of science teaches us that we must be our own saviors."
- Luther Burbank, expressed in the pulpit of a chapel at Santa Rosa

4. If you were trying to get a life or death message to EVERYONE on the planet, would you send ONE guy (the religious "savior" or "prophet") who only reaches a couple thousand in his life, and then leave the rest up to chance?

"Unconditional love is a characteristic of the Christian faith, such as that demonstrated by God in the form of a place of eternal torture for the unsaved." - Anonymous

5. Why create a heaven and hell for people to suffer because of their choices, which were made due to the free will you also gave them? Especially when the hell we endure on earth pushes many of us to follow the "wrong" path? How much of that is "fair"? And Why can't an omnipotent God destroy the invisible devil? And if he CAN but doesn't, why does he want his poor believers to continue to suffer?

"If you were taught that elves caused rain, every time it rained, you'd see the proof of elves." - Anonymous

7. If there is a scientific explanation for everyday phenomena (i.e., rain comes from the water cycle, the reproductive process produced children), why do we still have this "backwater" concept of God, a God who sends floods and gives and takes life? It's funny to hear grown, educated people speak on their God as what wakes them up daily. How simple-minded. Either your alarm clock or biological clock wakes you. The human body sleeps to wake up! That's the nature of the biological process we call "sleep." If you don't wake up, it's because you are dead. There is no Divine Intervention necessary in that process.

"Every man thinks God is on his side. The rich and powerful know he is." - Jean Anouilh

8. God does whatever you want him to do. People love to manipulate God's actions and intentions to fit the course of events as they happen. If someone has cancer, the believers say God will bring them out of it, and so they pray. But if that person dies, the believers say it was "their time" and "God knows best." C'mon now. If you pray for rent money, and get some money, you thank God. But if you don't get your money, YOU take the blame and believe God will do something else instead.

"The spectacle of what is called religion, or at any rate organized religion, in India and elsewhere, has filled us with horror, and I have frequently condemned it and wished to make a clean sweep of it." - Jawaharlal Nehru, Prime Minister of India

9. How does an omnipotent God allow so much evil and bloodshed to occur specifically in his name? I mean, it's one thing to let people kill and enslave, but why let people do it in your name?

"Religion. It's given people hope in a world torn apart by religion." - Jon Stewart, The Daily Show

10. Why does the same God allow for so many religions to exist (many of which predate the Bible), and even so many different versions of the Bible and Christian theology? Can't he just send his one true religion into our

brains? If the idea is that we must choose (free will), shouldn't God provide better evidence? Jesus was a great guy, but the Christian church also ordained slavery. Not very convincing. And there are tons of people who have never seen a Bible or Quran or any other scripture to this day, not to mention the billions of people who came BEFORE the organized theologies of the present age. What about them? And for those of you who believe God likes to "test" people, how come you'd let an invisible being play games with your life, but not a man or woman you're dating? Why the double standards? It makes sense because they're invisible?

"Gods are children's blankets that get carried over into adulthood." - James Randi

11. If we know Santa Claus is a myth with a purpose (behavioral control of children), why can't we conclude the same for the Mystery God (behavioral control of the masses)? As Bill Maher once said:

When you were a kid and they were telling you whatever you believe in religion, do you think if they had switched the fairy tales that they read to you in bed with the Bible, you would know the difference? Do you think if it was the fairy tale about a man who lived inside of a whale and it was religion that Jack built a beanstalk today, you would know the difference? Why do you believe in one fairy tale and not the other? Just because adults told you it was true and they scared you into believing it, at pain of death, at pain of burning in hell.

"Religion is excellent stuff for keeping common people quiet." - Napoleon Bonaparte

12. Isn't it curious that poor and disenfranchised people are the most religious? Meanwhile wealthy white folks don't wait for, or give credit to, God on ANYTHING. White folks go to church for SOCIAL reasons. The people that have the LEAST, pray the MOST. Hmmm. Everyone knows you can't get SOMETHING from NOTHING...except religious people. Religion is the ultimate pyramid scheme.

"People go to church for the same reasons they go to a tavern: to stupefy themselves, to forget their misery, to imagine themselves, for a few minutes anyway, free and happy." - Mikhail A. Bakunin (1814-1876)

13. Karl Marx said religion is the opium of the masses. We escape into believing in something that will one day relieve us of our daily suffering. Especially when you think about slavery and the religious ideas given to the slaves, and the religion given to people when white people take over their land.

14. Freud said religion provides an idealized "father figure" for people. Maybe you believe in a Mystery God because you need a better daddy, or a better "man." That would explain all the "Heavenly Father" and "Married to Jesus" references. But what about when he doesn't come through for you? How can you get over it so easily...but not with anyone else?

"No one saves us but ourselves, no one can and no one may."
- the Dhammapada of Siddhartha Gautama, one of many Buddhas

15. White people fear the rise of a "Black Messiah" from the ghetto (according to COINTELPRO documents). Black people are awaiting a

white Messiah from heaven. How dumb. Look in the mirror. You ARE the Son of Man.

16. In all history, the Black man has never seen, heard, smelled, tasted, or felt ANYTHING greater than himself. Ever. So good luck hunting.

17. Everything in the universe is caused by the Sun of Man/Son of Man. We are the creators of life and the universe. We wrote the universe in a language that perpetuates itself and there is nothing that occurs outside of our original programming. Knowing that, it's hard for me to give credit to something out of a fairy tale.

18. If you leave a group of kids in the woods and allow them to raise themselves without outside information, they WON'T pray or wait on a "god" for ANYTHING. That whole idea has to be TAUGHT.

> *"Faith in the supernatural is a desperate wager made by man at the lowest ebb of his fortunes."*
> *- George Santayana, Little Essays*

19. Then again, after some generations those kids may have made up a god or two to explain the things they can't figure out because of limited knowledge. But damn, we know WAY too much to have a God of fire, or floods, or prosperity, or of life and death (wait…maybe we don't?)

> *"I have never seen the slightest scientific proof of the religious theories of heaven and hell, of future life for individuals, or of a personal God." - Thomas Edison*

20. "Supreme Being" means the highest level of existence. Anything that exists can be measured. Even "unseen" forces like air pressure and magnetism can be scientifically measured. Spooks, spirits, and demons aren't real enough to be identified or measured. Within the bounds of reality, the Black man is the Supreme Being. But some of us are out of touch with reality. As Dan Barker, former preacher and co-president of the Freedom from Religion Foundation, writes in *Losing Faith in Faith: From Preacher to Atheist*:

> You believe in a book that has talking animals, wizards, witches, demons, sticks turning into snakes, food falling from the sky, people walking on water, and all sorts of magical, absurd and primitive stories, and you say that we are the ones that need help?

21. Finally, your God is your imaginary friend. You are free to believe in him. But damn, homey, you should know better by now!

WHAT HAPPENS WHEN WE DIE?
A CIPHER DISCUSSION ON THE AFTERLIFE
Moderator: Bismi Allah - Wisdom Victory (Huntington, WV)

Bismi Allah: What happens to your life force when your body dies? Does your mind also die? Where does all the intelligence and your inner self go?

Royal Star Allah - Allah's Kingdom (Anchorage, AK): This is one of those eternal questions. No one (old or young) really knows the answers.

Not with scientific certainty. Here is my take: WE ARE THE ESSENCE. We are just experiencing the physical realm. Period. When we decide (note that verb) to leave the physical realm to experience another realm, that is just it. Nothing to become emotional over. Death is just a transition.

Original Author Allah - Mecca (Harlem, NY): Your life force returns to the Foundation of all things, the Universe. It No Longer is 'your' Energy to control any more, that energy is now a part of the equality of universal law, that everything is in motion and every 'part' of it, is used to continue the motion. Since the PRINCIPLE of Energy is not created or destroyed, it goes through a refinement (change) and becomes Universal Energy that that keeps the cipher spinning. Your life force can 'Live' on by what you did or passed on through your seeds. Life force is simply wisdom that was expressed by the user. For instance, if you wrote a book that's the force of your life right there. You may be gone but the force that you created still exists. It's tangible, thus a part of life. This force is not consciously you anymore and has NO free will. It just 'lives' on through what actions and deeds you manifested. A life force is a basically a thought and thoughts of men have exceeded their own physical lives, whether its god or devil. It's why ADDING ON was is important in our ancient culture or the present one, before written word, these stories or Lessons passed on the wave lengths of energy(thoughts) from generations past. The same goes on today. The Bible says the Sins (forces) of the father will be passed onto the sons. We see the Errors of those who came before us, AFFECT us TODAY. The Pyramids themselves is a force of life. A force mathematically has STRUCTURE and thus can be DEFINED. Its definition lives on by what you BUILT. A force is an ACT UPON SOMETHING so the ACTS of men live on. Have you read a book by a person that is dead? Has that book 'moved' you? So your conscious life force simply returns to the foundation and is no longer 'yours' and it only exists by what you did.

Bismi Allah: What happens to your life force when your body dies? Does your mind also die? Where does all the intelligence and your inner self go?

Almighty Supreme Scientist – Born Mecca (Baltimore, MD) by way of Cream City (Milwaukee, WI): Check your 13th degree in the 1-40. Your mentality is the only thing that can be recovered. Therefore, if you teach, what you know can be seen in your Children and the people you teach and influence. The Culture is the continuity and leaves the best impression and representation of what you stand for and are about. If you can't go on personally, make sure your Culture does. Teach.

Aikuan Allah - Cipher Land (Oakland, CA): There are 3 ciphers that are intertwined and interdependent on one another. That's the cipher of the past present and the future. Our collective consciousness connects us together as 1 while at the same time we add our independent knowledge to the cipher. Thus standing on the shoulder of Giants. It's like when Elijah said "me and my people have been lost from home for 379 years" 11:40. Elijah wasn't 379 years old when he said that. 3+7+9= 19 (Self) which depending on the connotation can be me and my people. When our individual knowledge is born it has both a direct and indirect effect on forthcoming events. Cause and effect. Time immemorial through infinity is merely cycles of life going from Knowledge to Born and Back. This always has been and always will be the case.

Bismi Allah: Many think that the mind is Allah. Will you tell us to your knowledge is the mind Allah as it relates to the above topic? And where did 'it' come from? People are concerned with where the 'ego' goes after we 'die' yet are never concerned with 'where was it at' before we were 'birthed'. I also think it is appropriate that we define the terms on the table before discussing them. So for all I ask what is your definition of: life force, mind, intelligence and inner self?

Precise Infinite Peace Allah – Savior City (Syracuse, NY): Inner self? What is an inner self? Precise has one self. When my physical dies everything else pertaining to my physical dies with it. That was one of the most difficult things to come to grips with when I recovered from my blind, deaf and dumb days.

Islord Shabazz Allah – Victory Allah (Norfolk, VA): It is my understanding that all the above refers to my mind. The mind of man is the most supreme life force in the universe. I am the supreme life force manifested through mind as man. Intelligence is a product of the mind. The highest form of intelligence is that of the mind of man also. Inner self can only mean my mind. No one knows the inner you (your thoughts) unless you make knowledge born. There's a little more to this like the air we breathe and how it plays a part in the life of man. The mind and body of man won't work without air or oxygen. I could break this down myself but there may not be enough time/space for that here.

Truth Justice Allah - Now Cee (Durham, NC): I see the inner self as a figurative or metaphysical way of referring to the personal mindset of the individual. The source of one's thinking or ideas before being expressed or projected outward. The inner self can be looked at as the world within. The microcosm. The mind. The outer self being the reflection or expressions of what going on within. Seeing a person knowledge thru their wisdom. I see outer/inner self two aspects of the same coin, not to be taken on face value. Like when some gods talk about the lower and higher self, it's not to be taken literally as though the self is two.

Precise: I see you and I'm well versed in various schools of thought regarding the metaphysical makeup of man. The point I'm making is that regardless of the various levels, aspects, bodies, etc., that an individual has, they are all a part of the individual just like an arm, leg, leg, arm, or head. When the brain dies all of those things that compose the individual will die (become useless). In fact what we may call an individual is no longer an individual. What you are left with is a body without a control center which inevitably means it cannot sustain itself. Generally I don't use those neat names to describe self because they often make things confusing, especially for the novice. I imagine this is why Bish asked the question initially, because he's probably teaching a lesson to one of his students. Someone who has bought into the religious concept of life after death which more often than not translates into a fictitious spirit, astral or mental body that survives after physical death. Which in turn implies that once an individual physically dies there is some form of consciousness left of the individual to continue on, traveling on to new or different levels of reality. Basically the kind of sh*t an empty person can look forward to in hope of a better life because deep down they realize they've wasted and will continue to waste the life they have Now for their Nation to the End of what they can actually verify. All that sh*t about "the beyond" makes for great science fiction but cannot be shown and proven. Essentially just reinforcing the "mystery God" concept. This is a tactic used by the 10% through the vehicle of religion to keep people distracted so they don't exist in the NOW. So instead of being proactive in making for a better life and a better society based on freedom, justice, equality, truth, etc., people will be led to wait for something that will never be made manifest. The big LIE. The new beginning that something else (Jesus or some other religious figure) will make born.

Original Author: Same wavelength here god. Also mathematically, it should be Higher and lower THOUGHTS, not self. The Vibrations of all thoughts are not the SAME, but they all are manifested from the ONE self. You have to be able to recognize the speed of the thoughts. All thoughts rotate within the ONE cipher (self), just at HIGHER and LOWER speeds, not two different selves.

Bismi Allah: Has any one of you ever heard of or experienced what is called an outer body experience? Have any one of you been so close to death that you were thought to be dead for any amount of time? What is an "out of body experience"?

God Janal Allah - Medina (Brooklyn, NY): An "out of body" experience: As I lay in the bed looking up at the ceiling, tubes coming out from me every which way I suddenly began to feel something lift up out of me. It was as if they were two of me. Before I knew it I could see myself lying in the bed. I was a little scared for I knew what this was or what it was coming to, and it was not my time. I relaxed, tried to take composure and bring my body back down to me or wait until it rejoined. I have gone through this more than once. Another one is when you see bright white lights, and/or when you can hear everything yet can't speak or move...That's close.

Bismi Allah: It is called by some the parallel of lights. I was going to mention that but you did it first. Some say do not go to the light for you will not return but I went straight to the light that I saw and I am here. Can anyone else tell us about any related experiences that they had and can any of you give us a sensible reason for these things?

Truth Justice: There's a connection between the temporal lobes and religious experiences/mental illnesses. The brain produces neuro-chemicals during near death situations which produce pleasant feelings and a mental experience of a vision of a white light. It is these hallucinations that people talk about and feel were real.

Aikuan: I've had some interesting things take place that made me want to learn what caused them to happen. That's what initially got me interested in Shaolin and Qi gong. I think it would be easier to explain once a person learns some exercises that relate to Qi, prana or whatever term gods like to deal with. It's empirical though, until one experiences it first hand, an explanation doesn't really suffice. A lot of us haven't dealt with it and when that's the case a person is quick to think someone who has/does is on some mystery sh*t. Which may be the case sometimes. We have to deal with Actual facts before Solar Facts. B-u-t as they say "As it is above it is below."

Supreme Scientist: I lose no time SEARCHING. Etymologically, "search" means "to go in circles." I don't go in circles, I ADD ON TO THE CIPHER. There is a difference. See the Cipher and be Understood in the Cipher. Ain't no young, blind deaf and dumb people interested in the topics in this discussion. Y'all making your opportunity to trade with them disappear speaking all this crazy language. The 10% knows that when a man dies he will never come back to tell the living whether he lied or not. What happens after you physically die? No one knows. The only thing we KNOW about is...life. How about we talk about that? Most teenagers aren't ready to die. And that goes for the hard-headed and church-suited. They trying to get their LIFEstyle on. Money, good homes, and friendships in all walks of life. All that stuff Elijah had and Lil' Wayne now has. Supreme Mathematics beats Philosophy 101 class every time.

Speculation/Spectacular/Specter/SPOOK. They all share a common root etymologically. So does "Spectrum." Keep it within the limits of what you got optics and instruments to Observe. I Stimulate Life And Matter. If it isn't alive, then it doesn't matter. All of this "out-of-body experience" and soul and spirit and multi "self" disorder talk is just spooky.

Bismi Allah: I don't agree god. This topic is very important and the promise of an afterlife is what has many people worshiping a mystery. I was taught that it is that important to have sons so we can live on through them. I find this to be good sense, very realistic. Teaching that there is no mystery god to bring you back from the grave - students need to know this. What will they know about it if we do not prepare them our selves? They will be beaten with many questions that they can not answer. The Gods do not just accept words. They want facts and proof. They are not followers and that makes them stronger as individuals. They will unite and become one. I am simply part of the glue to be used to stick us together. Words at times get in the way. Words like "soul" and "spirit." This is because these words have been misused by the unknowing and abused by the unrighteous. Soul is not a mystery; your soul is your lining. It is your own true self, and your own true self is a righteous god, if you are a righteous god. A rock can be submerged in water for many years yet you can break open this rock and inside it is not wet. The inside of this rock is like the soul of you my brothers it is still dry, unscathed. It is still a rock inside and out but we do not judge a rock by its surface, a book by its cover, or a man by his looks from the outside. What Allah did, what he taught, what he lived for, and what he died for, is the soul of this nation and continues through this nation. You are composed of solid, liquid, and gas. Your body, your blood, and God Allah Self. It is not a ghost or a spook but who you are inside. That is your essence, from where you came and to where you return. Without breath you have no animation; that is also Allah. Allah is the source not no mystery or spook but the life force. How can you leave god and be god? Cause you are god and all in all is Allah. Spirit is not a little man inside of you telling you to do anything. It is your character and your motivation and a term used to express such. Some people are lazy or are not very spirited at times. Everything is real, but the 10% make things seem unreal. When you leave you can not take physical things but the glory of what you did and what you stood for. Who remembers you? Who carries your nation on? You live on in each and every one of us. God's cipher is divine forever, past, present and future. Always has been and always will be.

Supreme Scientist: Why focus on the afterlife? Why not focus on this life? Give a man a McDonald's filet-a-fish and he'll eat for a day. Teach him how to fish and he'll know that damn filet isn't really fish. In other words, switch the methodology. If a person is stuck on ONE belief, then freeing them from THAT ONE BELIEF isn't going to keep them from adopting ANOTHER Belief or Belief System. I know a cat who went from Muhammad to Jesus to Dr. York in one year. Do you think telling him there wasn't 72 virgins waiting for him after he died would've solved the problem? Probably not. Supreme Mathematics - If that doesn't answer the question, then what else can? Maybe the question can't be answered. That's alright, too. At least you won't place the same value on an assumption that you do Knowledge. And it's just that simple. A "promise" isn't Knowledge. A "story" isn't Knowledge. Epistemology. A lot of people don't know what Knowledge is. So, in turn, they don't know if a person's Word is Born or Bacon. The rod is what you Rule with. ROD = Rule Cipher Divine. The Rules are Supreme Mathematics. You can't beat that. Spare the rod and spoil the Child. Rotten Fruit has no Supreme Mathematics. I just keep it simple and supreme. There is no mystery god or afterlife because "that" I know not. I lose no time searching for "that" that does not exist. That makes you other than self. We need to focus more on THIS.

Aikuan: The etymological meaning of search is to view, watch, or see. There are some things the naked eye can hardly detect which require instruments such as microscopes, radar, x-ray etc. and perhaps the 3rd eye. There's a logical explanation for everything.

Supreme Scientist: Indeed, that's why I included "instruments to observe." The problem is, you can't make an observation of ANYTHING "after life." With or without optics or instruments. The only thing we (the living) know is a dead body. Why not just leave it at that? It's Spooky when you make an observation and then jump to a conclusion.

Bismi Allah: How do you gain the wisdom and the power to tell anyone why anything happens? You conquer the unknown. You look in all directions to find the truth. I use all information. When there is no one coming back to tell me about death (cause they will not return) I get all the details of life (past, present, and future). I use deductive reasoning, good sense and build to the best of my ability. The father died. Many of us never met him. Do we give up because he will not return? Do we act like religious fools? Or do we build in all directions like the eight points on our flag? Do we become supreme scientists by examine all past, present and future? Do we use Supreme Mathematics to open the door to reality? If we do not continue being a part of the collective existence. itself existing through our babies and our nation, then what is the point of being just and true and righteous? Does the father live in all of his sons (in us)? IS THAT SPOOKY OR REAL? IT IS ABOUT LIFE. IT IS ABOUT YOUR NATION, YOUR BABIES, ABOUT YOU BEING GOD, YET BEING ABLE TO DIE AND STILL EXIST THROUGH THEM.

Supreme Scientist: Propagating a person's MENTALITY via the reproduction of their teachings and physically via children: Cool. The only way you're going to see God again is to keep reproducing. That's what I said in my first response. I'm not going to attack anyone else's understanding. I'll just say I think some people believe in ghosts. Real ghosts. And ghostly things. When you PERSONALLY die, that's it. Finito. That's goes for Allah, too. That Man is dead and gone. His teachings aren't though. We can use euphemisms and figures of speech and say "he lives" blah blah blah, but that guy is dead. His influence isn't though. But he is. Now watch somebody reply with some more 'figure of speech' symbolic crap, like "The father and the son are one..." Whatever. People are scared to die and scared to live. It's better to keep his teachings alive, than to hope to live to see him 'live' again in all of these flowery ways. But anyway, I guess it's cool and interesting to wonder where you go after you die. I don't wonder. I have better things to DO, e.g. teach my Earth, teach my Son of Man and others, and do real things to MAKE SURE my Culture continues. That's why I brought up young people. Are we supposed to bomb them on Deuteronomy and science of Astronomy, but don't know a damn thing about the Economy? Most of them are struggling to find their place in the world and be self-sufficient. They aren't philosophizing. Why are we? They aren't too worried about dying. Why are we? That includes a 'belief' in the afterlife. It's just some peripheral sh*t to most people unless you're old, got a terminal disease, or some Heaven's Gate tennis shoes in your closet. That's real talk. And FYI: Physical death isn't just an Unknown, it's an UNKNOWABLE. There is a difference. If you are advocating you KNOW what happens to a person "after life," other than a cold body and a funeral/cremation, then you're lying. I'm not trying to jack up this discussion, Bish. As a matter of fact, my uncle just died a few days ago, so I'm speaking from experience. Maybe I'm just too outspoken and honest. I don't want to meet him again someday. I want to meet the REAL future, the children.

Truth Justice: You can hit a person up with mathematics, science, logic and reason, humanism, till you black and blue in the face. If a person hasn't conquered their fear, nothing you tell them is going to matter because their fear is always gonna bond them back to their mystery god belief and that's real. How many people you know are on a frequency where they can say "F*ck the Bible and Qur'an and all that bullsh*t!" and keep it moving? Negroes are scared to death of those books. From fear of death, to a hellfire, to a mothership picking you up, to being saved by "Sweet Jesus." Its fear that's going to keep them blinded to their belief systems, even if you can show and prove it with mathematics and science to be illogical or false. Most people believe out of fear more than anything else. In most cases they are scared not to. Someone being told since they were a child that they are going to hell if they don't believe in a fairy tale makes it hard for them to destroy those beliefs as an adult. The devil uses fear to keep people in a state of triple darkness. The 10% uses this to keep their sheep in line and make better slaves. And fear is what keeps a person from hearing you or seeing you. And that's reality. And the 10% know this.

"It is difficult to free fools from the chains they revere." - Voltaire

LIFE AFTER LIFE?
Sha-King Cehum Allah - Power Born (Pittsburgh, PA)

"In all the history of Islam, never has revealed anyone returning from a physical death. But there is a chance for the mental death…" - 13th degree Lost Found Muslim Lesson No. 2, 1-40

There are two major aspects of reality: the physical and the mental. Most religions, especially Western religions, pander to both of these concepts. They attempt to weave the two together by referring to the 'spiritual' reality. The term 'spirit' is used throughout the Bible and can be interpreted in many perspectives, especially since it was translated from other languages. This is very important to remember. Anyone who studies languages (a linguist) can affirm that languages aren't equivalent, which means that there are words or concepts in some languages that don't exist and can't be expressed in other languages.

The word "spirit" in religion usually refers to one's 'soul' or the essence of one's being. Some religious definitions infer that the "spirit" is the heavenly substance from which the mind, energy and matter derive from. I've even heard of the "spirit" being the religious equivalent to what scientists would call the 'mind.' The word comes from the Latin *'espiritus'* which means 'breath.' As in the Old Testament, when God 'blew the breathe of life' into man. It is seen as 'that' which animates the physical world.

This type of thinking is often a byproduct of a mindset that is unclear about life and death. Seeing someone and talking with them one moment, soon to find out that the life has left their body. This phenomenon mystifies and intrigues people who are often left to shrugging their shoulders and concluding that there must have been something else stimulating your physical frame. Thus, the idea of the 'soul.' The soul sometimes is envisioned as eerie mist or smoke rising out of someone's dying/dead body. And not wanting to accept that it's 'over,' we wish for more. We yearn so bad for there to be something else. After all, where did this person's 'life' go to?

It is very clear that the Old Testament does not claim life after death. For the Jews, the Kingdom of God is to manifest on Earth. The idea of life after death didn't come until the New Testament which is heavy laden with primarily Greek and to a lesser extent Roman influence. The Greeks and Romans, who at one time used to fashion theirs concepts of 'GODS' after the Egyptians, eventually broke from those ideas and began to propagate a God beyond human imagination. Formerly, all of their Gods and Goddesses had human characteristics and interaction. Eventually they moved towards an intangible, unviewable concept of an omnipotent being. Which seems more of a move to inspire esteem in their citizens. To detach the epitome of humanity from any association with Original people (ultimately because they knew they could never be 'Gods') and strategically placed God beyond where anyone could touch or see him. This later became a critical tool, militarily, for the conquest of people. Especially if the people were driven by the concept of their own divinity or relationship to the universal supreme mind. It should be noted that the concept of an afterlife is not found in the Old Testament. Nor was it an element of Jesus' teaching. Our righteous brother spoke Aramaic and Hebrew, was well-versed in the scriptures that later became the Old Testament, and held fast to their 'law.' For in John 10:29-36, he mentions that he did not come to 'change the law,' and questioning the persecuting Jews, he asks, "and is it not written and have I not said, that ye are all GODS?" Jesus, pardon self, *Yeshua ben Josef,* would have been familiar with the concept of 'no life after death' and 'heaven on earth.' So then what's this madness with this far off,

Never Never Land concept of heaven that we have been indoctrinated with?

Mathematically, there is NO SOUL or spirits. There is the MIND, which is NOT the brain. When you die, your body breaks down into its 99 natural elements. It's called 'atrophy' and it's a scientific principle characteristic of all physical matter in the universe. The 99 natural elements then bond with the elements and minerals in the soil. Keep in mind, as the law of conservation states in Physics, energy can not be created NOR destroyed, only transferred or contained. After millions of years of existence, people places and things brought into being and then destroyed, the Earth has never lost its mass. The energy is just converted. Your thoughts, which are really electricity (electrons) break from their current and dissipate, mixing with the other atoms of elements that exist in the atmosphere.

The 'spirit' as breath could at best be likened to 'Chi or Qi' in Daoism and Eastern religions. Also, Prana in Hinduism. B-u-t why such a mystical concept for a basic idea? Well one must understand the importance of 'breath.' Aside from your skin and intestines, a lot of substances are absorbed through the 'lungs.' The lungs are the organs responsible for the intake of 'air.' The air consists of a variety of elements, primarily Nitrogen, secondarily Oxygen and then a host of others from the top of the periodic table of elements. The particles of these elements, like others, consist of protons, neutrons and electrons that react and interact with other protons, neutrons and electrons. One atoms value to another is based in the electrons that they have in their outer orbits and how they are able to exchange and share them, creating a bond and then molecules, which eventually give way to another element or substance. The particles have components called 'ions' which are electrically charged (flow of electrons) and stimulate the cells in the body. By managing and controlling your breath you can control your blood flow. This means that you can control everything from your body temperature, to heart rate, to erections/orgasms. Because the air then filters (the oxygen) into your bloodstream. Your blood is a major carrier of vital vitamins and minerals which are dispersed to every cell and organ in your physical body. After your last breath (or shall we say if you held your breath until you 'stopped' breathing, your brain would still be functional, for the new 120 seconds, until it shuts down. And then you 'know nothing.'

By controlling your breathing you are exercising SELF MASTERY. By immersing ones' thoughts in concepts of 'spirits' and 'souls,' you open up the possibility for someone to control you. To master YOU. Because they lend your existence to a power greater than your own intelligence.

You can not resurrect the physically dead. However, you can resurrect someone from a mental death. By continuing to teach this truth daily, just as the Devil does with his lies. 'Physical life after physical death" is an illusion to keep us worried about the inevitable and naive to what is going on here and now. So we care more about a time we will never see rather than living righteous now.

THE POWER OF THE QUEEN IN CHESS
Emblem of Justice – High Cipher (Ohio)

I have stated in the past that I am a recovering chess addict: Power years clean and sober. The reason I don't get down on the chessboard anymore is because it becomes a clash of egos when man plays against man. Chess is a game that subconsciously says that "I am smarter than you, by way of strategy, tactics and cunning." It reeks terribly of egotism, and I want no part of it. However I do play against the computer on my phone, and in that context, it no longer becomes about my ego, as it is about building. The game of chess has been a part of my life since the age of  Equality. Early on, I fell in love with the game, but at a certain point I realized that I had to back off from human opponents. I did not want to proclaim with a resounding 'checkmate' that I was better, nor did I want someone to tell me via 'checkmate' that they were somehow smarter because they beat me in a game of chess. The male ego is crazy like that and consciously or unconsciously associates dominance in a given area with a complex of superiority. The ego of man manifests in some very strange ways, and chess is indeed one of them. Now I prefer a strong game against my Blackberry, no feelings of intellectual superiority or inferiority are involved, nor do I have the pressure of saying that I am better than someone else or they are smarter or better than me.

The game of chess is rich with many metaphors, and the greatest metaphor is the manifestation of the Queen on the chessboard. That wooden piece on the board stands strong and regal, she is free to zoom from one end of the board to the next. She causes opposing kings great anxiety, and she is prepared to die for her king. Interestingly enough, if she is taken, a pawn can elevate by climbing six ranks and become a Queen. The King is the most important piece on the chessboard and the Queen is the most powerful piece on the board in terms of movement. Yes I have learned to play without my Queen, needless to say it is very challenging, particularly if the opposing King still has his Queen. The fight without a Queen is brutal.

In many games of chess it is customary to castle within the first 15 moves either Queen side or King Side, regardless of the side of the castle, you must separate from the Queen. The King is usually protected in the castle, surrounded by his right hand man the rook, and three or four pawns, serving as bodyguards. The Queen from that point forward works in concert with knights, bishops, rooks and pawns to win the war. Chess is one of the most accurate game metaphors for life, and every man must ask the question, "Does my Queen have my back?" God directs her movements both at home and abroad. It is a grave mistake in chess to be careless with the movement of your Queen. Loosing her can be potentially disastrous. There is nothing worst than being forked, pinned, or skewered by an opposing piece and watching an opponent smile as he takes her off the board such is a heartbreaking sight for any true chess player. Some chess players gladly trade Queens, it slows the game down, and the game becomes a game that takes on a tactical tone. Her absence is felt in such tactical wars, and it is very similar to a man dealing with the world alone. I have dealt with life from both the aspect of having a Queen and not having a Queen, both have their pros and cons. That Wisdom degree in the 1-36, referring to coming to North America by yourself, is a very real journey in this wilderness, and the sense of loneliness can either make or break a man. Having a Queen is great particularly when you see that she has your back in the Wilderness of North America, and she is also on guard against your hidden and manifest enemies. Many Gods don't listen to their Earths when the Earth analyzes the character of men around her King - but believe it or not, the Wisdom is a 'Wiz' at peeping the nature of your so-called brothers and companions. She can determine via intuition the real from the fake, and see quickly into the treachery of so-called brothers and companions better than you can in a lot of cases. She is the field General after you have castled, and you must ask yourself can you trust those around you? Betty Shabazz is reported to have told Malcolm X that he was naive and that he was blind to the treachery around him. Needless to say, she was on point, and Malcolm X was shot numerous times by those who claimed to be his so-called brothers and companions. I have often stated that the 'Ear' is the key to the Earth, meaning you must allow her to build and listen to her! I listen to my Queen, and one of the things that I have noticed is that she speaks from an intuitive point of view, she can see into the hearts of men because she is a woman. She is naturally 20 miles outside of masculinity by virtue of the fact that she is a female. Yet the very nature of her femininity allows her to call masculinity like the Father called a dice roll. A woman has the capability to spot a b*tch move of a man. Men sometimes will act like b*tches, and she can see effeminate behavior in a man without that man realizing he is on some b*tch sh*t. I love asking what my queen thinks about a given cipher, particularly now that she has 120 on cap. She will bring a lesson to my attention that I was not necessarily focusing on. Such a collaboration of Yin and Yang, or "unalike attracting," is the proper order of things. Man and Woman combine to form the clearest, razor sharp view into a cipher and this borns understanding. Two men can advocate society, but two men can not born civilization, civilization comes by way of a woman. Whether it is the Wisdom degree in the 1-14 or the Knowledge God degree in the 1-40, both the meanings of "civilization" are inclusive of Wisdom. There was no civilization in triple darkness, because the way out was not manifested before time became time. Wisdom is the portal by which civilization is born.

A community of homosexuals only borns saliva and fecal matter. Two chicks born 'spit' and two men born 'sh*t'. Man and Woman are the root of civilization according to the Culture degree in the 1-14. Revelation 1:9 begins, "I John, who also am your brother, and companion in tribulation, and in the kingdom and patience of Jesus Christ…" Your brother and companion through trial tribulation just means that he's your rook in the cipher of the castle, and you're the rook in the cipher of his castle. Each man, however, is his own King. The most important elements of that Kingdom is teaching her how to act at home and abroad, after the Queen Side or King Side castle has taken place. After you castle, she is alone with your other lieutenants and private soldiers. When you close the castle doors - the Captain, or King, gives the orders for her to move either offensively or defensively on the chess board of life. Knowledge Wisdom in the 1-14 builds on the military training of men. She can tell you by being in the field which cats are for war and which cats need to get sent back to babysit the babies. Not every man is made for war, some men are made to stay back and gather berries, and weave baskets. She can peep the offensive postures and relay back to you necessary steps needed to deal with the impending battle. Our National Anthem, The Enlightener tells us that "Wisdom is the way." If you got a wisdom who is sharp with the math, connected with her innate intuition, and you have learned to listen to her, then the sky is the limit - better yet Pluto is the limit - better yet there is no limit!

Emblem was born in Philly, raised under the teachings of The Honorable Elijah Muhammad and attended the University of Islam as a child. In his late teens he discovered the teachings of the 5 Percent Nation. He's most noted for his fiction novel *Da God,* which is available on Amazon.com or at his blog: emblemofjustice.blogspot.com

THE GOD IN MAN
ALLAH'S SELF-CREATION
Knowledge Scientific Cipher - Birmingham, England

In the beginning of time there was nothing in existence but darkness. But this darkness was not the same darkness that you see at night-time

Because the darkness that you see at night-
time comes about
Because the earth is turned away from the
sun's direction.
This darkness was a true darkness
(A nothingness)
A darkness that contained within it the
power to create matter,
What we call Triple Stage darkness.
Within this Darkness, an atom of life
emerged

(Willing itself out of the darkness)
And came into existence, and when it came into existence –
Existence itself came into existence and TIME as we know it began.
Now the feminine is the receptive principle and the male is the active
principle,
And since this atom decided within its own consciousness to bring itself
into existence,
It was manifesting the active principle making it a male being.
And since it violated all scientific and natural laws
In being able to bring itself into existence without cause,
It showed and proved that it was a being
That was supreme over all things...the Divine.
And being a divine being, there is only one thing that that being could be:
The maker, the owner, the creator, the God.
Now the Supreme one decided that it was not just enough to exist,
So it decided to create.
And he created light and moisture, and from the interaction of these two
elements came millions of different planets,
Inorganic and organic, which were all made up from the same material
which grew from the creator.
The consciousness of the creator was right and exact, righteous and
supreme,
And existed as a force infinitely throughout time and space,
Until, as the Bible says in John, that 'the word was God and the word
became flesh and dwelt amongst men.'
Meaning that physical beings that were made up of the atoms which grew
from the creator,
And became the containers of the consciousness which had began all
things.
Physical beings which came in the form of the Arm Leg Leg Arm Head,
And who were direct descendants of the same one who made all things
And were made of the same material which had existed with him.
These beings were awakened to the fact of their true self

And could connect thoughts with the same thoughts and consciousness of
     God
And walked the earth doing everything right and exact, building pyramids,
     traveling throughout space and time
And manifesting knowledge that the greatest scientists in the world today
     could never understand.
They lived at the roots of civilization in the Nile valley in Egypt, which is
     properly named Kemet, and the Holy City of Mecca in Arabia.
Peace!

The above piece is a spoken word poem recorded by Knowledge Scientific Cipher for Baby J's *The Birth* album (Bomb Records, 1998). In 1996, Knowledge became interested in the teachings of the Five Percent through hiphop and traveled from England to Harlem to study at the Allah School in Mecca. In 2007, Knowledge used his 20 years of experience in the music industry (in both the business and creative sides) to set up the Sankofa Youth Academy (http://sankofacentre.co.uk), an accredited, independent multipurpose facility dedicated to providing education and enrichment programs to young people classified as 'at risk' in the West Midlands region of Birmingham, England. Sankofa works in partnership with schools and community centers that refer young people for participation in a number guidance and training programs. He is also head of Seven Entertainment, which features an extensive roster of artists, including Baby J and Moorish Delta 7 (myspace.com/officialmoorish), of which Knowledge is a founding member. Moorish Delta remains well respected as a significant contributor to the UK hip hop sound. Knowledge is also a full time father and trainer, running a boxing and weight training club for young people. He is dedicated to youth development, community development, economic development and making mathematics 'living.'

QUANTUM PHYSICS AND THE BLACK GOD
Divine Ruler Equality Allah - Godsboro (Greensboro, NC)

"I want to know how God created this world. I am not interested in this or that phenomenon, in the spectrum of this or that element. I want to know His thoughts; the rest are details."
– Albert Einstein

All things that exist are organized in statistical states of position (location in space) and momentum (the speed and direction a particle with energy travels) with continuous variation in the probability of what position or momentum is measured, and discrete intervals of energy based on the wave length of the particle or the wavelength of a medium through which a signal travels via its mass/energy density of the medium. It was once said by Einstein in his attempt to challenge the reality of quantum physics that "God doesn't play dice," when in fact, the game of dice only appears to operate by "chance" on a macroscopic level based on the lack of awareness or utilization of data to predict the outcome of a dice throw.

In reality, all dice throws can be predicted within a degree of certainty based on the initial physical conditions that led to the dice throw. Through the strengthening of the awareness of one's subconscious or autonomous functions, one can become very successful in not only predicting, but also DETERMINING such outcomes in a favorable conclusion. So in fact God can, has, and does "play dice" but in a manner that upon further study is in a deterministic fashion, when you are aware of the reality of God being none other than the Original Man, The Black Man, the Measurer of All Things. This is the same for the apparent dice playing on the particle level called quantum statistics.

The act of measurement, also known as Knowledge, collapses the mathematical model known as the statistical wave function, which produces a model that leaves either a certainty of position or certainty of momentum, which can be measured. This sets up a chain of collapsed statistical wave functions in the entire universe instantaneously of other particles, thus influencing the entire universe instantaneously, since the wave function of even one particle extends through the entire Universe.

The Black Man is the Original Measurer, biologically as well as electromagnetically. Biologically via dominance in genetics in the variable ethnicity of the biological species of the body of man, in addition to the volume of the population, and electromagnetically in relation to the length of time in possession of the management of the ensemble of photons, electrons and other mitigating particles that store and preserve the series of measurements and observations that have been made through out history.

The Original Mind or the Black Man is the total ensemble, collection or set of non-redundant mathematical comparisons. The brain is an organ that is modeled after the ensemble of these fundamental mathematical comparisons in the form of the exchange of photons and electrons in a neural network, a mixture of electrical and radiation circuitry in a biological form.

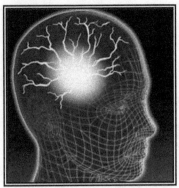

Not only is energy conserved, but also information in its fundamental form, that being the measurement of angular momentum (spin), charge, momentum (temperature), and other physical quantities, even through quantum mechanical evaporation of black holes and the preservation of spin statistics information of particles emitted from the event horizon with residual information that was absorbed by particles that pass the Black hole's event horizon. This conservation of energy plays into the dynamics of the so-called increase of entropy (disorder) in the universe being balanced out by the building and bonding of elements in the universe into an ordered state through the Intelligent Behavior of the Original Man.

Black Body Radiation is the study of the behavior of a body that absorbs all radiation incident on its surface and re-radiates it at a certain temperature, which is dependent on the wavelength and number of photons it emits. The behavior of the wavelength versus the temperature of re-emitted radiation is a testament to the success of the quantum physics model, and also parallels on the meso/medium scale, the reality of the Black Man being the optimum model for the element that absorbs almost all radiation, as the Being that has a Great Awareness and absorbs (analyzes) most forms of physical stimuli based on this Awareness. Due to measurements of the distribution of temperature of the cosmic background radiation, it can be deduced that the external Universe is casually moving from a state of increased order to decreased order, meaning from a state of greater complexity and organization to a state of less complexity and disorganization.

This points to the reality of the existence of Supreme Mathematical Thought and Greater Organization in earlier epochs of the Universe, more evenly distributed through the spatial medium. The apparent loss of organization over the spatial medium through the mechanism of "increase of entropy" is being compensated by the biological organism used by the Black Man/Primordial Intelligence undergoing vast campaigns of construction, organization, and archiving of observations. These acts of construction, organization and archiving manipulate the physical environment to cancel out the casual increase in entropy in the universe. Through the determined ideas of these endeavors of reversal of casual increase of entropy, physical reactions are produced which attenuate and magnify over time.

God is the Supreme Being. Supreme means Ultimate and Being means Existence. The Black Man has already been everywhere that exists, being that the photon is the fundamental particle that carries thought, and photons in equivalence principle of reference have already been everywhere that exists, i.e. "timeless," and these vary photons are what courses through the brain of the Black Man's biological organism which has lead to the manifestation of other forms of life in the Black Man's Universe. The highest density of these organized photons exists in the Black Man's Brain. This ensemble of radiation is causing and triggering all of the above phenomena in a determined fashion as opposed to just a casual fashion, when thought is applied, focused, and directed. The Brain is a multidimensional lens that the Black Man uses to channel our will into the biological organism, which then manipulates elements in the environment, which then produces magnified modifications of the larger environment over time. The strength and density of the photons in our brain allows us to unleash an everlasting modification of the entire environment through out space and time, thus showing that we are seen and heard everywhere. Thus this Supreme Modification of the Universe bares witness to our Existence, thus showing and proving we are the Supreme Being.

Divine Ruler Equality Allah earned his Bachelor of Sciences, immediately followed by a Masters of Sciences in Physics, both at Purdue University. Originally from Self Born, India (South Bend, Indiana), Divine currently resides near Greensboro, NC. He is a Technology Liaison for the Sciences at Elon University, an active member of ASCAC (Association for the Study of Classical African Civilizations), and past organizer of the Science Fair at the Nation of Gods and Earths' Annual Show and Prove. Divine is also the Founder and Site Administrator for www.allahsnation.net, the *5% Network*, the oldest site advocating the Nation of Gods and Earths, online since 1994.

THE KINGDOM OF GOD IS WITHIN YOU
Cappadonna – Wu Tang Clan

Wu Tang in the house! Stand up. This is Cappadonna, aka Original Tazim Great Mind. The science to my name is: C.onsider A.ll P.oor P.eople A.cceptable, D.on't O.ppress N.or N.eglect A.nyone.

As a child I realized that I was the true and living God when I realized that I had an arm, leg, leg, arm, and supreme head. I realized right from wrong and knew I had the power to make right or to make wrong. That's when I realized I was in control. The mind controls the body, not vice versa. Everything started from a thought, from one mind all appeared. Allah means all. There is no separation; even Yacub came from the original man. It all comes from one entity. All comes from the true and living God. We now must elevate. Now is the time to end all devilishment. The devilishment starts from within. It's our moods that cause rain, hail, snow & earthquakes. It's time to make a change. Pressure bursts pipes, and it's time to release all the pressure. We control all the signs and symbols. We make that. We're the reason for all of it.

"I am not a man, I am the Universe itself."- Morihei Ueshiba, Aikido and the Harmony of Nature

I feel like a disciple amongst people and the struggle. I have been around people searching for knowledge and I give them the cure. My knowledge allows me to walk freely in the land. That's when I can start healing and show the healing process is taking place. It must now start with one thought. Yeah there are casualties, but that's where that love, hell and right takes place. We start with the love and make sure through the hell we come out right. Now it's about getting in order, to get self in line. You may fall down, but you must get back up, quitting is not an option. You can knock me down, but can't knock me out. We came through muddy waters, bloody waters, which shows that there is no limitation to what we can accomplish as a people.

Don't fear the end of the world. The "end of the world" only means its time to end the B.S. It's time to introduce a new kingdom into the minds of the people. It's not a physical thing. All that means is that it's the end of how we seen the world before. The end of "the world" is a figure of speech, because the end of the devil's time is now. It's time to come out of this government and end all devilishment. Now is the time to create our own heaven. Heaven don't cost anything, because heaven is created in the mind.

Peace to all Gods and Earths, man, woman, and child. One more thing, you can't keep a good man down, cause after him there will be another one. Please educate all children equally, even divine evils. Let them know who the god of civilization is! P.roper E.ducation A.lways C.orrect E.rrors!

For most Hip Hop fans, the first time they heard Cappadonna spit is a treasured memory. It was in 1995, on Raekwon's now classic album *Only Built 4 Cuban Linx.* Cap had the last verse on one of the album's singles, "Ice Cream", and it blew everybody away. At that time, he was already a legend in the borough of Staten Island, but for fans worldwide it was a taste of things to come. In 1996, he appeared on Ghostface Killah's debut album *Ironman,* most notably for his never-ending verse on "Winter Warz." As the honorary tenth member of the Wu-Tang Clan, Cap appeared on the group's sophomore double-album *Wu-Tang Forever,* which was released in 1997. When the Wu-Tang Clan reunited for a third album, "Cappachino The Great" was promoted to official Clansman status. Cappadonna followed up in 2001 with his second album *The Yin and the Yang,* and in 2003 with *The Struggle.* At the end of 2007, he appeared on the Wu-Tang Clan's fifth studio album *8 Diagrams.* On January 27, 2009, he released his latest album, *Slang Prostitution.*

BIAN XING
THE MARTIAL LAW OF THE MARTIAL ARTS
PART 1: HEAVEN
Sunez Allah - Mecca (Harlem, NY)

Well now…So the perfection of physicality is to move the mind
where the Qi exudes beautiful brutality for love
and a vicious carefulness against hate.
The name of this training is Shaolin Kung Fu.
Its exponents are the true and living Gods and Earths.

Our root nature is emanated in the hidden breath from the toe to the crown, and expressed in 180 moves composing the Way. The Way is a wisdom of genuine usefulness, where revelations of clear principle teach one how to stand fully upright. With this understanding, the freedom of living perfection, our culture, is powerfully transmitted, as all flaws are refined into lessons. In the proper position, the warrior is powerful in the center. Equally the One and the All, the Supreme Being is reaffirmed in a rejuvenation of living metamorphosis. Through the building of natural potential with the destruction of its imperfection, the warrior is fulfilled. All this borns Self, in the cipher of *Bian Xing*: The Martial Law of the Martial Arts.

ALL BLACK

To see the supremacy of self as the One and yet of the All, as that indomitable mind that causes all - and will yet live and grow in the endless effects of these causes - is to be the Creator. In such awareness of Self as the maker and owner of one's reality, there is great humility. A humility that sees the relationship of Creator and Creation as simply *sharing*. In this sharing, there is education in identity through the process of merely *being*. If one is able to learn the Self in its fullness, then creation itself will manifest as an interactive fulfillment of one's core principle.

This revolving reality of our natural relationship (as Creator manifesting constantly with creation) is expressed by our ancestors in myriad ways, through countless mathematical systems. All these lead to our Supreme Mathematics. In our culture, we learn of self and live the Way. A Way where the mind learns, the body advocates, and all is promoted. In this, we embrace, enhance and exemplify the martial art of Shaolin Kung Fu.

The Martial Law is fulfillment of Self and All. Kung Fu is the martial art of Allah. With its corresponding foundation of fluidity (Tao), we express our nature as it is (Yang), interacting with all that will be (Yin). Truly, our lives are the Martial Art, with insightful Love, through the learning of all Hell, promoting the proper, Right principle.

180 MOVES ARE IN LOVE

Dr. Yang Jwing-Ming notes Kung Fu's etymological roots as *Ji Ji*, an attacking skill, but also as the way to "stop the weapons," or *Wuyi*, which developed into *Wushu*, the skill of the Martial Art. Kung Fu (or *Gong fu*) simply means 'hard work' and is applicable to anything. *Shaolin* denotes the association with the preserved foundation at the legendary monastery since the 5th century of the Common Era.

To embrace the art of Shaolin Kung Fu is to accept that we are endlessly engaged in the artistic study of our physical expression. To enhance this expression is to show our understanding of Supreme Mathematics, our declaration of self awareness as Supreme beings, and our performance of the way of perfection in Kung Fu: hard work. To exemplify this ancient Chinese art is to see that the truth of self has always been such and that the way itself is the display of the great principles that sum righteousness.

Our moves may be numbered 180, the foundation may be entrenched as *wing chun* and we may see the fighting styles of powerful tigers striking, sturdy cranes pecking, or even iron butterflies fluttering wildly. Yet, the number 180 symbolizes the fact that one motion will become many moves, as the study is never linear and finite. Instead, it is a cipher and wholly fluid. The learning of the ancients promotes simple practicality in our delivery, but our creativity makes it our own 180 moves.

This eternally unfolding revelation is reason for our exploration. The mastery of our microcosm of Self will emanate throughout the macrocosm of the universe. The quest for awareness using the tools of breath and love, generates a flow that navigates the internal body, offering healing and focusing strength.

We adopt a reality of preparation and performance, where one prepares to master the motions of his every muscle, bone and tendon, washing this with a mindful breath of *Qigong* (energy work), controlling our tempers, and channeling our full energy toward change. We are ultimately prepared to perform. Yet, it is this preparation that has recreated us, thus becoming the performance itself. In time, the cipher is realized to have no beginning nor end, as preparation and performance have merged...

These moments, twenty minutes daily, of 180 moves a day are the martial remedy of *Bian Xing* (metamorphosis).

3 TREASURES IN THE FOREST

Watching the self, we find three treasures in the forest of thought. It is a forest filled with a confusion that paralyzes, enemies that straddle our insecurities, and options of success that lead us astray from the bliss of enlightenment. With the desires of comfort, there arises the dismissal of hard work (Kung Fu). As comfort is appeasing, the art of life simply becomes a fight for mere preservation. With basic survival as our reality, the *outside* enemy is our only concern, and to kill for the next day is cause for celebration. This outlook towards the future gives birth to the beginnings of prayer's hopefulness. Thus marks the end of creation, as the Creator is now focused on a reality outside of Self.

Yet this forest is also the training ground where illusion can become a mastered science, thus extending the depth of awareness. It is here where one can turn tools of warfare into agents of creative expression, and where the mysterious hope that infects us can be ended, as it is channeled by an active wakefulness of the possibility of what is thought impossible, a reality that the Self, as Creator, alone can manifest. With this, the prospect of salvation becomes unnecessary.

We do not strike well or badly due to fear, but due to confidence in our control of the situation. We do not celebrate the destruction of a foe, but study what may be built the next time, without such carnage. In this way, what is necessary is done. So we will punch through opponents, have their limbs deflected and broken, and leave them with their organs tousled, as we tussle. Still, we mourn for the opponent, as a better tomorrow must also be learnt. The study of our martial art promotes living. In this, our need for peace is outwardly expressed in myriad ways.

Out of this forest, the 3 Treasures emerge out of self. We name them Heaven, Humanity and Earth - The mind, the people, and our home. This may be expressed as the 3 perfect principles of Originality, Honor and Full Uprightness. This Heaven is our Mind, the one that unites the All.

The metamorphosis, *Bian Xing*, of Shaolin Kung Fu is not the changing of the person, it is the person *being*, thus always naturally *becoming*. It requires that we move exactly as our mind has thought, share exactly as our heart intended, and create as freely as our culture speaks of the infinity of knowledge.

The above are not rules and regulations. This is the *Bian Xing* of the warrior soldiering in Shaolin Kung Fu for the union of Sun and Moon - a better tomorrow. This is the way of the 3 Treasures jeweled upon the Original family for posterity. This is the essence of the Martial Law of the Martial Arts. Peace.

PART 2: EARTH

Infinite Mind Allah – UniverCity (Union City, NJ)

"Brother, stop fighting, their changing their styles. You two traitors, you've mixed the Shaolin & Wutang together. No we have not, it's just that their the same. My lord, you misunderstand how Kung Fu works, it doesn't belong to anybody. It evolves!!!" - Shaolin vs. Wutang

"Teacher, what is this? This isn't Kung Fu."
"That's the highest form you'll ever see- the final form; you don't understand." - Enter the 36 Chambers

"I have three treasures,
which I hold fast and watch over closely." - Lao Tzu

Nature has patterns and cycles that have been recorded into numerous books by its students, our ancient ancestors. The author(s) of these books would study the three natural powers and their relationships. These three powers were measured by the energy they took in and expelled. Recorded within these books were the rules and cycles of nature's natural flow. Those who studied these phenomena realized that the rules never changed and the cycles repeated regularly. The people, (specifically the Chinese), used an understanding of these natural principles to calculate the changes within the energy field of the Three Treasures.

HEAVEN	EARTH	HUMANITY
天	土	人

The cyclic patterns in the motion of The Way gave birth to the Yin and Yang concept, which represents the duality and oneness of two opposing forces. Both Yin and Yang are represented by the ancient Chinese symbol: *T'ai-Chi*, which translates to "Diagram of the Supreme Ultimate." Its essence lies in the concept of darkness and light represented by the continuous circular movement of life. According to this Chinese philosophy, everything within the three natural powers deals with Yin and Yang forces, including an individual's daily routines.

One of the most influential books that recorded these patterns and cycles of the three natural powers was the *I-Ching: The Book of Changes*. It studies the various combinations within the Yin and Yang forces of the celestial bodies (Heaven), the science of geomancy (Earth), and the affairs of the people's everyday life (Humanity). The *I-Ching*, the first amongst the *Six Classics of K'ung Fu Tzu* (Confucius), is a system of eight trigrams that formulates patterns into sixty-four hexagrams based on Yin and Yang. It is a mathematically designed system used for preparation, prevention and self-development.

It is inevitable within the realm of all our sciences that we study mathematics to a more detailed description than just numbers. Mathematics is the key to unlocking the mysteries of the universe, the language of nature. Anything within the micro and macrocosm of life can be interpreted through mathematics. After trillions of years in studying mathematics we learned that these figures come together in a harmonious movement explaining a methodical and systematic process of development which can be translated into words of any language. This goes into more scientific depth than a mystified numerology theory.

SUPREME MATHEMATICS

1 \

2 - **Inner workings of the mind**

3 /

4 \

5 - **Principles of application**

6 /

7 \

8 - **Essence of bearing righteous fruits**

9 /

0 = **Whole (Universe)**

The proper scientific explanation of the martial arts provides the solid foundation for information and creativity and no longer mystifies the whole concept of The Way, but rather clarifies it. Bian Xing is a martial art concentrating on self-activation balancing the rigidity of its science with the flexibility of self-expression, while articulating through its philosophy.

The divine perfection of Bian Xing expresses Supreme Mathematics through the Science of Everything in LiFe. The art is the essence of bearing fruits, and knowledge of self is at the root of the tree. The tree growing and developing is the student maturing in his/her study. The ripeness of the fruit depends on the student's dedication, devotion, and discipline. The art becomes the ways of all things at the beginning, just like the seed within the fruit that is used to grow another tree.

"How do I know the ways of all things at the beginning? By what is within me." - Lao Tzu

To my understanding, the creation of life itself is Bian Xing. The movement of the universe is performed through 180 moves of Kung Fu where the martial artist engages in a cosmic dance of *BaGua* or *Capoeira*, whichever art you desire, orchestrated in the course of creation where conception plays the major role. It is a formless form constantly elevating at an ever-increasing rate with its master adapting to the environment around them utilizing everything within their cipher as a tool to change or transform their shape and form. The natural philosophy of the body guided by trained instinct moving in accordance with The Way of nature. Since we are constantly conscious of this way of thinking we apply this principle to all things in life.

To study every square inch of the body in order to build it, to know what you don't know and learn how to learn it; these are the characteristics of a martial artist, this is the Bian Xing of Allah.

"Real mastery is only achieved when technique is transcended and the art becomes an artless art growing out of the unconscious." - Dr. Fritjof Capra

---

Infinite Mind Allah is a teacher and Dean of Students at an alternative education high school in northern New Jersey. Holding a degree in Social Sciences with a concentration in Africana Studies (History & Political Science), he is currently pursuing his doctorate in Anthropology and Education, with a concentration in the African Diaspora. His passion is training and studying martial arts throughout the Diaspora. He is the co-author and editor of a forthcoming book, *The Three Treasures Manual.*

PART #3: HUMANITY
Nahlejj Eternal Allah - Medina (Brooklyn, NY)

"Man follows the ways of Earth,
The Earth follows the ways of heaven,
Heaven follows the ways of Tao,
Tao follows its own ways." - Lao Tzu

We are following our own Tao, boundless universal consciousness, the divine reasoning of the God(s) and Earth(s) executing Supreme Mathematics through the Martial Laws manifesting freedom on the material plane. Each and Every Way. The Three Treasures Martial Arts is the foundational gate to advancing the self through higher Martial Arts. Learning how to apply the martial precepts to everyday living and life's social endeavors. Maintaining the harmony in our daily conflicts or subliminal mental and spiritual battles in every walk of life.

HUMANITY-REN

The divine trinity of Man, Woman and Child. Humanity the rebellious child of Heaven and Earth representing the duality and constant struggle to co-exist society; never yielding to absolute peace.

Man being the medium or the bridge between Heaven and Earth (Father and Mother). Consisting of part Heaven (*Shen*: Mind-Spirit-God) and part Earth (*Jing*: physical-essence-elements) Man harnesses the power of the earth-elements to fulfill the totality of the infinite realization of Self.

All purpose is revealed by man and the universe is interpreted by him and is understood through the arts, through language, through music, the writings, the symbols and creativity. For as long as man exists through the eternal illusion of time the universe and the collective consciousness will continue to be made known to the unknown masters. Man being the essence of God, the transcendent power of his greatness or the central medium of the universal cohesion.

"The way of the superior man may be found, in its simple elements, in the intercourse of common men and women; but in its utmost reaches, it shines brightly through Heaven and Earth." - Confucius

HUO is the Chinese pinyin for fire, closely resembling the *Ren*, the character for Humanity. For Man is indeed the walking living fire in the earth-body emanating through the vehicle of bio-chemical transmutation, thus executing the *Jing* of Bian-Xing, changing all forms of life and atmosphere. In return, nature responds positively and negatively; simultaneously producing both yin and yang. It is measured and balanced by the Martial law of heaven and the mandate of heavenly order is given to those receptive incarnate soul-beings; *Shi* meaning God-Man. *Shi* is the root word to *Shifu* (Monk-Warrior-Scholar-Sage) who receives the vibrations of Harmony to be fulfilled on the plane of the lower earth society.

This being the reason why we meditate, study and practice the Martial Law of the Martial Arts, to build our skill (*FU*) through hard work (*GUNG*). As our ancestors and the enlightened Masters and high priest Shamans of the east, we are cultivating *Qi* so that we may effortlessly ward-off fear, ignorance, disease and unrighteousness. Finding peace through the refinement of Self; radiating light among the uncultivated souls of Humanity.

THE THREE TREASURES IN HEAVEN AND EARTH

"As it is in heaven, so it is below"

8 Foundational Lessons:

All things are parallel from the highest to the lowest equation. For example, let's look at the universe's numerical symmetry and similarities. Everything is symbolic to the Infinite Self in its complete definition.

1. In heaven there are the three great luminous jewels. The Sun, Moon, and Stars are the main component in recording the chronological history of the celestial movements and astrological laws written in the sky so that man may know himself. Anthropomorphically represented in ancient Kemet as the deities Ausar (Osiris), Auset (Isis) and Heru (Horus).
2. The human representation is Man, Woman, and Child.
3. Within the body there is the *San Cai* of *Jing* (essence), *Shen* (spirit) and *Qi* (vital life force).
4. On the Earth it is fire, water, and soil; the natural tools of the master builders of civilization.
5. Organically, on the plane of matter, it is protons, electrons, and neutrons.
6. In the mental aspect of master-scholar, *Shi* (God), the foundation of Knowledge, Wisdom and Understanding are the keys to unlocking inner truths and the lure of mystery, religion and philosophy socially executed through the state of freedom, justice and equality.
7. In the martial arts realm the three jewels of Shaolin Gung-fu is the *Gung* (work-practice), *Ge dou* (fighting-ability), *Taolu* (formless-form or Bian-Xing).
8. Then we have the three jewels of Buddhism. The first of course is Buddha (the highest spiritual potential in all beings), secondly is the *Dharma* (the teachings of Buddha), third is the *Sangha* (the community of the enlightened ones).

These are but a few parallel concepts that comprise the root origins of our natural culture where we practice and aspire to bring about a revival of the ancient arts.

No, we are not Monks.

We do various forms of meditation, fast and eat raw or healthy vegetarian foods and study holistic medicine, we cultivate our mind in the arts and sciences, practicing daily Gung-fu, Qigong and building on the universal concepts of Supreme Mathematics. Now is that enough to be considered a Daoist? Maybe. Who cares? Don't get caught up. Our martial arts existed since the beginning that never began. The Shaolin and the Wudang are our Chinese brothers who have perfected and preserved what our ancestors left for us. Our martial art dates back to the first civilization of Harappa and Mohenjo-Daro in the Indus Valley, the Cushitic (Black) tribe of Dravidian Dalits who practiced the first martial arts known to Asia, *Kalari-payattu*, itself deriving from Ethiopia. We have taken it upon ourselves to salvage all the teachings of the Martial Arts as well as elevate it in order to bring it back to the original people of the planet. All nations have developed their own forms of defense. Even the Young God(s) and Earth(s) in Harlem N.Y.C. who study Three Treasures Martial Arts are innovatively advancing the art to a supreme level. I hope no one takes offense to us not keeping it traditionally Chinese or Shaolin. Much love goes out to the monks and other Asiatics; we welcome all and respect all. Thank you for sharing a bit of your culture and now we will continue to advance ours.

GUNG- FU

Most martial arts masters would agree that there is more to the arts than just brutishly throwing blows and kicks. All sincere practitioners must take the time to contemplate the reasons why they are practicing martial arts, think about what they are really trying to accomplish, as well as consider the fact that they can get seriously hurt or cause someone else permanent injuries possibly resulting in the tragic death of another human being. Now can you sleep well after committing such a savage act?

In the process of learning martial arts one is always going through introspection to weigh and judge self circumstances so that the heart and soul will remain pure and balanced with the right intention. So the main emphasis should be placed on the self-awareness of the martial arts practitioner in his/her early stages. The Higher Self will then automatically confront the lower Self when it is acting in disaccord with the Martial Law of the Martial Arts. Self analytical questions are then posed by the Higher Self such as: do you really have to fight? Do you just want to take your frustrations out on another human being, simply because you can? What level of force should you use? Do you have a choice? Do you have something to prove to yourself? This is the internal duality that can make the difference between life and death. Again, we are made of *Shen*, the Divine Spirit that makes us in the likeness of the Buddha.

> "Your mind is the Buddha. Don't use a Buddha to worship a Buddha."
> - Bodhidharma, The Zen Teaching of Bodhidharma, as translated by Red Pine

Let us understand the time and sacrifice that it takes to master the skill of making split-second decisions effectively for the purpose of preserving life. True defensive fighting starts with the mastery of the third eye. One must have the utmost sincerity and dedication to be able to advance in the martial arts so that you will be strong and able to fight the temptations known as "the spirit of the flesh" as taught to me by Sigung Bobby Lee Whitaker. The flesh complains about being tired and hungry, wanting to fulfill its pleasures. The flesh is weak and tries to persuade the mind to be weak by tempting the mind to stop practicing the rigorous training of the soul. The body is affected by the mind and the mind is affected by the body. The ultimate goal of the sincere practitioner is that the mind would become the absolute master and the body the complete servant. The body effortlessly carries out the will of the mind. This is where reaction is psychically demonstrated. There is no thought, just absolute knowing-the complete execution of the laws and techniques. Qi is produced in precise amount bringing forth the just balance in the universal equilibrium. Life can then continue its cycles; and the harmony is again maintained within the social state of man. The inner peace and humanity is temporarily at rest as long as there is the natural control of the forces of Self duality.

Peace Omitofo!

Nahlejj was born on August 17, 1976 to two Latin Music nightclub performers, one a Puerto Rican mother of Moorish lineage and the other a Dominican War refugee. Nahlejj grew up in the countryside of Cayey, Puerto Rico until age 6. His Old Earth brought the family to El Barrio, Spanish Harlem where he was raised, soon learning English, Hip Hop, the Streets and the Knowledge of Self. This is also where he met Sigung Bobby Lee Whitaker who taught him the Martial Arts. He has been a resident of Brooklyn for 11 years now where he educates youth and imparts the teaching of the Martial Arts.

'TIS THE SEASON
C'BS Alife Allah – New Heaven (New Haven, CT)

Ecclesiastics 3:1
To every season there is a time

Tis the season
Tis the season

while some are lighting menorahs I
    sit at home playing my kora
fasting from gluttonous feasts
moonset to moonrise
like I need mistletoe to show my
    godly affection
most beneficent, most
    compassionate, most merciful
no I don't crave snow for I B
    tropical, equatorial
insomniac
dreaming not of a white Christmas
how about a right Christmas
being that a right Christmas would
    B no Christmas
anointed Palestinian messiahs have
    limited connections with this
    mess
bough breaks, thus falls Christ's
    cradle
whirlwind dreidel
tricknowledge picture of three wise
    men, mary, joseph, baby jesus in
    a manger

cunningly slipping past Herod's
    abortion hanger
for the first born
little drummer boy pound on the
    djembe drum
pa-rum-pa-pa-pum
how dumb that sitcom vision B
truthfully, royal family B amongst
    camel spit, cow pee, llama feces

burn kwaanza candles instead of
    barbecuing yule logs, or gorging
    bellies on the intestines, feet,
    heads of hogs
caress skulls
gaze, gander Hamlet's eyes,
    holding Yorick
i knew ye well
while obese consumers sit around
    worshiping colored lights on
    Christmas trees
blind deaf, dumb and blind have
    yet to hear about the infamy
blinking lights symbolize the heads
    of Nimrod's enemies
son of Cush, Nimrod
slept with his mother so he
    would B
God
the father,

God
the son
comes back on Christmas eve as
the holy ghost in your eggnog
toast

CHILDREN IN THE
GHETTOS ARE
BEING LIED TO

here chimneys lead to furnaces
which only work half of the time
B suspicious of any fat white man
in a red suit who is climbing on
your rooftop

at this time I would like to thank
my mom and my pop for never
lying to me
let me say that again

NEVER LYING TO ME

the Truth,
the greatest gift a child could ever
receive

others forget their voyages on
slave ships, bind their selves to
merchants, swipe their magnetic
strips
caught now in the abyss of soured
credit, wallowing in this X-mess

It's now secular
excuses of religious folks
listen to facts given by Asiatic
astronomers charting the night
sky with telescopes
longest night of the year B on
Christmas
known to all scientist as winter
solstice

reorientation of the Earth on her
axis pole
sacred illustration of I, Sol
Controllers perfect control

A mean one
great grinch grab stocking off of
mantels, a jolly face mask
murder Santa Claus in malls,
church halls
Santa Claus B the tip of Satan's
Claws
stripping all of charity

jingle
the bell tolls for those who blindly
follow, don't bother to know
sheep slaughter sheep slaughter
PLEASE put coal in my sock
I B that black rock, call me the
Ka'aba, that transforms under
pressure into diamond
tiptoe around me seven times
while many are hypnotized,
mesmerized by the 25th of
December
i remember that goodwill is to B
executed all 365 days of the solar
year
paganistic foundations have no
place here
besides the Pope is the one who
set Christ's Born Day on that
date hundreds of years after his
death
not catholic/ just God/ so it isn't
that hard/ for me to do away
with italian religious
proclamations from the Vatican
Same place that sanctioned slavery,
the Holocaust, and genocide of
the Native American
So Saint Nick
U can suck my....

And to all a good night

The above poem is one of many in *Perihelion Baby,* C'BS Alife's second book of poetry reflecting on life, love and loss, available at www.AsiaticLight.blogspot.com

WHAT DO YOU LOVE?
Original Author Allah - Mecca (Harlem, NY)

What is Love? We use that word often, yet for as much as we use it, do we really understand it? It seems doubtful, considering all the issues that plague our communities today. To start off, Love is a bond. A bond is that which links two things together. Usually in today's world we hear stuff like "I Love you, but" there is no "but" after Love. To Love is to have RESPECT. If you respect your mate, would you creep behind their backs and do things that would hurt them? Love UNIFIES the cipher. It makes the Two become the One. You and I become U N I. This unification shows you that you should treat others as you wanted to be treated. I have yet to meet a person who says they like to be treated unfairly.

To start giving this kind of Love, we must Love ourselves first. It's the only way we can extend it to someone else. If people hate themselves, how could they Love you? What do they have to offer? Could I give you 5 dollars if I have zero?

If we plan to make changes as a people, we must move as ONE right? Can we change the world by liking each other? We can't change the situation of original people in North America by liking each other or ourselves. A "like" is not supreme. Supreme means the highest form of anything. What we saw happened in the 60's was not based off a "like" for our people. The Black Panthers did not protect and feed the communities because they had a liking for their people. The Gods did not protect NYC from riots after MLK died because they liked their communities. It was Love that was the healing and protecting factor in the pains of what we went through in North America.

In the last 40+ yrs, we as original people have lost the "Love Connection" through digesting the wrong foods (mentally and physically). Do you notice when the white man kept us away from him, we had more Love? We fought and marched and took all kinds of abuse, always sticking together…just to go to his schools and eat in his restaurants and use his bathrooms…and once we had all that, we LOST the Love. Now, was the trade off worth it? The closer we got to his way of life, the emptier we became in our Love for our people. In many ways we started to Love him more than we Loved ourselves, and that's the ULTIMATE recipe for the destruction of our people.

Love is not an emotion. It is the highest form of understanding for each other. We are born with the understanding of Love. Emotions are more learned behaviors. We have to learn hate, greed, and jealousy, etc. A baby does not need to be taught Love.

What Makes Love Supreme? It crosses Space and Time. You can still Love a person that no longer lives or whom you have ever met. I was adopted yet I still can say I have LOVE for my birth mother. I never met her a day in my life. I understand why she had to put me up for adoption, yet after all that, we STILL have a bond. Love is the reason why most adopted children seek out their parents; there is a chamber of Love that needs to be filled. Filling that void with Love (and not desire) results in PEACE.

I had a lot to learn about Love. Yet when I finally came to that understanding, my life and what I wanted to do became perfectly CLEAR. Love is the Windex for your vision. Because Love helps clarify your vision, it helps define your mission in life. This Love is also the fundamental principle of righteousness. So show me a righteous man or woman and I will show you a person who had a LOT of Love to give.

So what do you like and what do you LOVE?

OPTICS
Divine Ruler Equality Allah - Godsboro (Greensboro, NC)

Today's Mathematics is Understanding Cipher, all being Born to Understanding. Sight is related to Understanding, and Cipher is our Environment. Today I composed some literature on Optics, to further illustrate the relationship of Understanding (Sight) to our Cipher (Environment).

The following treatise is on the relationship of Optics to the Universal Science of Life. Optics is the study of Electromagnetic Radiation, and its manipulation and behavior in various mediums. Electromagnetic Radiation is essentially Light, in various forms, whether it is visible light, infrared, radio, ultraviolet, microwave, x-ray, and various other forms of radiation of varying frequencies. The Full Range of Frequencies of Light represents the Fullness of Allah or the Black Man, in his Mathematical Form. Light is Energy, and therefore Eternal, since Energy is neither made nor destroyed, but transformed from one medium to another.

The constituent particle of light is the photon. Strong enough photons can manifest all forms of matter in a process called pair production. This is related to the Energy of the Photon, the mass of the particles created, and the speed of light, or light travels at 186,000 miles per second, or approximately 300,000 kilometers per second. This is expressed as $E = mc^2$ or Energy = mass times the speed of light squared. So we can say that Light are the parents of particles and vice versa, in an ongoing cycle. It takes two particles with mass in order to form at least one photon, but singular photons can manifest 2 particles. When particles of opposite and equal states combine, it is called annihilation. In fact matter and antimatter combining is the most efficient form of energy production in the Universe.

In reality, the Original Man's first or Original Form is electromagnetic fields. It is PHYSICAL, even though it does not have a rest mass, because we are never at rest (dead) or have never experienced a REAL DEATH other than mental death, via being BLOCKED from matter. We travel throughout our Universe via Light and pair production which can later be used to resurrect ourselves again into Light. Even though we do not have a rest mass in our Original Form, we have ENERGY and Momentum, and therefore can shape and direct activities in our Universe.

The sum total of the patterns of electromagnetic signals going through the universe is included in what we, civilized people, call the Mind. The Mind is the Highest form of LIVING Mathematics. Light is the active medium, and Matter is the more passive medium. The combination of the two brings about the Family of Energy and Material, which in the Equilibrium state brings about Life. Light in and of itself does not have any effect unless absorbed and re-emitted by Matter. This is why Light underwent pair production and continues to do it today, in its more energetic forms.

Within the Universe of Optics there are two forms of transformation, emission and reflection. Emission represents the masculine principle, and reflection represents the feminine principle.

The Greatest Lights in our Immediate Universe are the Sun, Moon, and Stars. These are Planets, either Grown (The Sun and other far Suns, known as stars) or Made (Gaseous and Terrestrial Planets, such as the Earth/Moon, Venus, Jupiter, etc.). The Sun and other Stars EMIT Light, and the other Planets Reflect Light. This is Manifest in the Black Family by the Man, Woman, and Child. The Man is symbolized by the Sun, the Woman by the Moon/Earth, and the Children by the Stars, or little Suns and Planets.

In the world of optical devices, there are two forms which correspond to the male and female principles. Lenses are male, and mirrors are female. Lenses help to directly focus and shape electromagnetic radiation. Lenses can either be convex (focusing) or concave (defocusing). The measure of a lens's usefulness is related to what is called its focal length. In order to maintain and successfully manifest optical engineering we must use a combination of both focusing AND defocusing to relate to different situations. Too much focusing can cause a beam to be too strong which can be destructive, so it must be tempered with defocusing, to make the intensity relevant and manageable to our targets. Too much defocusing causes us to lose the picture, so we need a focusing lens to bring things into view. This is related to the functions of our brain, which in reality is a FLEXIBLE LENS, with focusing and defocusing properties. Our brain in reality is an organ that is an EYE. This is our 3rd Eye. We use it to break up information and scrutinize it (left brain, analyzing, concave, defocusing) and merge it back together and integrate it to get a clear picture from its combination (right brain, synthesizing, convex, focusing). The dual properties of our lens system called the brain is known as bicameralism.

Mirrors are polished surfaces that have the same shapes as lenses, only instead of re-emitting light, they reflect it. Effective mirrors must maintain a polished surface, or otherwise they will appear dull. Consequently those that are Reflecting Light (Earth) must renew themselves by cleansing and regenerating mentally and physically to maintain a superb reflection. This occurs in the personal life cycles of the Black woman as well as the terrestrial life cycles of the planet Earth, in the same manner.

A prism is a form of a lens, which not only focuses or defocuses, but also breaks up various constituents of frequency into separate forms. Rain drops, oily puddles, triangle shards of glass or polymers, can serve as prisms. These are how rainbows are formed. In the personal body of the Original Man and his Family, we are able to see in the visible spectrum 7 major divisions. These go from Violet, Indigo, Blue, Green, Yellow, Orange, to Red. This is a sign of the harmony of the quantity 7, which is used to symbolize God, and correspond in our bodies to seven harmonic notes in our cycle of hearing, and also the seven mediums of the endocrine system in our personal body. The range of the 7 major visible colors is a manifestation of our larger body or Environment, the Universe, for in our Universe, the Stars, in the main sequence and major populations, range through these colors. The Stars represent the Babies, whether they are Suns far off in distance or Planets that reflect the Suns they orbit. Of course, the absorption of all forms of light results in the origin of all, Black.

The process of splitting up light into constituent frequencies is known as diffraction. This is a method of SEPARATION. This is the same method which can lead to DEVILISHMENT in human affairs. This is because the light loses coherency (Knowledge of Self), and begins to compete with each other and manifest what is called destructive interference.

Although the speed of light is 186,000 miles per second, there are VIRTUAL phenomena in the light which have a greater magnitude of speed. The 186,000 miles per second is what is called the GROUP velocity of light. However within the light "beam" itself, along its path of travel, you can have PATTERNS within it that travel faster than 186,000 miles per second (some say 24 billion miles per second). This is what is called a PHASE velocity of the patterns within the beam. HOWEVER, these patterns are USELESS, unless the people that intercept the beam ALREADY KNOW WHAT ELSE IS COMING. This is related to the science of prophecy and prediction.

The Mind - covering all expanses of time and space - does not have a rate of travel. Thus, KNOWLEDGE is an instantaneous phenomena that does not have a group or phase velocity. This is the phenomena of "Mind Detect Mind," or "telepathy" or "foresight," etc. It is not a communication, it is only KNOWLEDGE, based on knowing a past initial condition for a mechanical system. From this principle of KNOWLEDGE, you will see that two particles which evolved from the same photon will exhibit similar behavior, such as spin and polarization, INSTANTANEOUSLY, even though they may be several billion miles away from each other. This is related to a phenomenon known as "causality." Nothing happens with out a cause, which is related to the conservation of energy. Energy does not come just from nothing. There is no mystery god.

Holography is a science of manifesting a 3-dimensional image using a combination of two dimensional surfaces. A holographic photograph, in reality contains a representation of the ENTIRE photograph in each individual pixel on its lattice, only each lattice has a different perspective of the ENTIRE photograph. The combination of light being reflected off these pixels creates constructive and destructive interference of light, which manifests itself as a 3-dimensional image. In reality, our brains are a holographic photograph of our Mind. We store memory in the ENTIRE brain, not just parts of it. If you cut away small parts of the brain, we will still be able to retain some memory, although not as quickly, or as clearly as before, of individual instances. In fact, we can use our entire environment as a memory storage device. We use mnemonic devices, such as strings around fingers, index cards, notches on wood or trees, to increase our chances of recall of memories that we have recorded, not just on our brain, but in the entire Universe. This is why the Universe is designed with countless reminders of its Creator. (See "The Greatness in Man")

The field of vision for the heads on our personal bodies is 120 degrees. With optical instruments we can increase this to a full 360. We can use periscopes, digital monitors, rear view mirrors, etc., to multiply 120 by a factor of 3, to get 360 degrees or the full cipher. This is the same way we can use supplementary literature, education, experiences, and interaction with other people, to get a full and holistic (Cipher=whole) perspective of the Knowledge and Wisdom of the Original Mentality.

THE INTERNET: A BLESSING AND A CURSE

C'BS ALife Allah – New Heaven (New Haven, CT)

This is the super-secret history of the Nation on the internet. Well, not super-secret. It's just unknown to a lot of people.

Long ago, in a time before many of us had even thought about knowledge of self, there was the virgin territory of the world wild web. This was the era of AOL chat rooms, usernet, listservs, static web pages, and flame wars. It was the early 90's and the few who were online were the science nerds in colleges.

In terms of the Nation, this was an interesting time. There had always been Gods and Earths who had gone to college since the time of Allah, yet in the early 90's you had the first generation of Gods and Earths who were exposed to the 5% primarily via the golden age of Hip Hop (circa 86-91). Outside of the Gods in the military, this is one of the major ways in which the ideology of the Gods and Earths got spread abroad. In this landscape, a few Gods that were online made their presence known mainly by posting their build on the day's mathematics in various forums dealing with hip hop, black culture, and politics. The names I remember from this time include Divine Sun, Divine Ruler, Knowledge Born, the Earth Rukiya, and Melanasia, among others.

I was just getting acquainted with the net at that time, and it was good to see the budding of the Nation online. I connected with the true and living and it was around this time that Divine Ruler noticed the growing population of online Gods and Earths and those who were interested in our Nation. Thus he set up the first Nation of Gods and Earths web page and set up the first Nation listserv (basically an email group). One of the first things that we did was to resolve to meet each other face to face at the Show and Prove. There I met Divine Ruler, SciHonor Devotion, CeeAaquil and a few others. That was ALWAYS the rule. Because if you were claiming true and living status and you didn't endeavor to meet people at the root or face to face, then you were labeled a fraud.

Jump ahead literally almost two decades to the modern internet era – the era of the so-called "social network."

Let me digress for a minute before I address this. There was a recently an online newspost about how Norway's Prime minister was stuck at Kennedy Airport due to the Icelandic volcano's eruption. Yet dude was still running the government via his iPad. This is the level that the white man is utilizing technology and media. Yet when you look on most social networks of Original People you will not find them utilizing this technology in any way other than literally "socializing." Every Original organization that is represented on the internet should take a long time to review how they are represented on the net and how they can use the internet to expand their values.

Specifically, with the Nation of Gods and Earths, the internet is NOT where you learn our curriculum. Just like you will not learn our curriculum by buying this book. Let me say this again. You can NOT learn this culture from the internet or a book. At most, the internet is a place to become familiar with some aspects of our value system. What you want to do with the internet is use it to network with someone with whom you can connect to *in the real world.* That's where you can *really* learn this culture. After all, this culture is an oral tradition passed from mouth to ear.

I guarantee you will have no problem finding 1001 different Myspace and Facebook groups advertising themselves as the true "spot" for the Gods and Earths. You will find Twitter accounts and blogs from many who seem to be the sterling example of a God or Earth. And we aren't saying that you won't learn *something* of value from these places. Yet, many times, all you'll find out is how the Gods and Earths *are NOT*, because many of these people never went through the proper rites of passage for this Nation. Some of these people online don't even EXIST in real life, if you know what I mean.

In fact, there's really no culture that you become a part of online. You connect with people of a particular culture by meeting up with them. You see how they talk, how they eat, where they hang out at. You do not construct a virtual fantasy world for yourself online. This truth is set up to change your life. It is not set up for you to create a veil to hide the issues that are plaguing you. With that said, **if you don't know any True and Living Gods or Earths in your area who are qualified to introduce you to this culture correctly, reach out to us at kos.anthology@gmail.com and we will direct you to someone who can.**

CHOOSING A POOR RIGHTEOUS TEACHER
C'BS ALife Allah – New Heaven (New Haven, CT)

Looking for a good enlightener/educator is like looking for a good college, mate, job, etc. You have to put in some work and work with some guidelines. Here is my top 20 things to look out for. Most of these should be instant disqualifiers.

1. They ain't taught nobody.
2. They haven't made any change in their own life since knowledging 120 and they clearly aren't about anything.
3. They are an isolationist. The push isolating you from any God and/or Earth.
4. They don't know any history about this Nation
5. They're rushing to teach you 120 without any examination of your background, your needs, and your present conditions.
6. They don't have one good word to say about one God or Earth.
7. You don't know if they know 120 or not.
8. They can't answer any question about 120, break it down, draw it up or show you how to connect it to life.
9. They're always talking about what an Earth is supposed to do and be and ain't got one/never had one. They're always talking about

saving the babies yet ain't got one and they're never around any babies.

10. They either worship ALLAH or shit on his name. Either polarity is unbalanced.

11. Nobody in their physical family, in their hood, at the job, etc knows that they're God or Earth.

12. They're clearly using the universal flag to shield some type of dirty activity that they're involved in.

13. They want some type of an immediate trade for this knowledge (sex, gold, submission, etc.).

14. They always down this science and try to graft other things onto it.

15. They're stuck in whatever year they got it.

16. They don't challenge you on dumping your own bullshit (presuppositions) that you're trying to bring into the science.

17. They live in opposition to their name. For example Gods named Sincere who lie all of the time or Earths named Serene who are always causing a ruckus.

18. They're always referring to a "creator", "the most high", "being God with a little g" or calling every woman who they exchange fluids with Earth.

19. They accept you not giving your all to the journey of walking through 120.

20. I don't know them, of them, or know someone who knows them. No, for real. This Nation is like one degree of separation and if no intel on a person can be drawn up by the true and living pass on that person.

AFTERWORD

Then what happens? You've read about everything from prison to quantum physics, from the minds of individuals who – collectively – have seen, done, and studied nearly everything in life. You've read about God, the Earth, the devil, and the universe. You've also explored an approach to life that only 5% of the world can handle. It is a difficult path, yet it is also the most important. It is the 5% who preserve the integrity of humanity.

In reading, you've certainly also noticed the various paths a person can take to come into the knowledge of him or herself. Many of these writings let you know what landmarks you should see along your journey, while others identify some of the many resources you will need on this long road, and still others present the obligations one has along the way. Yet, with all this, this book alone is not a sufficient roadmap for a journey so serious.

Then what happens? Many people gather information around the clock. However, many don't separate good information from useless information, and even those who know the difference often still do nothing with this information. They sit on the corner and talk. They sit in classrooms and talk. They sit in boardrooms and talk. The one thing that all of those groups have in common is that they sit. And guess who they usually talk to? People who agree with them. Thus nothing changes. A mind that doesn't change is dead. A life that doesn't change isn't worth living. So are you the type who sits around and does nothing to change your situation? What about our situation? Locally? What about globally? What will be your life's legacy? How will you be measured 100 years after your life is over?

If nothing else, are you satisfied? Or do you want more out of life? Are all of your questions answered? If not, what's the next step? We're not preachers, and we're not into "conversions" so what you do is up to you. Just think big. And think better, because what's been tried is not always what's true.

Then what happens? This part of the book is called the afterword. The question is what are you doing after you have gotten the word? Of course we want you to start applying the ideas that make sense to you. And we highly recommend you read Supreme Design Publishing's other books for more insights. But we don't want you to think that everything can be found in books alone. Or that this particular book's purpose is simply to provide you with some interesting ideas. Our mission is bigger than that.

Our goal has been to help make our culture more accessible to people everywhere. The diversity of the authors and their contributions is intentional, with the aims of bringing about understanding in as many different readers as possibly. You may *already* be one of the five percent of people who think differently, seek the truth instead of accepting the lies, and work for the betterment of humanity. So this book may be the confirmation you needed. Or maybe you're still "fighting the feeling." Even then, somebody, somewhere in this book has said something that resonated with you. And that one thought may spark the change you're meant to make. Unfortunately, that can't be accomplished by reading alone. Book knowledge is a good start, but it's simply not enough to produce the revolutionary change needed in ourselves and our world. That requires something else. So take the next step. If you're reading this book and finding yourself wanting to know more, contact someone in your area. If you're unable to connect with someone close to you, consider taking a trip to visit the closest Parliament or Civilization Class. And if you don't know any True and Living Gods or Earths in your area, reach out to us at kos.anthology@gmail.com and we will direct you to someone qualified to speak on what we're about. Then ask your questions. Decide your path. Hitting one of us up does not obligate you to do anything other than be honest and sincere.

What Else Can I Do to Promote this Book?

You're done already? Great. Now relax. Breathe. Let everything sink in. Reread whatever you think you need to look at again. Don't get all excited and start slapping people in the face for not knowing half of what you know now.

Instead, here's what you can do now:

- ☐ Tell people about this book and the ideas in it.
- ☐ Send copies to people who need this in their life (check out our great wholesale rates online at www.supremedesignonline.com).
- ☐ Put the lessons in this book into practice in your daily life.
- ☐ Develop a plan for how you're going to create changes in your life and the world around you.
- ☐ Look for lessons from this book in your daily life and the lives of others you know.
- ☐ Start eliminating your bad/weak habits, beginning with those most destructive to you.
- ☐ Build your leadership skills and destroy your fear.
- ☐ Think about constant themes found throughout this book (ideas or facts that keep coming up) and ask yourself why?
- ☐ Pick up our other titles (see the back) to learn more.
- ☐ Sending us your praise, comments, or suggestions for improvement.
- ☐ Post quotes or links related to this book on Facebook, Twitter, etc.
- ☐ Leave positive reviews of the book at Amazon.com and other sites.
- ☐ Request this book at your local Borders and Barnes and Noble.
- ☐ Create a promotional video on Youtube or share one of ours.

FAQ

1. What is your Official Name?
We don't have an "official" name yet we do have names which resonate with and are most commonly utilized by our community. These two names are the Nation of Gods and Earths and the Five Percenters.

2. Is this a religion?
No, we are not a religion. A religion is a way of life that utilizes belief as its system of operation. A belief system doesn't require that you verify any of the information yourself via the five senses. It operates utilizing such things as faith and hope. Our way of life is Mathematics, which is sometimes referred to as Islam, because of its original meaning: A state of peace. Our way of life IS NOT the religion of Islam.

3. Are you Muslims?
No, we do not consider ourselves Muslim. Although the word Muslim technically denotes "one of peace," the commonly understood meaning of "Muslim" is one who submits to what he believes is a higher power in order to find peace. The Blackman is the *Sole Controller* and is the author of peace.

4. Are you a part of the NOI?
We are not members of any organization, nor do we follow any such leadership, nor are we a sect, branch, or offshoot of any organization. However, in terms of the original meaning of the term "Nation of Islam," everything belongs to the Nation of Islam. That is, Islam – in its original sense – is Mathematics and has no beginning nor ending because it is the fundamental structure of the Universe.

5. Are you an organization?
We are not an organization in the sense that we are classified within the structure of United States government. We are a Nation who has within it various different organizations (such as the Board of the Allah Youth Center, Earth Committees, G.O.D. Committees, etc.)

6. Do you have temples?
We are not religious peoples so we do not have temples. What we do have are schools which are outreach centers for the youth.

7. Do you have a headquarters?
Our primary headquarters in terms of the preservation of our history and the continuation of our determined idea to save the babies is at the root of Civilization in Mecca (Harlem) known as Allah's Youth Center.

8. Do you have leaders?
Each man is his own leader. By critical examination of the history of Black people in the U.S., you can see that anytime a leader galvanizes our people, he is assassinated or rendered ineffective. In fact, this was attempted with us

by the assassination of Allah, the Father. Yet he prepared this Nation to survive after his physical death by removing the "office" of leader, and pushing us to realize that we all need to utilize a sovereign mentality and come together as one. This is exemplified in our governing process which is called a Parliament. Anyone is able to address the whole body, offering direction and suggestions. From this governing body, we then organize committees to carry out the agreed upon idea. We also have elders within our Nation whom we respect as transmitters of our oral traditions.

9. Do you follow the Qur'an or Bible?
We don't "follow" any text. We do realize that such written texts are a collection of history, moral directives, and mythology of the Original Man. By critical analyses we can assess which portion of the texts are relevant to our current conditions in the Wilderness of North America and which portions are being utilize to oppress, confuse, and stagnate us.

10. If Black men are Gods, why aren't Black women goddesses?
We recognize that the duties of the Blackman and Black woman are different within our Nation. When one titles the Black woman as a "goddess" then one is implying that the only difference is gender, yet that the duties are the same. Therefore we have a title more suited to the state of being of the righteous Black woman which is the Earth. "God" and "Earth" clarifies the fact that the duty of the Blackman and the duty of the Black woman are different, yet complementary in nature.

11. Is only the Blackman God? / Is only the Black woman Earth?
Yes. However, by Black, we are referring to all the shades of Original, i.e. Black, Brown, and Yellow.

12. Do you hate white people?
No. We are not pro-Black or anti-white. Many white people come to us to study the truth of themselves and this world. There have been white Five Percenters throughout our history, most notably Azreal, who was taught by Allah in our early days. We do not seek to integrate or separate, but to develop our communities without the interference of outsiders.

13. Are all of those rappers really "Five Percenters"?
The majority of the "rappers" who are identified as "Five Percenters" primarily utilize our language to magnetically attract audiences. Most of them are not true and living. Fulltime rappers are a minority in our Nation. Our Nation has many more Gods and Earths who hold other professions, such as educators, entrepreneurs, doctors, lawyers, construction workers, authors, architects, janitors, carpenters, soldiers, etc.

14. Are you a gang?
No. A gang is a group of people organized for criminal activity. There are those who have used our flag to shield their dirty practices by coming in our name and using our language as code. We are civilized people whose duty it is to teach Knowledge and Wisdom to all the human families of the planet Earth. Because we actively engage and educate those who are in the streets,

some individuals inevitably have a hard time leaving their "old ways" behind them. However, if we don't teach them, who will?

15. What's up with that hand sign?

The peace sign is not a gang sign. It is the exact opposite. The two fingers held up together is the correct hand gesture for peace. It has been utilized for thousands of years by various cultures such as the Nile Valley Civilizations, India, China, Japan, and even early depictions of Christ. Our universal greeting is peace. It is utilized by all civilized cultures in their own languages, i.e., *Salaam, Shalom, Hotep,* etc. Peace is the absence of all confusion. We walk the earth in humility, so we greet the people in peace.

16. Isn't it just as good to be involved with any religion or culture focused on improving our community?

While it IS good to be involved with improving the community, and we DO work with people and organizations from all walks of life, it is important to consider what it is that our people really need at this point. Offering the people more religion, or a new religion, will not "free" the people. Also, simply making the people more militant or politically-oriented will not "save" the people if they don't have the full knowledge of themselves and the nature of who/what they are up against. Finally, an escape to Africa, or a withdrawal into the seclusion of holiness will not help the larger community. While many other groups paved the way, we teach what is needed now, which is why we came when we did.

17. Do you have a problem with other groups?

Allah taught us to respect any flag, even the flag of the United States government. Allah also taught us that religious people tend to talk about each other, so we shouldn't engage in the same. So the answer is no, we have no "beef" with other cultures, groups, or organizations, unless they are clearly about bloodsucking the poor. Even then, we are opposed to the corruption of the leadership, not the misdirection of the followers. We are here FOR the people, all people.

18. If you have more truth, why don't you all have more money?

It is quite easy to collect funding and develop large projects if you have a hierarchy in place, along with a body of followers who will respond to external authority. With associations of freethinking individuals like us, however, you are less likely to find enough slave labor to build a pyramid, but more likely to inspire widespread changes throughout the world. The latter has always been our primary aim. While many Gods and Earths have established incredible for-profit and nonprofit ventures, this receives less attention than it would among groups that actively seek recognition.

19. How do I become a Five Percenter?

Find an educator who is qualified to teach (knows 120 degrees by heart, has a good reputation among the NGE, etc.) and travel, if necessary, to start studying in person. As we've explained elsewhere, this culture has to be learned through direct interaction with credible individuals.

GLOSSARY

10%: Those who know that the Blackman is God yet conceal this fact. They manipulate the poor and get rich off of the poor's labor, as the poor allow themselves to be exploited in pursuit of an elusive concept of happiness and heaven.

5%: Those who know that the Blackman is God, teach that fact, and work to bring about freedom, justice and equality for the masses.

85%: In general usage, it refers to non-members of the Nation of Gods and Earths. Technically, it refers to 85% of the population that does not know the truth of God, who do not think for themselves, and who are thus easily led in the wrong direction but hard to lead in the right direction.

Allah School: Usually refers to the street academy in Harlem and outreach center for the youth located at 2122 7th Avenue, NY, NY 10027. However, when used in connection with the name of another city, the term can refer to that cipher's local street academy (e.g., Allah School in Medina, also known as Akbar's Community Center, at 318 Livonia, in Brooklyn, NY)

Asiatic: Term utilized to show the oneness of Original People. "Asia" is one of the first terms used to express a 'world' consciousness (outside of national boundaries). "Asia" is also synonymous with concepts of the former supercontinent Pangaea.

Black: Used collectively to refer to any non-white person (Brown and Yellow being shades of Black) and not regulated to just African descent. Also used in conjunction with "seed," "shade" or "soil" to refer to those of the darkest shade of any non-white ethnic group.

Breaking it down: Taking a complex lesson and reducing it to simple concepts. From the highest to the lowest.

Brown: Used in conjunction with "seed," "shade," or "soil" to refer to those of a medium shade of any non-white ethnic group.

Build/Building: Constructive communication and/or tangible work.

Cipher: When the Gods and Earths come together to Build.

Civilize: To teach someone how to adhere to codes of conduct.

Devilishment: Wicked and/or oppressive/exploitative behaviors or systemic practices. The opposite of righteousness, or behavior opposed to righteousness. SYN. devilment, devilishness, deviltry, deviltry.

Drawing it up: Taking a simple concept and adding more layers of depth. From the lowest to the highest.

First Born: Used by itself, the term refers to those who were selected by ALLAH to represent his teachings. Used in relation to a city outside of Mecca, the term refers to the first group of people to take on the knowledge in that city (e.g., the First Born of Medina).

Fruit: A term used by some to refer to those whom they taught. Related to the term "Tree." Also can refer to one's physical children.

Graft: To remove something from its original state through a process (like selective breeding), producing a weaker end result.

Honorable Elijah Muhammad: Leader of the Nation of Islam from 1934 until his death in 1975. Referred to as the Messenger of Allah and also under the acronym of T.H.E.M. (The Honorable Elijah Muhammad).

Master Fard Muhammad: Founder of the Nation of Islam in North America. He led the Nation of Islam from 1930 until 1934 when he mysteriously disappeared. He is also referred to as the Prophet.

Muslim: A term used to refer to those who follow the religion of Islam. Muslim means one who submits to the will of Allah. The Gods and Earths do not consider themselves Muslims.

Muslim son: Within 120 degrees this refers to a white male who climbs the ladder of Freemasonry and then becomes inducted into the Ancient Arabic Order of the Nobles of the Mystic Shrine also known as the Shriners. Nowadays it has been used more loosely to refer to white males who knowingly study various sciences of the Original Man.

Mystery god: The concept of an invisible, intangible 'god' that supposedly dwells in the sky.

Original: Used synonymously with Black, refers to any non-white person or group of people.

Parliament: The gathering of the Gods and Earths where Nation business is conducted. There is one monthly Universal Parliament in NYC and local Parliaments that happen across the United States.

Rally: Whenever the Gods and Earths gather together. Every Parliament is a Rally yet every Rally is not a Parliament.

Savage: A "savage" according to 120 degrees refers to someone who has lost all knowledge of himself and is living a beast way of life. In common usage the term refers to an often illicit lifestyle characterized by indiscretion.

Seed: Man or boy.

Soil: Woman or girl.

Tree: The way in which some members of the Nation trace their lineage to ALLAH through one of the first born.

Word is bond: The concept that one's word is as binding as any promise or legal signature.

Yellow: Used in conjunction with "seed," "shade," or "soil" to refer to those of the lightest shade of any non-white ethnic group.

How to Get Our Books

To better serve our readers, we've streamlined the way we handle book orders. Here are some of the ways you can find our books.

In Stores

You can find our books in just about any Black bookstore or independent bookseller. If you don't find our titles on the shelves, just request them by name and publisher. Most bookstores can order our titles directly from us (via our site) or from the distributors listed below. We also provide a listing of retailers who carry our books at www.bestblackbooks.com

Online (Wholesale)

Now, you can visit our sites (like www.supremeunderstanding.com or www.bestblackbooks.com) to order wholesale quantities direct from us, the publisher. From our site, we ship heavily discounted case quantities to distributors, wholesalers, retailers, and local independent resellers (like yourself – just try it!). The discounts are so deep, you can afford to GIVE books away if you're not into making money.

Online (Retail)

If you're interested in single "retail" copies, you can now find them online at Amazon.com, or you can order them via mail order by contacting one of the mail order distributors listed below. You can also find many of our titles as eBooks in the Amazon Kindle, Nook, or Apple iBooks systems. You may also find full-length videobook or audiobook files available, but nothing beats the pass-around potential of a real book!

By Mail Order

Please contact any of the following Black-owned distributors to order our books! For others, visit our site.

Lushena Books
607 Country Club Dr
Bensenville, IL 60106
(800) 785-1545

Afrikan World Books
2217 Pennsylvania Ave.
Baltimore, MD 21217
(410) 383-2006

Special Needs X-Press
3128 Villa Ave
Bronx, NY 10468
(718) 220-3786

www.ingramcontent.com/pod-product-compliance
Lightning Source LLC
LaVergne TN
LVHW090608090325
805223LV00001B/5